Praise for

OLYMPIC PRIDE, AMERICAN PREJUDICE

"*Olympic Pride, American Prejudice* sprints and soars as the story of these unforgettable athletes takes readers on a gripping moral journey and a by-the-second, heart-pounding race of grace and grit. It is at once powerful and tender, as the athletes emerge as champions in the face of Hitler and the Jim Crow South. Ever timely, *Olympic Pride, American Prejudice* is a must-read for anyone concerned with race, sports, and politics in America."

—WILLIAM C. RHODEN, columnist, writer at large for
ESPN's *The Undefeated*, and *New York Times*
bestselling author of *Forty Million Dollar Slaves:
The Rise, Fall, and Redemption of the Black Athlete*

"*Olympic Pride, American Prejudice* is a marvel of perseverance and inspiration. Deborah Riley Draper, Travis Thrasher, and Blair Underwood have done the world a favor by bringing into the sunlight the unknown story of eighteen black Olympians who should never be forgotten. This book is both beautiful and wrenching, and essential to understanding the rich history of African American athletes."

—KEVIN MERIDA, editor in chief of
ESPN's *The Undefeated*

"Cutting across disciplines, this stirring remembrance of athletes who have long been overshadowed will resonate with anyone interested in the Olympics or the history of civil rights."

—*Publishers Weekly*

OLYMPIC PRIDE, AMERICAN PREJUDICE

THE UNTOLD STORY OF 18 AFRICAN AMERICANS WHO DEFIED JIM CROW AND ADOLF HITLER TO COMPETE IN THE 1936 BERLIN OLYMPICS

DEBORAH RILEY DRAPER
AND **TRAVIS THRASHER**

ATRIA PAPERBACK

NEW YORK   LONDON   TORONTO   SYDNEY   NEW DELHI

ATRIA
PAPERBACK

An Imprint of Simon & Schuster, Inc.
1230 Avenue of the Americas
New York, NY 10020

First Atria Paperback edition September 2021

ATRIA PAPERBACK and colophon are trademarks of Simon & Schuster, Inc.

For information about special discounts for bulk purchases, please contact Simon & Schuster Special Sales at 1-866-506-1949 or business@simonandschuster.com.

The Simon & Schuster Speakers Bureau can bring authors to your live event. For more information, or to book an event, contact the Simon & Schuster Speakers Bureau at 1-866-248-3049 or visit our website at www.simonspeakers.com.

Manufactured in the United States of America

1   3   5   7   9   10   8   6   4   2

Library of Congress Cataloging-in-Publication Data has been applied for.

ISBN 978-1-5011-6215-2
ISBN 978-1-5011-6216-9 (pbk)
ISBN 978-1-5011-6217-6 (ebook)

CONTENTS

CONTENTS

PART THREE

INTRODUCTION

THE MIGRATION OF African Americans out of the South begins in earnest during World War I. Rampant racism, coupled with Jim Crow laws and lynchings, drive many black families to look north and west. Between 1880 and 1950, an African American was lynched more than once a week, and many of these atrocities remain unrecorded or undiscovered. The call of the opportunity to earn a living wage and the promise of a better, safer livelihood in cities in need of laborers to work in manufacturing and industrial production is answered by Southern African Americans. Ninety percent of African Americans live in the American South in 1910; for the next six decades 6 million African Americans would leave the South, cutting the population in half. And, ironically, by the time America elects its first African American president, African Americans are returning to the South and once again reshaping American demographics, economics, and political base.

John Brooks's life benefits from the opportunities found north. Born in Vidalia, Louisiana, on July 31, 1910, he won't remember much about his birthplace after moving to Chicago. But one memory does stand out. He recalls the feel of the Vidalia fields under his bare feet as he constantly ran around the small town. His feet are

African Americans stop near Shawboro, North Carolina, on their way to New Jersey, to pick potatoes. July 1940.

tough and his legs are strengthened. Track becomes a natural passion for John. Later he not only becomes an elite athlete but a coach too when he meets a local girl by the name of Tidye Pickett. John knows that a young African American girl in the United States will not be afforded the same training and coaching as her counterparts. Brooks's life changes in his seeking refuge 839 miles to the north.

In the 1920s, the Albritton family, too, leaves the South. David Albritton is just seven years old when his family moves from Danville, Alabama, to Cleveland, Ohio. He barely remembers the lanky kid he met one Sunday afternoon when he was five years old watching his brother play baseball. David has no idea this boy who lived in the next county over will eventually become his best friend and fellow competitor.

Albritton meets Jesse Owens again in junior high school. Even-

African American going in colored entrance of Crescent movie house on a Saturday afternoon in Belzoni, Mississippi Delta, Mississippi, October 1939.

tually both will board the SS *Manhattan* to compete in the Berlin Olympics.

Saying good-bye to the shackles and shadows of Jim Crow, the Brooks, Albritton, and Owens families are among many who refuse to settle for separate seating and even different Bibles from their white counterparts. The laws down South require African Americans to attend segregated schools and churches, to enter "for colored only" bathrooms, to eat in a designated area of a restaurant, and to always sit at the back of a bus.

By 1936, despite escaping the racism in the South, these families will be in a country grappling with the Great Depression. There is real worry for thousands of African Americans that they will never be able to obtain the American dream. The country, still many years before the civil rights era, does not consider African Americans as full citizens.

Hope is often found in athletes like John Brooks, David Albritton, and Jesse Owens. They are among the eighteen black athletes who journey to Berlin to compete in the 1936 Olympics. They will eventually grow up to become soldiers, scientists, principals, and politicians. Sixteen men and two women who take their memories and their medals from Berlin and allow them to become a springboard to combat segregation and racism back home in America.

At the most notorious sports event ever staged, eighteen African Americans challenge discrimination on the world stage. Their presence in Berlin is a blow to racial prejudice on both sides of the Atlantic. The unprecedented effort is largely unknown, and their stories forgotten.

The most unlikely of figures foreshadow Hitler's defeat and a shift in American civil rights in the most spectacular of ways. Yet the world remembers only one of them, by the name of Jesse Owens.

This is the story of the others.

PART ONE

CHAPTER ONE

THE GIRLS ARE FAST
1923

F OR MANY AMERICANS in 1923, times are good. The United States and the rest of the Western world roar through the twenties with their moving vehicles and motion pictures. The New York Yankees play their first game against the Boston Red Sox in "The House That Ruth Built," the newly opened Yankee Stadium. Bessie Smith, "The Empress of the Blues," sings her soulful hits on the radio. Magician Harry Houdini mesmerizes crowds with his stunts and tricks. The country unexpectedly inherits a new leader when President Warren G. Harding has a fatal heart attack on August 2 and Vice President Calvin Coolidge becomes the thirtieth president.

Yet amid an economic boom that doubles America's wealth from 1920 to 1929, racial unrest only intensifies as Jim Crow laws take hold of the country, spurring the revival of the Ku Klux Klan, whose membership grows to 5 million people. The public becomes accustomed to Klan members, adorned in their hooded white robes and carrying American flags, marching down main streets in parades, proudly included as part of the festivities.

The Great Migration continues from the previous decade and manifests itself with a sea change in the culture and the core beliefs in the black community. Big cities such as New York, Chicago, Philadelphia, St. Louis, and Detroit become highly attractive, and very soon black neighborhoods significantly impact metropolitan areas. The change of environment and the chance for new beginnings spur a creative cultural event known as the New Negro Renaissance, or the Harlem Renaissance as it's more commonly called, where the worlds of literature, music, cinema, and theater all open doors to African American artists and voices.

Popularizing the phrase "the New Negro," Alain Locke sums up this revolutionary era in a seminal essay with the same title. A Harvard graduate and the first African American Rhodes Scholar, Locke writes that "So for generations in the mind of America, the Negro has been more of a formula than a human being—a something to be argued about, condemned or defended, to be 'kept down,' or 'in his place,' or 'helped up,' to be worried with or worried over, harassed or patronized, a social bogey or a social burden." Locke sees a sweeping change occurring where "the mind of the Negro seems suddenly to have slipped from under the tyranny of social intimidation and to be shaking off the psychology of imitation and implied inferiority. By shedding the old chrysalis of the Negro problem we are achieving something like a spiritual emancipation."

With this renewed self-respect and self-dependence, the life of the Negro community is bound to enter a new dynamic phase. The Cotton Club opens in Harlem, the heart of New York, in the same year. The nightclub for white clientele will showcase many famous black performers. Duke Ellington, Louis Armstrong, Bessie Smith, Ethel Waters, and many others come to grace the stage. The year also sees the publication of *Cane*, Jean Toomer's hailed collection of poems and stories highlighting the African American experience.

The ripple effects of the Harlem Renaissance can be seen not only in the world of art, but also in the hearts of young African

American kids growing up with a new sense of hope and promise. Two of these are Tidye Pickett and Louise Stokes.

. . .

"Go!" Charles shouts, loud enough for his voice to echo down the block of their Southside Chicago street.

Tidye Pickett's eight-year-old limbs begin to sprint though she remains a few feet behind her older brother. With the sun shining on her face, Tidye moves as quickly as a breeze, catching Charles. For as long as Tidye can remember, she has been racing her older brother, trying to keep up. She's never beaten him before.

Young Tidye knows she's fast, and today she proves it by reaching the finish line by the tree several steps ahead of Charles. As they catch their breath, Tidye's cheeks climb her face, stretching into a smile. From that moment on, she will always be the fastest in the family.

Tidye Pickett and her brother, Charles, on their tricycle, Chicago, Illinois.

The first time Tidye Pickett attends the Newsboys Picnic in Washington Park across the street from her home, she can't imagine just how much she'll learn about her speed. The *Chicago Daily News* hosts the picnic for its newspaper delivery boys and will do so twice a year. She and Charles turn their attention to the park, where box lunches are provided and they can play games and run races all afternoon. Tidye might be short for her age, but it doesn't prevent her from entering the races.

Her neighborhood of Englewood is a thriving community with plenty of department stores and is home to one of the largest theaters around, Southtown Theater. It's a time before the Great Depression and severe redlining policies that will drastically change the neighborhood in the near future. Tidye's father, Louis Alfred Pickett, works as a foreman in a foundry for the International Harvester Company, and her mother, Sarah, is employed as a factory clerk.

By the time Tidye is born, Chicago has more than seventy playgrounds and parks along with a few beaches and pools. The city's park system contains a number of facilities that become home to athletic programs and citywide tournaments. Kids like Tidye compete in a variety of sports such as skating, softball, and track. It is no coincidence that some of the country's best track and field athletes of the twenties and thirties are products of Chicago's athletic programs.

The first day at the picnic, Tidye enters one race and wins a baseball cap. Then she wins another. After emerging victorious in the third race she is awarded a camera. When she arrives home that evening, sweaty and tired from all the races she's run, her mother sees her loot and demands an explanation.

"They had some races at the picnic in the park," Tidye says.

"So, how'd you do?" Sarah Pickett asks her daughter, still not understanding where the hats and cameras came from.

"They give you a prize every time you win a race."

Her mother looks at the winnings with amazement. It won't be the first time the petite girl surprises someone with her speed. It is, however, the first time Tidye realizes she enjoys seeing that sort of reaction. Especially from someone she loves.

· · ·

Louise Stokes steps onto the tracks and stares down them. The railroad stretches a quarter of a mile before intersecting with Pleasant Street in Malden, a Massachusetts town just north of Boston. The winter morning is cold enough for snow, but the skies are clear, her jacket too light to keep her warm from the steady wind. It doesn't take the nine-year-old long to reach her school from her house at 55 Faulkner Street, especially when she runs part of the way. She sprints and steps over every single railroad tie, sometimes counting how many she crosses but eventually losing track after a few hundred. Louise practices every morning before school, and knows she's becoming fast. Morning after morning, she returns to these tracks. Running feels as natural to her as breathing.

The tracks directly intersect the railways at Malden square, the downtown's center, where F.N. Joslin's Department Store (known as the Big Store), the Granada Theater, and the First National Bank are located. Louise's grammar school is downtown as well. As a hub for manufacturing, Malden wields a population of more than sixteen thousand people, many who use the Boston & Maine and the Saugus Branch railroads to connect to Boston, four miles to the south.

Born in Malden, Louise is the great-granddaughter of slaves and the oldest child in a family of six girls and one boy. Her father, William H. Stokes, holds numerous jobs, including gardening and tending to the lawns of the wealthy in the summer while stoking their furnaces in the winter. Her mother, Mary Wesley Stokes, works all day as a housekeeper. Louise's job is to pick up her younger brother and sisters from the nursery and take care of them until her parents return home.

Like most children, Louise longs to play basketball or run along the tracks instead of babysitting her siblings, doing chores, and prepping for dinner. Running along the tracks outside offers Louise

Louise Stokes sitting with her sister.

an escape. For a few fleeting moments, she can even outrun her own thoughts and memories, though she can never lessen the pain of losing her younger sister, Alice. Running doesn't allow her to escape the memory of Alice's sweet smile, nor can it take away the guilt she carries as the older sister. The fire that took four-year-old Alice a year earlier will always be in her memory. Her sister was playing with matches when she lit her nightgown on fire, dying a few days later.

The morning sprint to school is usually no different from her afternoon trip back home. Louise, who keeps to herself and is quieter than most others she knows, runs everywhere she can. After school, she routinely dashes over to Genevieve O'Mara's house in Salem Place, rushing through the front door without knocking and calling for her friend to come outside. Then she and Genevieve dart over to Amerige Park, where they will spend an afternoon playing.

Today, she can't avoid the sneers and the scorn from the neighborhood boys.

"You're not that fast."

"Who are you running away from?"

"Why don't you race us? You can't beat us."

They've done this before, belittling someone younger and smaller than they are. Maybe it's the fact that she's a girl, and maybe it's because she's a black girl. It doesn't matter. Louise knows better than to respond to their banter. She also knows the only way to silence someone's scorn is to prove them wrong. Beating them won't make them like her, but at least they could no longer make fun of her.

"I'll race you," Louise says to them.

The race is over seconds after someone shouts "Go!" The boys are too big, too quick. They all sprint ahead and finish long before she does. Now the energy behind their mockery only seems to intensify.

Louise knows she's fast, but so are they. This isn't going to slow her down, however. One of these days, she'll be old enough to beat them. In the meantime, she keeps her feet fast to the pavement.

ACROSS THE NORTH *Atlantic Ocean in a country decimated and in decline, an unlikely leader, average in appearance and unimpressive at five feet nine inches tall, attempts to overthrow both the German and the Bavarian governments. His name is Adolf Hitler.*

As Germany reels from the crushing defeat of World War I five years earlier, turmoil and chaos consume the country. Almost 20 percent of the male population of Germany are casualties of the war, and by the twenties the downward economic spiral bottoms out. A dollar is now worth 4.2 trillion marks, as opposed to only 90 marks two years earlier. A single loaf of bread costs 200 billion marks. Communists and socialists alike riot over food shortages and political unrest. In the center of the violence and upheaval lies Bavaria with its Nazi Party, led by Hitler.

A year earlier, in October 1922, Benito Mussolini and his Fascist Party rise to power after a successful insurrection, the March on Rome. The following year, Adolf Hitler and the Nazi Party plot to seize control of the government and march on Berlin in a similar manner. His goal will be to take command of the Bavarian government and military in Munich, thereby forcing the hand of the state's top officials, Gustave Ritter von Kahr, Otto von Lossow, and Hans Ritter von Seisser. The result leads to the famous Beer Hall Putsch.

On the night of November 8, 1923, as several thousand people fill a beer hall for a rally being held by the Bavarian leaders, Hitler and his uniformed men storm into the building and burst through the thousands. Hitler jumps onto a chair and stands in front of the crowd, firing off a round from his Browning and commanding everyone to be silent.

"The national revolution has begun!" he shouts.

With the crowd watching in silence, Hitler informs everyone in the beer hall that they are surrounded by six hundred of his storm troopers (the Sturm Abteilung, or SA) and that no one can leave. He then declares the Bavarian government deposed and the armed forces now under his command. He is both lying and exaggerating.

A standoff ensues. However, Hitler is unsuccessful at convincing the state's officials, Kahr, Lossow, and Seisser, to join his side. He calls on the truly captive audience in the hall, pleading for them to join him in the German revolution. Being a master orator, Hitler wins over the crowd and temporarily regains momentum.

Before the night is over, however, the furor dissipates, leaving Hitler with few options. He decides to appeal to the public by marching with three thousand of his men in the streets of Munich. They sing songs that proclaim "Deutschland! Deutschland!" as they proceed through the stone streets. Once again, he feels confident this will work. Yet after they are met with resistance that includes both the police and the army, a skirmish turns into gunfire, leaving four policemen and one Nazi dead. Hitler narrowly escapes death himself, with the man next to him shot in the chest.

As quickly as it began, the rebellion is now over. Two days later, on November 11, Hitler is arrested, accused of committing high treason.

The deposed leader of the Nazi Party is sentenced to five years in prison. Soon Hitler sits in a cell, his hate only fueled by his confinement.

"The right to personal freedom comes second in importance to the duty of maintaining the race," he writes.

CHAPTER TWO

A SINGLE INCH, A CROSS ON FIRE

1924

T HE CLEAVER CUTS through the fish head with ease, the sharp blade sticking firmly into the wood. The fourteen-year-old moves fast, getting rid of the waste with one hand and placing the cleaned fish among the others. This April day on the south side of Chicago is hot, but the tall teen has barely broken a sweat after an hour of work.

Ralph Metcalfe no longer thinks about the smell of the fish even though the scent will linger on his hands the next day at Wendell Phillips Junior High School. It doesn't bother him when one of the girls teases that he reeks. Cleaning and chopping fish in the market pays well, and they let him start in the afternoon once he is released from school. He finds himself skillful with his hands, though his legs will eventually become his claim to fame.

Work comes natural to Ralph. From the time his family moved from Atlanta to Chicago in 1917, when he was seven years old, he

Ralph Metcalfe Tilden High School track team photo, Chicago, Illinois.

has found jobs in the city and has grown to know his way around the streets. They relocated to the quaint Douglas neighborhood, where it only took eight minutes for Ralph to walk to Doolittle Elementary School, half that time if he jogged. When he worked as a delivery boy for a variety of the merchants near his house, he ran all over the city. That's how everybody began to realize he was fast. They would give young Ralph something to deliver, and he would be back at their door moments later, awaiting another package.

Born in Atlanta, Georgia, on May 30, 1910, Ralph Horace Metcalfe is separated by two years from his older brother, Andrew, and younger sister, Lucy. Ralph's father, Clarence Metcalfe, works in the stockyards while his mother, Maria Attaway Metcalfe, sews dresses, both of them doing what they can to support their three children. As the United States enters World War I in 1917, the Metcalfes leave Atlanta for better opportunities in Chicago.

Ralph still holds vivid memories of Atlanta, where he and Andrew were confined to their yard at home for play, with not much space to run around. Chicago is different. They finally have a playground nearby, one where they can spend hours playing every kind of sport. Metcalfe is a natural at them all—football, basketball, and baseball—and because of his speed he earns the nickname "Rabbit."

Dreams of pursuing a career in sports seem foolhardy, since there are few examples he can follow. It will take Georgia native Jackie Robinson another twenty-three years before integrating major league baseball. In professional football, there are only a few black players, such as Fritz Pollard, Sr. And between Jack Johnson in 1915 and Joe Louis over two decades later in 1937, no African Americans will be allowed to participate in a heavyweight championship boxing match. Despite the racial barriers, Metcalfe believes that someday his athletic abilities will lead him somewhere special.

On this day working at the fish market, Metcalfe loses his concentration and watches the cleaver cut into his left index finger. Fortunately, the sharp blade gets stuck. Human bone is a bit more solid than the skin and flesh of a fish. He doesn't yell very loudly, but he quickly raises the instrument and sets it down to tend to his finger. His palm and wrist are already soaked with blood.

The good news is his index finger remains intact, still attached to his hand. But the pain rips through him as he rushes to find his boss and tell him he's leaving a little early today. Only he will be going to the hospital nearby instead of heading back home.

Metcalfe considers himself lucky for not chopping off his finger. He discovers he severed his extensor tendon, the tendon on the top of the finger that helps to move, grip, and let go of things. After he wears a splint for what seems like years but is only a few months, Metcalfe's injured finger will never be the same. There will always be a noticeable crimp.

This doesn't affect Metcalfe a bit, however. It only reminds him to be careful in all matters. And it tells him that sometimes a single inch can make all the difference in the world.

. . .

"God's not gonna let that fire come inside this house," Mallie Robinson tells her children as they look out of their second-story window onto the burning cross on their lawn.

Earlier, Mallie's son Mack watches his little brother Jackie as he zips down the sidewalk on his bicycle. Jackie chases after their older brother Edgar, twenty yards ahead on his roller skates. Their other siblings, Frank and Willa Mae, play near the steps to the house. As the five-year-old tries to take a corner, the bike skips off the cement and stutters to a halt, tossing Jackie onto the grass. Nobody worries because they know he is tough, but Mack rushes over regardless just to make sure nothing is broken.

"You okay?" ten-year-old Mack asks as he grabs Jackie's hand and pulls him up.

His brother gives him a mischievous grin and says he's fine. The sun is hot on this July Saturday in Pasadena. An elderly man across Pepper Street walks his driveway, glancing over at the group of kids playing, then heads back into his house without any sort of greeting or acknowledgment. Mack is used to it by now. He assumes the old man is the same person who called the police on Edgar because of the supposed noise he made while skating. The policemen suggested that his mother keep him and his siblings inside, but Mallie Robinson told the officers her children weren't making any more noise than the other kids in the neighborhood.

They have been in the neighborhood for only less than a year and have been living in California since moving four years ago from Cairo, Georgia. Mack, only six at the time, recalls the sharecropper's farm they lived on and the trip west with his family in 1920. Sometimes the memories find their way into his dreams at night.

He'd see his father coming in after working in the fields for barely any pay and then one day never coming in again. Moving into that smaller cabin and Mom being forced to find any work possible. The

Mallie Robinson and her children. Seated: Mallie Robinson. Standing, L to R: Mack, Jackie, Edgar, Willa Mae, and Frank.

thirteen of them packed in a dark and cramped train car headed west.

His mother comes from a family of fourteen children, with Mallie born right in the middle. Growing up in Georgia, she'd lived on land her parents owned and made it all the way up to sixth grade in school, two rare accomplishments for an African American child growing up in the South at the turn of the century. Her parents were slaves, and they stressed the value of education to their children. More than that, the McGriffs instilled in their family the value of faith, so much that Mallie, only ten years old, taught her father how to read the Bible. She will eventually do the same with Mack and her four other children, living out the importance of her Christian walk and the unity of their family, both necessary for a black family living in the South.

After marrying Jerry Robinson, much to her father's displeasure, Mallie finds her husband being taken advantage of by his boss at the plantation. She speaks up, fighting for Jerry and their family. Instead of paying paltry monthly wages, the plantation boss allows the Robinsons to become sharecroppers. The scraps they have been living on soon turn into a bounty of hogs, chickens, turkeys, cotton, corn, sugar cane, and more. Yet with the provisions they are now beginning to accumulate thanks to Mallie's efforts, Jerry looks elsewhere in both his life and his marriage. Twice he leaves Mallie and the family, and both times he comes back to open arms. The third time is his last, however, with Jerry telling his wife and five children good-bye at a train station on July 28, 1919. There are rumors of an affair known by many; Mallie eventually learns Jerry was employed at a sawmill and living with another woman.

Matters become worse when her husband's boss discovers she willingly helped Jerry leave, resulting in the Robinson family's being forced to move two times into smaller, unacceptable houses on the plantation. Exhausted by the constant moves and by the oppressive nature of sharecropping, Mallie decides to leave Georgia. In May 1920, along with her young sister, Cora Wade, her brother-in-law, and their two sons, the Robinsons make the pilgrimage to the hope and warmth of California where Mallie's half-brother lives.

"If you want to get closer to Heaven, visit California," Burton Thomas, her half-brother, tells her.

Burton, Mack's uncle, eventually persuades them to move West. After the two families share a cramped apartment for a few weeks, Mallie and her children move into a more spacious home along with Burton. Mallie, having saved up enough money from her job as a domestic worker, is able to pool her money together with Cora and Samuel Wade to buy a house at 121 Pepper Street. The large two-story house in the all-white neighborhood contains five bedrooms and two baths. Mallie purchases the home from a black man who managed to buy it with the help of a light-skinned relative. When the Robinsons and Wades move onto the street in 1922, the neighbors petition for them to leave and threaten to burn the house down.

Mallie Robinson prays for strength and wisdom daily while attempting to gain respect by working for those in the neighborhood at no cost. Yet, in a couple of years' time, matters still haven't improved. Every now and then a rock is thrown at them or they find something on their property vandalized. Kids in the neighborhood bully the Robinson and Wade kids, though they fight back, especially Mack. The neighbors attempt to buy them out, yet that eventually goes away after someone says the Robinsons are decent neighbors. In 1924, the Wades move to their own home, at 972 Cypress Street, a few blocks away.

On a summer's day like today, Mack and his siblings stay outside playing and easily lose track of time. With the sun starting to fade, Mack hears his mother calling for them just after he has assured himself that none of Jackie's bones were broken from the fall. He looks and sees his mother on the porch leaning on the railing and watching her children. It's time to come inside for dinner.

Later that night Edgar's screams awaken the family. He is shouting as he stands by the narrow window, staring down to the front of their house. Mack nudges in beside his two older brothers to see bright flames on their lawn. A burning cross lights up their yard as the blaze cuts through the black night like intertwined torches. Mack watches in wonder. Who in their neighborhood would do such a thing? Has the kind of evil they experienced in Georgia followed them to California, or is it simply standing by at every corner of the world waiting to greet them?

Mack doesn't hear his mother until she is behind them, watching the same ugly sight on their property. She puts her arms around the boys.

"We didn't come all this way to let someone scare us. Especially like this."

Mallie Robinson guided her family across the country to end up in this house, so Mack knows she isn't going anywhere anytime soon.

For the Robinsons, especially Mack and little Jackie, life will take them much further than 121 Pepper Street.

———————————

IN THE BAVARIAN *town thirty-eight miles from Munich called Landsberg am Lech, Adolf Hitler sits in the Landsberg Prison, writing out his great magnum opus on a Remington portable typewriter. For nine months in 1924, he remains in the special wing of the prison known as die Festung, or the fortress. The prison is nothing more than a two-story building resembling a dormitory, with the inmates serving under "honorable imprisonment" conditions with minimum security. Hitler's time at Landsberg Prison, which he will consider his "university education at state expense," turns both his career and the Nazi movement around.*

Following the failed Beer Hall Putsch of 1923, Hitler rises to national acclaim with a trial that serves more as a showcase for his extraordinary speaking gifts. The opening speech from Hitler at the trial lasts nearly four hours and consists of his telling his story, a biography, filled with anti-Semitic beliefs along with his acceptance of bringing salvation to the people of Germany. After receiving the lightest sentence possible of five years, Hitler moves into a small bedroom on the second floor, containing a bed, a lamp, a couple of a chairs, and a small desk on which he can write.

Every day and night, next to five-foot-high windows, Hitler works on his autobiography, a declaration reaching far beyond personhood that becomes the manifesto Mein Kampf.

On December 19, 1924, Hitler is released from prison. The New York

Times *writes a small article summing up his time at the fortress and how they view Hitler.*

"Hitler Tamed by Prison"
Released on Parole, He Is Expected to Return to Austria.

Berlin. Dec. 20 (1924)–Adolph Hitler, once the demi-god of the reactionary extremists, was released from imprisonment at Fortress Landsberg, Bavaria, today and immediately left in an auto for Munich. He looked a much sadder and wiser man today than last Spring when he, with Ludendorff and other radical extremists, appeared before a Munich court charged with conspiracy to overthrow the government.

His behavior during imprisonment convinced the authorities that, like his political organization, known as the Völkischer, he was no longer to be feared. It is believed he will retire to private life and return to Austria, the country of his birth.

Most of the world doesn't know of the contents of Mein Kampf, *which spells out Hitler's views on race and its effect on history. Perhaps if they did know, they would be more fearful of the intentions of the man who views world history as a struggle among races. Laid out in his book are three categories in which he organizes races: culture-creating races like the Aryans, culture-bearing races like the Japanese that neither create nor destroy, and culture-destroying races like the Jews.*

Of course, Hitler's racist beliefs don't end with the Jews. He also shares his beliefs about African Americans in Mein Kampf, *sentiments that many Americans unfortunately share with him at the time:*

"The Jews were responsible for bringing Negroes into the Rhineland, with the ultimate idea of bastardizing the white race which they hate and thus lowering its cultural and political level so that the Jew might dominate."

CHAPTER THREE

DISCIPLINE AND HEART

1928

ARCHIE WILLIAMS CAN'T find his tie. The twelve-year-old wears one only for special occasions and can't remember where he put it the last time it hung around his neck. Archie knows he doesn't want to be late for the sixth-grade graduation ceremony at Peralta School, the third school he's attended.

He might've still been at his second school, Washington School, if it had been big enough for all the students. Peralta had just been built on nearby North Street by the time Archie switched schools. There aren't any black kids in his class, but that isn't much of a surprise since there are hardly any black families in the part of Oakland where he lives. All his friends are white, except for George Suzuki. George once told them that his last name is as common in Japan, the place where he was from, as Smith is in the United States.

"Come on, Archie!" Mom calls outside his room.

"Okay," he says, checking under his bed and discovering a lot of toys and books he hasn't seen in years. But no tie.

It would be sad not to have gone to Peralta. He loves the school and all his classmates. Kenny Bradshaw, his buddy who lives right down the street. Bobby Earhart, Irving Mahoney, Jack Martin, Dick Kruger, Jack Mayer, and Robbie Chapman. Principal Bradley. And of course, Annie, the sweetie of the class.

He'd already lived in west Oakland while attending his first school, then he and his family moved to north Oakland. Moving has been a thread of life for Archie and his brother and sister, especially when their father was still alive. Dad's interest in real estate prompted the moves, something Archie didn't mind because he enjoyed making new friends.

There it is.

The red and black tie lay buried amidst black socks in a drawer. He quickly clips it onto his collar while looking in the small mirror on his beat-up dresser. He sees a faded picture of his mother and father and stares at it for a moment, wondering what Dad would think about today if he was still around.

Wadsworth Williams passed away a couple of years ago when Archie was ten, but it feels to him like one of his moves—as if it happened in another lifetime. Dad fell sick with pneumonia and was never able to recover. Archie heard about people dying all the time from things like scarlet fever, diphtheria, and the flu. He'd see people wearing masks or large, red signs in front of houses that said they were quarantined. It scares Archie anytime he sees those signs, forcing him to cross the street to walk on the other side. He doesn't want to get sick like his father; getting sick is deadly.

It's not as though his father wasn't tough. Archie remembers the stories Dad told them, like the time he worked as an elevator man for the U.S. Mint and got his skull cracked open after a pallet of gold fell on top of him. Or once, before Archie was born, when his father worked on a ship that traveled along the coast. After an accident, the ship sank and left his father in the middle of the ocean drifting with only a log to keep him afloat. He was finally rescued when another ship came along and spotted the young man in the water.

"Hey, boy. What the hell you doing out here in the middle of the ocean?" one of the seaman had asked his dad before fishing him out.

His father had originally hailed from Chicago, and after moving to Oakland met and married his mother, Lillian. Along with his interest in real estate, his father also owned a grocery store near their house at Twentieth Street and Telegraph Avenue. They certainly weren't rich by any means, but at the same time Archie doesn't feel they were poor. He can still recall the new car smell of the first vehicle Dad bought for them. It was a Model T Ford, and he paid around one hundred dollars for it.

"Archie!"

He sprints out of his bedroom and follows his mother and siblings out the front door. Copies of today's *Oakland Tribune* sit in a pile on his porch, the remaining papers from his morning route. He glances down at Telegraph Avenue where the running car waits for him, and for a brief moment Archie looks beyond the street to see the top of Sather Tower, otherwise known as the Campanile. The 307-foot-tall tower sits on the campus of the University of California. As he has many times before, Archie wonders what it would be like to attend CAL. He knows there are lots of great sports teams at the university, especially the California Golden Bears football teams that won championships in '20, '21, '22, and '23.

Climbing into Mom's car, twelve-year-old Archie doubts he will ever go to college for any kind of athletic reason. He likes playing sandlot ball and basketball at the park with the other kids, but he just isn't particularly great at anything. Maybe he will study engineering since he loves to build things, like the sailboats he made with his neighbor Kenny Bradshaw. It was Kenny's idea, in fact, when he came over to Archie's house wanting to construct the same sailboats that were shown in the *Popular Science* magazine he held. After collecting a bunch of boards at a nearby friend's house, Archie and Kenny build a pretty decent sailboat. One good enough to put onto nearby Lake Merritt.

"Did all of you brush your teeth?" his mother asks the three of them.

They all say "yes" at the same time. Florence and Fritz sit in the backseat. His sister is eleven years old and Fritz is ten. His real name is William, but since he was born during World War I, the family said he looked a little German. They will later learn that one of their kooky uncles devised the name.

His mother's parents owned the house they live in now on Telegraph Avenue. His grandfather served as a sergeant in the army and was in the Spanish-American War. After he met his grandmother, a young woman from Tennessee, they eventually moved to the Presidio in San Francisco, where his grandfather was stationed. After he left the army, they eventually moved to and stayed in Oakland.

Maybe Archie would be like his grandfather and serve in the army or another branch of the military. He would love to fly airplanes one day. It doesn't matter if anybody thinks he is crazy for imagining that he might be able to do so. Maybe they will tell Archie he can't be a pilot because of the color of his skin. He knows lots of people have problems with black folks, and though he doesn't like it, that's just the way things are. It's no different from the Boy Scouts.

All his buddies wanted him to join their Boy Scout troop, but when they took Archie to sign up, they were told he wasn't eligible, for obvious reasons. It's the same in the restaurants, theaters, and swimming pools that he and his family are not allowed to enter. Even the YMCA, which is nothing more than a broken-down house with a couple of pool tables in it, tells him he is not welcome.

As he adjusts his tie and then rolls down his window, Archie knows this is simply part of life. He resents it, however. He would like to one day show people that he can indeed be a Boy Scout. Or maybe the star of a football team. Or maybe the builder of great big boats. Or maybe, just maybe, a famous pilot who flies all over the world.

• • •

Almost four hundred miles away on a warm Los Angeles morning, James Ellis LuValle begins his last day at McKinley Junior High School. He carries victory in his hand and remains determined to proudly display it. This isn't about bragging or proving that he is smarter than anybody else. James knows he isn't. But he can still remember the girl's words and how they stung. He took them home with him and pinned them front and center in his mind.

The girl didn't just mock him. She issued a challenge, one he hasn't forgotten two and a half years later.

James was born in San Antonio, Texas, on November 10, 1912. His father, James A. LuValle, is a minister, while his mother, Isabel Ellis, teaches music. Along with his younger sister, Mayme, the LuValle family briefly spent time living in Washington, D.C., before heading to Southern California, where they will stay. They aren't alone, either; during the 1920s, California sees its population grow by 66 percent, with over 2 million people settling in the Golden State to bring its total population to 5.7 million. The last time for such high growth was during the California Gold Rush in 1849.

The report card James carries into the junior high school isn't completely unexpected. His parents signed him up for a library card as soon as he could walk, and James grew up reading as many books as he could. But that doesn't mean he did not like hanging out with his friends, goofing around, and avoiding his homework. So when he entered McKinley Junior High in sixth grade, his grades and study habits weren't good.

Then he meets the snotty-nosed girl who changes everything.

One day in sixth grade he spots Rachel staring at him in class as if she is standing on top of a statue looking down. Her conceited eyes and condemning gaze say enough, but Rachel backs them up with words.

"You know, you're dumb like all of the other fellows," she tells him. "I'm much brighter than any of you."

She is technically right, since Rachel is the so-called smartest one in the class and always eager to show off her quiz scores. But on this day Rachel isn't so smart. She doesn't know James. She doesn't know a single thing about him. All she can see is that he is a boy, and a black boy at that.

Those words aren't received as just some simple criticism. They are starting blocks he will use to push off and begin a competition. One that lasts for two and a half years.

At first, James struggles to find the time to do his homework. He reads less for fun and more for school. He still takes part in all the different athletics the school offers, but he isn't serious about any one sport in particular. The subjects in school, however, are areas where he really discovers he has talent. He excels at math and English, but his favorite subject is science. It has been his favorite since he was eight years old and his parents ignited his imagination one Christmas morning.

On Christmas Day, 1920, James spots a large present for him under the tree, unwrapping it to find a chemistry set. Some kids might have balked at the gift, but not James. He tries out every experiment in the box. Unfortunately, one unexpectedly fills the house with smoke, making his mother force him to do the rest of his experiments outside on the porch.

James enjoys not only being able to do experiments at school, but being able to get them right the first time. Always making sure Rachel sees his accomplishment. Always having her words in his mind telling him he is "dumb like all the others."

On his final day of eighth grade, James shows his report card to his so-called dumb buddies. He knows Rachel will be curious to see it as well even though, by now, she is aware of how smart he was. Motivated by Rachel's challenge, James worked hard these past couple of years; in the fall he plans to enroll in L.A. Polytechnic High School, one of the area's top high schools.

With the Olympics approaching that summer, James has no idea how these games will one day change his life

. . .

On May 19, 1928, there is no hint of a breeze to be found around the track in Champaign, Illinois. The annual high school track and field state meet is being held at the University of Illinois campus, and the day could not be more perfect, with a temperature in the mid-seventies and the humidity not yet oppressive, as it will be in a couple of months. All eyes converge on the tall sophomore sprinter from Tilden Technical School.

When Ralph Metcalfe walks onto this track, the looks from the other teams tell him everything he needs to know. The other runners are nervous about the black kid from Chicago they've been hearing so much about. Some have already raced him this season. So far very few have beaten him, however. And he has only gotten better as the season goes on.

The mostly white Tilden Technical School turns out to be more than a change of scenery from Metcalfe's previous overpopulated and underfunded junior high school. It's become a valuable place to learn track.

"You have to put daylight between you and your nearest competitor," Metcalfe's track coach at Tilden told him the first time he began to race.

Ralph realizes the reason why: If the race comes down to him and a white runner, there will be no question who receives the gold medal. That's why any victory must be absolutely convincing. And to achieve this, Ralph will have to train with more discipline and heart than he ever has before. He will need to try a little harder with every single thing in the race. Starting, for instance. Ralph knows he isn't the fastest starter out there, so in those crucial first couple of seconds, those thousands of milliseconds in the race, he needs to make them count and force himself to catch up to his competitors.

Seventeen-year-old Metcalfe lines up for the 100-yard dash, the tougher of the races, since his style of running is building up speed for every ten yards and every single second. The 100-yard dash doesn't give him much space or time to make up ground on fellow runners. On this day, he starts quickly and bolts down the track, finding himself in the clear with nobody around him.

He easily wins the race, but not only that, Ralph breaks the state record in the 100-yard dash by two-tenths of a second. The old mark of ten seconds flat has been standing since 1905, but now thirteen years later he has put sufficient daylight between him and that mark with a 9.8 second finish, matching the national record.

The extra 120 yards in the 220 display Ralph's running style in proud form as he starts slowly but runs with smooth, long strides, overtaking the rest of the runners easily until breaking into the last straight stretch and shattering the national record by a whole second in 21.1 seconds.

The day isn't over for Ralph. He completes the track meet with another win and another broken record in the 880-yard relay, with Ralph taking the baton last to sprint home to a time of 1 minute 32.4 seconds. Ten days before turning eighteen years old, Ralph steps out onto the Champaign track and demolishes the former race times.

The next day the *Chicago Sunday Tribune* describes him as "flashy," but perhaps it is simply summing up his performance.

It will be a long time before that flash begins to dim.

IN 1928, THE *Summer Olympics is held in the Netherlands. The host city of Amsterdam welcomes athletes from all over the world with an opening ceremony on July 28 and a closing ceremony on August 12. For the first* time in Olympic history, women can participate in something more than archery, golf, swimming, and tennis. Track and field is finally open to female athletes when the International Amateur Federation allows them to compete in the following events: the 100-, 400-, and 800-meter relay, as well as the discus and the high jump.

One of those competing is Betty Robinson, a sixteen-year-old Chicago-area native. Born in Riverdale, Illinois, a town fourteen miles south of Chicago, Betty calls herself a "hick" who grew up knowing nothing about track and having no idea women ran in events. Spotted by an assistant track coach when she sprinted to catch her train one day, just three weeks later, she entered her first race and finished second behind the U.S. record holder in the 100-meter race. In her second race, she matched the world record in the event, then went on to make the Olympic team in only her third track meet.

The young girl's long journey to the Netherlands that summer results in one of the most surprising victories of the 100-meter race ever. The Chicago Tribune reports her victory over a formidable runner.

"Halfway down the lane [Robinson] pulled up on even terms with Fanny Rosenfeld, the Canadian champion, and, going stronger with each stride, gained a foot advantage, which she held as she breasted the tape. The time of 12⅕ seconds bettered by one-fifth of a second the accepted world record mark."

Along with the gold medal she would win, Betty also wins a silver with the relay team for the 4x100-meter race. She arrives back home to ticker-tape parades in both New York and Chicago, then goes on to receive a warm welcome from Riverdale along with the gift of a diamond watch from the town and a silver cup from her high school.

Betty Robinson's unlikely odyssey surely stirs the hearts and spirits of young girls everywhere. Women can finally run and compete in the Olympics.

Without knowing it, the 1928 Olympic Games opens a door that ushers change into the sport. African American athletes will have many years and miles to go, but the charge is set.

CHAPTER FOUR

DETERMINATION
1930

T HE SUN BURNS above Louise Stokes while her shadow keeps
close by her side, always moving in a fluid motion. The sixteen-
year-old runs alongside train tracks once again. This time, she has
company, jogging in a pack of high school girls, all part of the Onteora
Track Club. While it doesn't bother her that she is the only black girl
on the team, she does feel excluded by not being able to practice on
the smooth surface of the high school track. It is reserved exclusively
for the boys' track team. Since the nearby parks don't have enough
flat ground to practice sprinting, the girls must run over a cinder and
gravel path between two sets of tracks that service a local commuter
train traveling from their town of Malden to the town of Saugus.

"All right, take a break," Coach Quaine calls out as he finally
stops their warm-up jog.

The April afternoon pauses with them, the clear Massachusetts
sky stretching out with blue for as far as they can see.

"We're going to work on your starts today," the coach informs the
girls as they stand catching their breaths.

Kathryn Robley walks next to Louise with her hands on her hips, her face flushed from the jog. Louise feels great and hasn't started to sweat yet, but she doesn't want to show off. She gives her friend a smile as she waits for the coach to begin the next drill. Kathyrn joined the track club first, telling Louise about it afterward and encouraging her to join. They played basketball together, and Kathryn knows how fast Louise can run. The coach, William Quaine, works at the post office along with his duties as one of Malden's park commissioners. He's been involved in sports since he was a kid. Quaine started the Onteora Track Club to allow girls like Louise and Kathryn the chance to participate in track. When Louise contacted him, she quickly realized the coach wasn't interested in the color of her skin. He noticed Louise's speed and seemed impressed.

Practice is held every day after school. Coach Quaine enjoys running himself, and he always guides them in a couple of long runs each practice. The trains pass at the same time daily, and now the familiar passengers not only wave but call out from open windows, encouraging them to keep going and to run faster. It's always fun for the girls to see if someone yells out anything and what they say.

For half an hour on this sunny afternoon in April 1930, Coach Quaine shows the girls the proper technique for starting a race in a sprinter's crouch, demonstrating it himself and then getting the girls to do it one by one. Louise has no problem bending into position and then launching herself forward. She's already been doing something similar for years now.

After practicing a dozen starts, Coach Quaine measures off fifty yards and has the girls run sprints while he times them. Louise wins the first run by several yards. She sees Coach Quaine looking at his watch, then giving Louise a puzzled stare before glancing at the stopwatch again in amazement.

"Good work, Louise!" he calls out. "That's your best time yet."

Louise loves to hear any sort of cheer, whether it comes from the crowd when she played center on the basketball team at Beebe Junior High or from Coach Quaine during practice. These afternoons are a welcome break from reading and studying at Malden High School or doing homework later at night.

The coach has the girls run multiple sprints so he can record their times. Louise runs as hard as she can, yet she still has enough inside her to charge the next time they race. She wants to be ready when she finally steps out onto an actual track and lines up against other runners. She doesn't expect to always be the fastest on her team, but so far, it's difficult for anybody else to keep up with her.

Louise imagines what it must be like to run in front of bleachers full of spectators. Will they cheer if she wins, or will they cheer if she loses? How will it feel to compete? To race others not just down the street or over train tracks but between the lines on a genuine track?

．　．　．

"A little thing like you doesn't have a chance."

Tidye Pickett can't believe her cousin's comment. What does size have to do with how fast you can run, she thinks. It matters in basketball and volleyball but not with track and field. At fifteen years old, Tidye already knows she can outrun others her age. She can also outplay them on the basketball court as she's done so often as a member of the Englewood High School basketball team. So why can't she compete and beat other sprinters?

"You know I'm not the shortest person on the basketball team," Tidye reminds her cousin.

She isn't quite five foot three, but surprisingly there is another player shorter than her on the team. Her height doesn't matter. Neither does the fact that she doesn't even weigh more than a hundred pounds. You don't need to rebound a ball if you make your shots.

On this bright and warm spring Saturday, Tidye takes in her surroundings. She realizes she wouldn't be at this track meet in the first place if someone hadn't noticed her speed.

After becoming accustomed to winning those little races at the

Louise Stokes poses with her Malden High School Basketball Teammates. Malden, Massachusetts.

Newboys' Picnics held in Washington Park, she catches the eye of her gym instructor one day on the Carter School playground. Miss Pearl Greene notices Tidye dash past her, seeing firsthand the young girl's quickness. Greene knows speed when she sees it since she is the director of the girls' athletic program for the Chicago Board of Education Playground Programs. She asks Tidye to join a team, and soon afterward Tidye becomes a part of the Chicago Park District's

Tidye Pickett sports her uniform. Chicago, Illinois, early 1930s.

South Park track team. Instead of just running and jumping against others in a park, she is now being trained by knowledgeable coaches.

Tidye quickly forgets her cousin's comment. This Saturday marks the first official meet for her. She tugs at the South Park jersey that she's still getting used to wearing and glances at the many other girls she will be racing against. Some of them wear medals they've won over their chests. Those are the girls her cousin pointed to.

"See that girl in the red?" her cousin asks. "The tall one? She's had the record in the 50-yard dash for years."

Standing across the track from the girl, Tidye studies her for a long time, watching how she walks with confidence and how casual she appears around the other competitors. Tidye observes those long legs that probably move as smoothly as a cheetah's. It's obvious how familiar the girl appears to be with this course, warming up at the starting line.

On this particular day, Tidye isn't the tallest or the fastest runner. Nobody notices her. Nevertheless, later in the season, she will set records in these same sprints.

By the end of the season, people will be singling her out the same

way her cousin pointed at the girl on this first track meet. The first
of many.

• • •

"Why can't I try out for sports?" Mack Robinson asks his mother.
"There's nothing wrong with me."

Mallie Robinson shakes her head as she sorts through the breads
and pastries the local bakery just delivered. It's become a tradition
for the bakery to give the Robinson family the day's remaining
goods. They even let the Robinson boys take away treats on Saturday
evenings. They have been receiving so much that Mallie is starting
to spread the wealth and give neighbors some of the baked goods.

"I'm the fastest kid in eighth grade," Mack says.

Since he was ten, Mack has realized he's a gifted athlete, along
with knowing he's fast. It especially showed when he and his friends
played Chase the Fox, a game where they all lined up in a large circle
and then stood still until one bolted free, causing the rest of them
to try to catch them. Whenever Mack played the role of the fox, he
was impossible to tag out. With his athletic ability, Mack excelled
in baseball and basketball. Then came his annual physical in sixth
grade that told the school and his mother otherwise.

"We discovered a heart murmur," the doctor stated.

Heart murmurs in children are common, Mack will come to
understand, and they usually go away by the time kids enter school.
After more tests, however, the murmur appears to become more serious, enough to ban him from participating in any more sports. All
of them—softball, basketball, baseball—suddenly stop. All because
doctors heard some sort of strange fluttering in his heart.

Mack Robinson entered his first year at Washington Junior High
unable to compete in school athletics. Refusing to be a bystander,
Mack worked hard on convincing his mom to allow him to play
sports.

"Just let me try," he pleads. "You're always tellin' us never to give up."

"That's right. And we shouldn't. But God also gave us common sense."

Mack Robinson refuses to take no for an answer, and he believes his mother will understand. How can she not? That's the way she approaches life herself. He can still remember the time she surprised Mack and the rest of the kids when they teased that she couldn't ride a horse. His mother defiantly hopped onto the horse, sitting side-saddle on the large animal in her dress, then confidently galloped down the field. This showed Mack there were many sides of Mom he didn't know.

"I'm going to work hard," Mack promises. "My heart's going to be fine."

From the very start of his career, Mack will face higher odds than others with his heart condition. His stubborn, relentless efforts finally pay off when his mother relents and goes to the school to make a case for him to compete. After explaining the situation, Mallie and the school will come to a middle ground regarding Mack and his murmur. He is allowed to participate only in noncontact sports, leaving track as the lone option. His mother is forced to sign a letter that prevents Washington Junior High being held responsible if something happens to Mack.

As a teenager, Mack soon discovers just how fast a fox he truly can be. He competes in the 100-yard dash, along with the 220 and 440. He also tries out for the high hurdles, learning the proper form of jumping over them and how many steps he needs to take between them. Many hurdles are overturned, and his arms and legs are scraped from the tumbles he takes, but by the end of his first season he excels in his races. He is so confident that he begins to eye the broad jump. Perhaps Mack will start competing in that next year.

Young Mack Robinson didn't just inherit toughness from his

mother. He also has the same faith she carries inside her. Perhaps it's something that Mallie Robinson instilled in all her children.

———————————

THE ROAR OF *the twenties silences in 1929, when a recession starting that summer along with rising stock prices bursts the stock market's bubble in October. "Black Thursday" on October 24 builds to "Black Tuesday," on which day 16 million shares are traded amid a surge of panic on Wall Street. Stock values plummet, leaving many shares worthless. Half a month later, an estimated $30 billion in stock value is gone.*

By March 1930, the unemployment rate more than doubles in the span of five months, going from 1.5 million before the crash to more than 3.2 million. President Hoover tries to reassure the country by saying the toughest days of the employment drought are behind them, but the worst is yet to come. For the next decade, the United States finds itself in the Great Depression, with the rest of the world feeling the impact as well.

That same year, as New York City street corners eventually become occupied by unemployed thousands selling apples, the Nazis go from being the smallest political party in Germany to becoming the second largest, ensuring 107 seats in the German Reichstag. With Germany suffering from the effects of the Great Depression and its decline since World War I, political instability only adds to the malaise and uncertainty. Adolf Hitler knows it is time once again to make an appeal to the German people.

A year earlier, Hitler chose Josef Goebbels to be his minister of propaganda. The campaign Hitler and Goebbels wage in 1930 is relentless, with Hitler speaking to the crowds and Goebbels employing slogans and imagery, both of which begin to win public support for the Nazis. The onslaught of newspapers, leaflets, and posters is impossible to ignore.

On September 15, 1930, a day after the election, thirty-three-year-old Goebbels records the triumph in a diary entry:

"I am shaking with excitement. The first election results. Fantastic.

Jubilation everywhere, an incredible success. It's stunning. The bourgeois parties have been smashed. So far, we have 103 seats. That's a tenfold increase. I would never have expected it. The mood of enthusiasm reminds me of 1914, when war broke out. Things will get pretty hot in the months ahead. The Communists did well, but we are the second-largest party."

The following day, Hitler speaks in Munich, inspiring the masses and moving ahead toward his ultimate goal of seeing the Nazi Party reigning over all, envisioning himself as the world's savior. His words motivate people living in misery, men and women desperate for something more.

"From blood, authority of personality, and a fighting spirit springs that value which alone entitles a people to look around with glad hope, and that alone is also the condition for the life which men then desire."

His speeches continue to be calls to arms for the German people.

CHAPTER FIVE

DASHING TO THE TAPE
1930

THE LETTER OFFERING Ralph Metcalfe a college scholarship remains in a drawer in his dresser, unacknowledged and unanswered. He waits to tell his mother about the offer. Metcalfe knows he will, but he holds back and takes it slow. It's not like him to hesitate, but a part of him knows what she will say. Metcalfe fears it won't be the right decision to make.

Marquette University is a Catholic institution, and it's one more reason the college interests him. He's always held a casual interest in the Catholic Church, especially after seeing his mother become a convert herself. His mother is impressed with "their sincerity of purpose, their zealousness, their calmness in travail because of their religion."

Competing in track and field at Marquette University will open doors for him, yet Metcalfe considers the cost of going off to college. Even with a scholarship, there will be books and meals to pay for. He also wonders how he will be able to help support his family in Chicago when he's studying for classes in Milwaukee, Wisconsin.

Times haven't gotten any easier for folks in the country, not now in 1930. Almost a year after the collapse of the stock market, the nation suffers at the start of its Great Depression. To attain any sort of education is now a luxury. Several thousand schools have either shortened their hours or shut down completely. Around 3 million children from kindergarten to high school age drop out of school; many of the older high school kids flee to search for jobs by hopping on railroad trains or any by other means possible. Attending a university seems almost unworldly to a young man like Metcalfe.

One evening at home that summer, Ralph decides to ask his mother what she thinks about his taking the scholarship and starting school at Marquette. At first, she can't believe he didn't tell her, then she looks him directly in the eye with an intensity he has never seen before.

"Boy, if I've gotta get on my hands and knees and scrub these white people's floors, you are going to college."

With an answer like that, there's no longer a question or choice about Marquette University. Ralph not only has his mother's blessing. He also has a slight kick in the butt for entertaining any other option.

· · ·

"Jimmy! Come over here."

James LuValle looks over at Coach Eddie Leahy and wonders if he's going to be asked to leave the track. He decided to come out here this afternoon just to kill some time before heading to work at the library. On most days he walks over to the library right after classes end at Polytechnic High School and works until ten o'clock every night. The last thing James expects is to be singled out by the track coach.

"Jimmy, I want you to run the 660 against Sam," Coach Leahy says.

LuValle smiles and shakes his head. "I don't know how to run a 660."

Sam is a very good half-miler, and LuValle knows he can't keep up the pace with the guy.

Leahy pats him on the shoulder. "Just run it."

"Okay."

The seventeen-year-old knows nothing about track and field. Outside of his job at the Los Angeles Public Library, LuValle spends his time studying and earning straight As. Chemistry is his passion and love. He's no runner. But for some reason Coach Leahy wants him to race.

LuValle starts the race running alongside Sam. He doesn't know how fast or slow to go. He simply keeps the pace, and then when the end approaches, he has enough in his tank to beat Sam in this 660. Both Coach Leahy and Sam appear surprised at how well he ran the race.

"You're a quarter-miler," the coach tells him as he tries to catch his breath.

"What do you mean I'm a quarter-miler?" LuValle asks.

"You need to join the team. We have a meet in two days."

LuValle wants to object. He's never competed in a 660 or a quarter-mile, and he has his job at the library every evening. But Coach Leahy is convincing. For Leahy, LuValle's running is a no-brainer, since he obviously has some talent.

He has played basketball and football, but James doesn't consider himself a fast runner. However, he is curious to see what might result from at least trying. As with any sort of science experiment, you have to first try out different combinations and attempts in order to reach a goal. Maybe Coach Leahy is right; maybe LuValle can run the quarter-mile.

Two days later, LuValle represents L.A. Poly in a track meet alongside another newcomer to the team, Sinclair Lott. Coach Leahy suggested the quarter-mile for Lott as well. Moments before the race, LuValle asks the coach the only question on his mind.

"How do I run this race?"

The grin on Coach Leahy's face should've given it away, but Lu-Valle doesn't yet know the man is a bit of a joker.

"Boys, get out and run as fast as you can as far as you can, then start sprinting."

Later in life, LuValle states the obvious about the race. "Both Sinclair and I were stupid enough to believe him."

A quarter-mile is 440 yards. Sprinters run as fast as they can with the 100 and mostly with the 200, but not with a distance slightly over one lap around the track. Young James LuValle and Sinclair haven't learned those facts, however.

When the race begins, both bolt from their starting positions and don't slow down a bit. The other competitors are surprised or amused by the rookies in the race. Sinclair and LuValle stay side by side for most of the quarter-mile, both of them believing they should be able to run as fast as possible and then sprint to the finish line. Their gasping, flailing sprint at the end is more of a rocky slowdown, but the two runners are so far ahead of everybody else that they easily win, staggering across the finish line with LuValle barely edging out Sinclair.

Kneeling on the track after the race, sucking in air and feeling as though he might die, LuValle doesn't notice Coach Leahy at first. He instead sees bright lights every time he blinks, and it seems as if his lungs have temporarily stopped working. Once he can clearly look up he notices his coach.

"Now that's not the way to run the quarter-mile, is it?" Coach Leahy asks, laughing as if he just heard the world's greatest joke ever.

* * *

Marquette University might want Ralph Metcalfe to attend its school, but it seems America doesn't want someone of his color, at least not yet. As he marches into Soldier Field on September 3, 1930, representing his country along with fellow athletes and citizens supporting this international track meet versus Great Britain,

Metcalfe sees only two other African Americans along with him: John Lewis, the quarter-miler from University of Detroit, and Gus Moore of the Brooklyn Harriers. There is also Eddie Tolan, whom the forty thousand spectators want to see, but they will have to wait until his event starts. Tolan was held out of the procession around the field in order to be fresh for the first big event of the evening, the 440-yard relay.

Memories of the last few years and how he's arrived at this point flood his mind. In three short years, Ralph has been instrumental in leading Tilden High to three state titles in track. From 1928 to 1930, he wins both the 100- and 220-yard dashes. At the National Interscholastic Meet and the University of Michigan Interscholastic Meets, he runs record times in both events. Competing for the Chase Park Athletic Club, Ralph wins the Amateur Athletic Union (AAU) junior championships in both sprint events and places fourth in the national senior AAU 220-yard dash. Success has come as fast and as furiously as his sprints.

Metcalfe now enters the competition at Soldier Field with a healthy combination of excitement and uncertainty. The *Chicago Tribune* announced the competition two days before it began:

"Sixty-six athletes were chosen yesterday at Pittsburgh, PA, for the 54 places on the American track and field team which will meet the stars of the British empire at Soldiers' Field Wednesday night. It will be the fourth series of international meets and the first held in the United States."

Running against high school students in Illinois is one thing, but against international running stars? This will certainly be a test of things to come for Ralph, not only because it's an international competition, but also since he'll be competing in front of thousands of onlookers.

Metcalfe imagines that all of the fanfare surrounding the event— including a speech by Secretary of State William R. Castle, and the grandeur of the band playing "The Star-Spangled Banner" and "God Save the King"—must be what parading into an Olympic Stadium feels like. The Summer Olympics are less than two years away.

The anticipation for this event was dampened a couple days before it began when Metcalfe and the rest of the black athletes were forced to stay at a colored hotel while the rest of the American teams lodged at the Illinois Athletic Club. However, the black athlete on Great Britain's team, Phil Edwards, was not discriminated against, being able to stay with his team at the Medinah Athletic Club. Edwards competed on the 1928 Canadian Olympic team, and being from British Guiana, he was allowed to play on the British team. Eddie Tolan considered not competing in the meet because of the segregation, yet after hearing his mother's admonition he decides to run.

The track meet organizers might treat the black athletes in a different way, but the sea of spectators they compete in front of holds no reservations. Along with cheering for Eddie Tolan, the crowd also stands and applauds Metcalfe. The two black men won't race each other in the 100-yard dash since Eddie focuses solely on the 220-yard sprint and the mile medley relay, but many future meets await them.

The *Chicago Daily Tribune* announces the results of Ralph's race in a very big way under the front headline "United States Beats British Athletes, 9-5." The photo front and center show a strong, tall black kid outrunning a pack of strong, tall white kids. The contrast in the black and white photo can't be any more prominent, yet the newspaper is still sure to pinpoint the winner for their readers.

"Ralph Metcalfe, Chicago Negro, dashing to the tape in the special 100 yard race at the international meet at Soldiers' field. Metcalfe, third from the left, beat a field composed of some of the greatest sprinters in the world."

The *Pittsburgh Courier* writes of Metcalfe's victory a few days later: "He won it, for his race and for America. The thousands rose and cheered him, ignorant and unmindful of the back-room insult that had been given to Metcalfe and his race."

The same question Eddie Tolan faced when deciding whether to compete will return often in the near future, as black athletes begin to wrestle with athletic progress and racial standstill, a question the *Pittsburgh Courier* poses:

"Was the glory of winning worth more than the opportunity to indicate in a big and convincing manner his high and determined resentment against any and all means employed to discriminate against him in 'the land of the free'?"

———————————

ON MAY 24, *1930, the entire country of Germany begins its campaign to bring the Olympics to Berlin and finally fulfill the mission that started at the 1912 Games in Stockholm when the International Olympic Committee (IOC) awarded the 1916 Olympics to Germany. All the preparations that had been underway were soon interrupted by World War I. Germany hadn't forgotten; indeed, the German Olympic committee has made preparations unlike those of other groups before them. On May 24, 1930, members of the Olympic Congress are treated to a spectacle that ensures their confidence.*

Gathering in the town of Grünau, a community located on the west bank of the Langer See, the IOC members stand alongside the Regatta Course southeast of Berlin as they are welcomed by the Germans. Boat races of all kinds have been held on the waters around Grünau since 1870, when Kaiser Wilhelm II constructed a summer pavilion for his family to watch the sporting events. At two thousand meters long and with room for six lanes, the Grünau Regatta Course held its first official regatta on June 27, 1880. Since then, numerous rowing clubs had sprouted up in the community, making Grünau the ideal setting for the Germans to show their rowing prowess to the rest of the world.

What the Olympic Congress members observe this day is nothing short of breathtaking. A procession of rowing boats glide across the racetrack, the eight oarsmen wearing all white, contrasting with the dark red cedar wood of their sixty-foot-long shells. The long, narrow wood blades move in unison, driving into the water and then swinging back again. Soon the entire course resembles the stars in the sky on a clear night as the procession of two thousand German rowing teams advances across the tranquil waters. The influential IOC delegates are invited on the rowboats to personally take in the proposed course for the future games.

With the popularity of rowing in the 1920s and 1930s, the Germans make a wise choice to show off the course at Grünau along with their rowing teams. At the time, it is one of the favorite spectator sports in the Western World, drawing thousands of people to watch the events. As the IOC members gather at the final reception on the grounds of the German Sport Forum, most have already decided Berlin and the Germans are ready.

CHAPTER SIX

THE UNDERESTIMATED

1931

T HE CROWD SPILLS out of the stands, lining the field and crowding one another along with the 235 women preparing to compete. Fifteen thousand spectators have flocked to Pershing Field in Jersey City, New Jersey, to watch the ninth national track and field championships, which includes eleven defending champions and eight Olympians. Most are eager to watch the phenom from Texas who has captured the attention of the entire country.

"There she is," Coach Quaine says to Louise, pointing toward the track at the pale girl in the bright orange outfit.

Louise stares at the nineteen-year-old woman she has heard all about on the four-hour drive from Malden, Massachusetts, to Jersey City. Warming up for the 80-meter high hurdles, Babe Didrikson doesn't look like some unbeatable superstar. Her cropped, straight brown hair makes her look tough, but she isn't towering or imposing in size. Her demeanor stands out, however; there's something about the way the girl carries herself. The slight grin on her lips, resembling almost a smirk, appears confident, maybe cocky, and perhaps downright contemptuous.

She looks like she's already won her races.

Coach told the girls that Babe Didrikson excelled in all types of sports. Baseball, basketball, golf, swimming, tennis, and boxing. She has barely won any track events, but people are still there to watch her and to see if she will live up to the hype.

The Saturday in late July is cloudy but humid, perhaps adding to the pressure building on the sidelines. The crowd crams into the makeshift stands and squeezes along the field, edging out onto the track itself. Police mounted on horses march over the grass to control the crowd. Louise watches the spectacle in amazement, not just at all the onlookers but at the popularity of the event. She has come without any expectations, but her anxiousness grows as the events unfold.

Louise notices one of Babe's teammates getting her water, as if she is already the star receiving preferential treatment. "Babe" is the nickname she took from the famous baseball player after she hit five home runs in a game during her youth. Born in Port Arthur, Texas, Mildred Didrikson is the sixth of seven children born to Ole and Hannah Didriksen, immigrants from Norway. As with so many families, money is tight and scarce, so Mildred worked many part-time jobs when she was young. What she loves, however, is playing sports with her brothers and competing against boys. It's always a sweet victory when she beats the boys.

Bold, outspoken, and already known for having a foul mouth on her, the Texan never doubts her abilities. Never has this confidence been displayed more than on this day. When Babe's first race finally begins, Louise watches in fascination just like everybody else. Didrikson doesn't get off the line as quickly as the others; in fact, she has the slowest start of the field. Yet she swiftly makes up the distance and never slows down. Running the steps between the hurdles with clocklike precision, gliding inches over each obstacle, Babe breaks away from everyone in a blink, swatting away the 80 meters as if it is only 50 yards. Everybody, including Louise, finds themselves amazed.

Babe sets a world record in the hurdles race with a time two-tenths of a second faster than the world mark. At the end of the event in Jersey City this day, Babe leads all scorers with three victories. Along with 80-meter hurdles, she easily wins the long jump and also sets a world record in the baseball throw.

The hype has been justified. Didrikson really is a phenomenon. And the country will continue to hear about it. Arthur Daley of the *New York Times* writes about Babe the following day on July 26:

"A new feminine athletic marvel catapulted herself to the forefront as an American Olympic possibility at Pershing Field in Jersey City yesterday when 19-year-old Miss Mildred (Babe) Didrikson of Dallas broke the world's record for the 80-meter high hurdles, shattered the American mark for the baseball throw and topped off her activities with a victory in the running broad jump."

Never mentioned is Louise Stokes's fourth-place finish in the 50-yard dash, as it shouldn't have been. She is still starting out and is not in Babe's league. She is simply thrilled to be at an event like this. The thought of doing anything more, such as breaking records, being a national champion, and heading to the Olympics, is absurd to Louise.

Coach Quaine, on the other hand, is a believer. He knows he has someone as special as Babe running and training for him. He just needs to make Louise believe that about herself.

• • •

James LuValle can still picture his second-place finish in the quarter-mile race behind Carl Satterfield in the city meet. With his eyes closed for a moment while recuperating in a hospital bed, he remembers nearly beating John McCarthy in the state meet in Visalia that year. The difference between first and second place is only a foot. Barely twelve inches from winning. As he finally opens his eyes to see the familiar bare walls and muted colors of the hospital room, the eighteen-year-old realizes victory in any sort of sport is now miles away.

In his senior year at L.A. Polytechnic High School, LuValle takes for granted how fast he can run, and where that speed can take him. He receives a scholarship offer to play football at Notre Dame, as well as an offer to both play football and run track at USC. With decisions to make and a future set to begin a few months from high school graduation day, LuValle finds himself in agony on a June day at the start of the summer. A sharp, burning sensation suddenly tears through his lower right abdomen. Every time he moves or takes in a deep breath or sneezes or barely coughs, the pain intensifies. He feels sick to his stomach, eventually vomiting, the ache unbearable. When he finally goes to see a doctor, his ruptured appendix is discovered. Not only that, but peritonitis sets in, causing an inflammation of the tissue that lines the abdominal wall.

The worst part for LuValle and his family comes after he slips into a coma, one that lasts nearly a month. Appendicitis and peritonitis in the 1930s are very, very dangerous and life-threatening, especially since there are no antibiotics to treat them. Instead, all they can do is flush out his insides every day with chlorine water. Altogether LuValle spends the next six months in and out of the hospital.

With college only a couple of weeks away, LuValle finds himself trying to figure out what to do. Sports is out of the question, at least in the coming months. Being forced to go into the emergency room and being unconscious cause James to face the reality that tomorrow is not guaranteed. He can't help asking himself a question:

What do I really want to do?

Ultimately, he decides he wants an education. That is more important than pursuing something fun like football or track.

Realizing he won't get the sort of education at Notre Dame or USC that he can receive at other places, LuValle considers Caltech, the California Institute of Technology. He had the grades to get into the school, but he doesn't have enough money to afford it. When he gets out of the hospital, he goes to talk to the advisors at Caltech. They encourage him to go to UCLA for a year and then eventually transfer.

LuValle takes their advice and enters the University of California in Los Angeles. No one from the athletic department knows LuValle has enrolled. They all knew about his offers from the other schools and assumed James had taken one. There are no track scholarships offered at UCLA at the time. All he can do is continue to make stellar grades and continue to work, saving up his money.

LuValle finds a job in the chemistry department that year. Competing in track is still a possibility when the time comes for the season to begin the following spring. First LuValle talks to Dean Cromwell, the track coach at the University of Southern California, and asks what will happen if he joins their track team. Coach Cromwell knows exactly what he'll do with LuValle.

"We'd get you out and run you on the track," the coach tells James.

LuValle then approaches Harry Trotter, the UCLA track coach, with the same question. He hadn't spoken to the coach until after he started classes, and there has been no pressure on LuValle to compete during his freshman year.

"Well, what do you think you should do?" Coach Trotter asks James.

"I don't think I'll try to run for a year," LuValle says. "I think I ought to build myself up slowly."

"If that's what you want to do, that's what you'll do."

LuValle appreciates the response from Coach Trotter and feels confident about his decision to stay at UCLA. Since there is no scholarship for James at UCLA, he doesn't push himself to go out

James LuValle UCLA student photo.

there and perform on the track. At the end of his first semester, LuValle works hard enough to earn a regents scholarship. This along with his job in the chemistry department makes him completely independent from the athletic program.

The desire to run remains, pumping through him like the blood flowing through his heart. Some things in life might rupture, but the passion to run isn't one of them.

. . .

Louise Stokes makes the other girls nervous. She can tell by the way they look at her, steadily watching her stretch on the grass and then jog on the track at Fens Stadium. None of the other girls paid much attention to the black girl from Malden until she set a New England record for the 100-meter race at a meet at Norumbega Park just two months ago. Louise broke the former mark by a second, finishing ahead of longtime favorites Olive Hasenfus and Marie Wendt by three or four yards. The paper went on to say that "the Negro girl was practically unbeatable."

Now all the girls on the other teams know. Their coaches tell them to pay attention to Louise. To watch out.

Four hundred people fill the stands on this nineteenth day in September to watch seventy girls compete in Mayor James Curley's Day Races. Eyes watch as hopefuls for next year's Olympics in Los Angeles will emerge. Louise is already being talked about as a potential Olympic candidate. Today is a test to see if she can repeat her earlier success.

Louise barely has a chance to breathe after arriving at the stadium. Since she is competing in three events, she must transition quickly from one heat for the 50-yard dash, to another for the 100-meters, then finally to the broad jump. She makes the finals for all events.

Before the start of the 100-meter race, Louise learns that Mary Carew is a scratch for the event. Carew, one of the national champions, has created a lot of buzz with the two of them finally competing against one another. Louise wonders if perhaps Carew is nervous about getting beat by someone else. By a "Negro girl."

Wearing a white, sleeveless shirt and black shorts that match her running shoes, Louise steps up to the line. Spectators kneel and stand close to the track to watch her. Well-dressed men and women, young boys and girls. Black folks mixed in with white folks. She moves into position and readies herself, awaiting the crack of the gun.

Then she is off.

Mere seconds separate Louise from the starting line and the finish, yet somehow seventeen years seem compressed inside them.

One second.

She pictures her beloved sister, Alice. Sweet, young, four years old, and always following after her. Always at her back and eager to chase, clutch, hug, and tug. Maybe Alice watches her from Heaven. Perhaps she is helping her out, blowing her along.

Two seconds.

She visualizes her parents, William and Mary Stokes. Her father's pleasant demeanor and her mother's hard-working spirit. The man twenty years older than the woman he asked to marry. They watch with the rest of her siblings. Louise doesn't have to see them on the sidelines to know they are there with her. Rooting for her. Running in spirit with her.

Three seconds.

The image of those streets and those train track ties in Malden she used to run over passes through her mind. She sees the boys she eventually outran.

Four seconds.

She hears Coach Quaine as he gives the team instructions while running the path along the rails, or as he encourages her one on one. His words of motivation affirm that she is the fastest one out there.

Five seconds.

An image flashes through her mind of the masculine girl who has captured the nation's attention earlier that year. Known to all as Babe.

Six seconds.

Somewhere Olive Hasenfus is close to her on this track, gliding as she always does, though Louise can't see anybody on either side of her.

Seven seconds.

The faces, cheers, applause, and eyes all pass by as she blasts toward the finish.

Eight seconds.

Tomorrow's *Boston Post* will write, "the dusky Louise was here, there and everywhere in the meet."

Nine seconds.

Another paper calls her "the flying mercury from the Onteora Club."

Ten seconds.

She knows she will win the race. The question will be how fast did she run?

Eleven seconds.

She sees the finish line right there, right in front of her.

Twelve seconds.

Plowing forward with her arms moving and her head straight, Louise crosses the line, winning with no competitor near her. The winning time of 12 and ⅗ seconds sets a New England record by a girl in the 100-meter event, breaking her own mark earlier that year.

By the end of the day, Louise earns second place in the 50-yard dash behind national champion Mary Carew and third place in the high jump.

While misspelling her name, the *Boston Post* states that "Miss Louis Stokes . . . easily proved herself the star performer of the day's happenings and was awarded the Mayor James M. Curley Cup for the athlete furnishing the greatest all-round performance . . . no one could deny that she was entitled to the beautiful trophy."

Along with earning three medals, Louise wins the two-feet-tall bronze trophy with her name inscribed on its side. They photograph

Louise Stokes with trophy, 1931.

her sitting, in a long dress, smiling wide as she holds the Curley Cup in her hands. A beautiful young girl arrives on the scene and the public takes notice. She will have her own nickname very soon as newspapers begin referring to her as the Malden Meteor.

．　．　．

"Go on, Archie. Let us grown folks talk."

His grandmother, Fannie Wall, and the other ladies are eating ice cream in the family room and don't want fifteen-year-old Archie Williams hanging around. His grandmother's friend, Mrs. Mary McCleod Bethune, is in attendance, so it's a very important meeting. The ladies discuss civil rights, education, and raising money for various causes. Since his grandma runs the Fannie Walls Home for Children, she is always organizing a lot of meetings to raise funds for those in need.

As Archie leaves the room and heads into the kitchen, he picks up a magazine one of the ladies left on the counter. Bold letters at the top say *THE CRISIS*. He's never read a magazine before, so Archie opens it up and thumbs through the pages. What starts as mere curiosity suddenly becomes consternation as Archie sees a vivid photo of two black men hanging from a tree while a crowd of white folks mingle underneath, some even pictured with smiles. He's shocked that a magazine would publish a photo of a lynching.

Later, Archie will come to realize that *The Crisis,* a quarterly magazine published by the National Association for the Advancement of Colored People (NAACP), was founded for this very purpose, to shed light onto the darkness polluting the country. W. E. B. Du Bois, who was the first editor for the magazine and was instrumental in its publication, stated his goal with *The Crisis* was to "show the danger of race prejudice, particularly as manifested today toward colored people."

His grandmother, Fannie Wall, is invested in the movement but she's even more concerned about the lack of care the kids in the city receive, near neglect. That's why she started her home for children. Sometimes Archie visits to play with the kids. Some of the children were orphans or came from broken homes. The community supported Fannie Wall by helping to raise money for the children's home. People up and down the state were involved in securing the home.

There are many in need of help as the Great Depression begins, though Archie Williams and his family in Oakland don't know that term just yet in the spring of 1931. His mother, Lillian, works in San Francisco as a home cook, with hours that include the weekends. Just like everyone else they knew, the Williamses are simply surviving. Everyone around them was broke, with few possessions and fewer opportunities. To pitch in and help, Archie cuts lawns, shines shoes, or sells papers, whatever it takes.

They are more fortunate than others in the country. Archie's friend George has a father who works as an electrician. Al Hobs-

Fannie Franklin Wall, grandmother of Archie Williams. Circa 1900s.

worth's father is a butcher, and so is Norman Wagner's dad. Nielson is a grocer. They are all considered middle-class Americans, working long, hard hours to endure these times.

After finishing at Edison Junior High, Archie first attends Berkley High School as a freshman. Up till then, he's enjoyed playing baseball and soccer just like the other kids, but he never sees himself as an athlete and never has any illusions about developing into one. He becomes interested in track his first year of high school, yet Archie underwhelms them to death, winning one or two times but mostly coming in second and third in most of his races. He enjoys running, however, always approaching each race with the same attitude. *Today might be my day and it might not.*

Eventually, when Archie switches schools and goes to University High, he will be the third man on the relay team that will win the city track meet. It will be a small victory, but for Archie, it will be enough of a spark to make him believe that he can continue to run, that he has a future in track.

"I was told not to aim too high because I was going to fail," Archie will one day say. "My idea is to aim twice as high as you think you can go—then maybe you will get there."

HISTORY HAS SHOWN *us the power of underestimating individuals, whether they're prophets, politicians, or performers. Two remarkable interviews with Adolf Hitler illustrating this will bookend 1931. The first shows up in* The Jewish Criterion *on January 23, 1931. The editor remarks that this interview is "the only one which Germany's antisemitic leader has ever granted to a Jewish journalist." In the article, Hitler makes his hatred of the Jews very clear, yet much of the Western World at the time still pays little attention to the leader of the Nazi Party.*

"Our program is to purge Germany of all such elements as hinder its re-

turn to normal conditions," Hitler says. When pressed to be more specific, the future dictator obliges the reporter. "The Jews have infected culture and German politics with their views," he says, then later states Jews "are a real menace."

While being frank and open about his stance on Jews and other races deemed inferior to the great Aryan race, Hitler also deliberately lies about his intentions.

"I intend to do nothing against the Jews except carry on the educational campaign I have prosecuted during the last few years. I do not have to go into details. My views are known. I am the only German leader who is not afraid to speak out. I am concerned with the Jews only in so far as they obstruct the realization of the ideal German Reich."

Hitler knows the world underestimates him, so while being vocal and spreading propaganda of hate to the German people, he also remains sly and deceptive. The Jews have plenty to fear from this malevolent figure. So does the rest of the world.

Though this doesn't prevent Germany from winning its bid for Berlin to host the 1936 Olympics. With Rome and Barcelona competing with Berlin to be the host city, the final vote turns out to be forty-three for Berlin and sixteen for Barcelona. The Germans are ecstatic with the results. The Reich Commission for Physical Training announces their celebration with an official statement including the following promise:

"The world expects the German nation to organize and present this Festival in an exemplary manner, emphasizing at the same time its moral and artistic aspects. This means that all forces must be exerted, that sacrifices of a physical as well as financial nature must be made, and there is no doubt but that all expectations will be fulfilled for the advancement of the Olympic ideals and the honour of Germany."

At the end of 1931, one of America's most respected foreign correspondents, Dorothy Thompson, is granted an interview with Adolf Hitler after years of trying. She sums up her first impression without mincing words. "When I walked into Adolf Hitler's salon in the Kaiserhof hotel, I was convinced that I was meeting the future dictator of Germany. In something *less than fifty seconds I was quite sure that I was not. It took just about that time to measure the startling insignificance of this man who has set the world agog."*

Throughout the interview—published the following year in the March 1932 issue of Cosmopolitan—Thompson concludes that it is "highly improbable that in this case (Hitler) will succeed in putting through any of his more radical plans." Though it seems another part of her realizes the truth:

"Looking at Hitler, I saw a whole panorama of German faces; men, whom this man thinks he will rule. And I thought: Mr. Hitler you may get, in the next elections, the fifteen million votes which you expect.

But fifteen million Germans CAN be wrong."

CHAPTER SEVEN

QUALIFIED AND CONFIDENT
1932

C HICAGO, THE GRITTY metropolis by the lake, finds itself in desolation by the third year of the Great Depression. With its dependence on manufacturing, half of the working force in this sector becomes wiped out by 1932. The African American and Hispanic communities that flocked to the Windy City for better opportunities are now recoiling. Mexican workers leave to find better conditions, while 50 percent of the black laborers find themselves jobless. By February 1932, the emergency relief funds for Chicago are gone, and the churches and charities in the city become strapped, with few resources to help those in need.

However, even among the financial turmoil of the country and the world, the jubilant spirit that sports summons has not diminished. In every game and race there is always the same possibility: the hope of winning. Deep in the heart of a frigid Chicago, this hope ignites a young man who knows he has just seen pure gold running in front of him.

John Brooks realizes the petite girl is special. He doesn't have to hear about the four-year-old record she tied while winning the 60-yard run today at the indoor track meet. All he wants to know is the girl's name and where she lives. An idea has already sprouted.

I want to coach her.

Standing in the newly completed Naval Armory located on the lakefront at Randolph Street, Brooks comes to this Olympic preparatory meet in the three-deck Gothic building to observe the most talented women athletes from Illinois and Wisconsin compete. Just thirty days into the new year, naturally the event needs to be held indoors. Brooks walks over to talk to the small teen girl who is running for the Board of Education playground team.

"Good job out there," he tells her as he glances down and catches her gaze.

"Thank you."

"What's your name?"

Tidye Pickett with John Brooks on the practice field.

"Tidye. Tidye Pickett."

"You're fast, Tidye Pickett," Brooks says, offering to shake her hand. "I'm John Brooks. I'm on the track team for the University of Chicago. I do the broad jump."

He studies her dark locks pulled back in a ponytail and her steady, strong eyes looking at him.

"How old are you?" Brooks asks.

"Seventeen."

Even though she is petite, he can tell she is muscular and fit.

"And where do you go to school?"

"Englewood High."

"Let me ask you, Tidye. Have you ever thought about being in the Olympics?"

If she hasn't before, she will start to now. Despite the *Chicago Tribune* publishing a photo of a pretty white girl jumping over a hurdle in Tidye's win, the headline reads "New Playground Star Ties National 60 Yard Record" as they remind readers that Tidye is a "colored sprinter from Board of Education."

Days later, John Brooks visits the Pickett household across from Washington Park intent on persuading Mrs. Sarah Pickett to allow him to train her daughter. For a while, Brooks isn't sure it will happen. He explains the value he brings as a trainer and the years of experience he has competing in track and field. Not to mention that Tidye will be competing to make the Olympics, too. Brooks knows that as a young African American girl, Tidye might not be afforded the coaching and training she deserves. He wants to give that to her.

Mrs. Pickett knows the impact a black girl going to the Olympics for the first time can make. She can't just ignore the issues that plague the African American community. She listens to the young man talk about how confident he is in Tidye's abilities.

When Sarah Pickett finally gives Brooks her permission, he feels a great sense of pride and excitement. There is something about this tiny Tidye, something he knows other athletes don't possess. There is a furious spark deep inside her, a strength that allows her to explode when she begins to run. He wonders how he might fan that spark and how much he can help build her strength.

Before Brooks begins to train Tidye, he decides to give her a gift. He buys her proper running spikes and a new sweat suit to replace the ones she had worn for years. Brooks makes it clear that he is committed to doing whatever he can to build her confidence and speed.

• • •

There are two things Ralph Metcalfe's mother tells him before he heads off to Marquette University his first year.

"Go get an education," she says, "and become the world champion, too."

He starts his track career at Marquette in 1932 with a loss in the 40-yard dash to a teammate, John Tierney. This is definitely not the way to become a champion, much less to begin a running career. It will, however, be the last race he ever loses while wearing the white shirt with the Marquette name across it.

By the spring of 1932, track season is in full swing. Metcalfe does double duty as an athletic trainer and a runner. He earns forty dollars a month assisting the athletic program in multiple ways, enough money to pay for his room, transportation, and books. The work also allows him to get to know a lot of students, and it doesn't take long for him to become a well-known face on campus.

By the time May and June arrive with important meets determining who goes to the Olympics, Metcalfe has forgotten what it feels like to lose. At the close of May, he has won both the 100-yard race, in 9.6 seconds, and the 220-yard dash, in 20.4 seconds. Now, in mid-June, he competes at the ninth NCAA Championship held on the track of the University of Chicago.

As a sprinter, Metcalfe knows the anomaly of his size: At five feet eleven inches and 180 pounds he is more suited for football. News-paper reporters already remark about his stature, with one calling him "a mass of rippling and perfectly coordinated muscles." His sole concern is improving his start. It's the weakest part of his race, something he and Coach Con Jennings have worked on repeatedly. It takes some experimenting but Metcalfe eventually finds an effective start that works for him.

Metcalfe lines up for the 100-yard dash and readies for the start. Keeping his big frame coiled as tight as possible, he bolts out of the starting position with his feet running close, his hips high. After several steps he finds himself ahead, finishing with a victory and a time of 9.5 seconds, equaling the world record. His coach compliments Metcalfe on how hard he drove in the race, digging his spikes into the track while propelling his arms ahead and leaning forward.

The 220-yard dash allows him to truly use his full strength, running with a steady velocity as smooth as a freight train. The great Jesse Owens confirms this himself years later when the two begin to race each other. "Ralph Metcalfe was a locomotive. If you were ahead of him, you had to worry every second wondering about how fast he was catching up with you. And if you were behind him, you lost."

With more track to accelerate and work with in 220 yards, Metcalfe ends up leading the pack easily down the home stretch. The grandstands at the University of Chicago field are full, men and women standing to watch and cheer. A crowd capturing a hope that isn't as evident in their day to day lives of survival. The white hurdles rest on the grass next to the track, with reporters, coaches, and officials wearing suits and ties watching carefully. Metcalfe's powerful legs push his quick pace, yet he forces nothing and holds no worries about winning. As his chest catches the tape at the finish line, he neither struggles nor strains. Behind him, the faces and the bodies of his competitors say it all. The runner from Ohio, right next to him, reaches the finish with a grimace of pain. Another runner looks

Ralph Metcalfe on the track at Marquette University.

as if he will topple over. One runner faces down, everything in him having given up. Two others on the side battle over fourth and fifth place, both with coiled muscles in their legs, arms, and neck trying to find every single available inch.

Metcalfe is happy with his time of 20.5 seconds. This time he doesn't tie the world record. He breaks it.

His day isn't over, however. By the end of the meet, Metcalfe not only cements his footprints onto this track in his hometown but also confirms his place in history with the reporters of the day. Newspapers all across the country announce his greatness. The *Star Tribune* from Minneapolis: "Metcalfe, in one of the most sensational individual performances in track history, shattered the world record for the 220 yard dash, the 100 meters, the 200 meters and the accepted world record of 9.5 seconds for the century. Metcalfe's performance, topping an afternoon of record breaking, was hailed as the greatest achievement since Charlie Paddock broke the world records for the 100 and 220 in one afternoon back in 1921."

Metcalfe is running better than anybody in the country at the right time. The 1932 Olympic trials are a month and a half away, and the only surprise the trials might bring is who will be competing for gold against Metcalfe in the games held in Los Angeles.

Unfortunately, speed isn't the only determining factor in making it to the Olympics. He still has to find a way to pay for some of the expenses for the trip cross-country.

* * *

At the Olympic trials for the women, the sun seems to dare anyone to be outside for too long on this summer day. The men's and women's trials are held in separate locations, with the female athletes competing at Northwestern University in Evanston, Illinois. As Louise Stokes walks across the field at Dyche Stadium, she notices a girl from another team being carried by her coach. The girl looks exhausted and dehydrated, her face red, sweaty, completely drained. The races are already taking their toll on some of the athletes, with the seven heats of around eight racers followed soon after with the semifinals. Coach Quaine isn't about to carry her from event to event, but he does stress one thing over and over again.

"Conserve your energy for the finals," he advises.

Quaine never doubts Louise's ability to make the finals. With the success she has had leading into the Olympic trials, Louise herself remains confident she will be among the finalists.

Louise has taken home the Curley Cup for the second year in a row along with winning the 100-yard dash at the New England Amateur Athletic Union. She also wins the National Junior 40-yard dash championship. Her accomplishments don't stop there. Louise breaks the world record for the women's standing broad jump at the end of 1931, jumping 8 feet 5¾ inches. However, there isn't a standing broad jump event for the Olympics, so Louise only competes in the crowded 100 meters.

I can't believe I'm actually here, Louise thinks throughout the course of the day.

From the moment the coach tells the Stokes family that Louise is invited to the trials, a sense of doubt fills Louise. Her parents' reaction is mixed; they are thrilled they have a daughter who is going to do something they never dreamed of, yet they are sad this is something they just don't have the money to make happen. Her siblings know this opportunity means they will have to do more than their share of chores. Louise doesn't worry about the chores and who has to do them, but she's anxious that Coach Quaine won't be able to raise enough money to send her to the trials.

At the very last minute, her track club figures out a way to sponsor Louise, giving Quaine permission to take her to the trials. After a long trip from Boston to Chicago, Louise and Coach Quaine arrive a little later than the other girls. This prevents her from having time to practice on the track. Many of the other top-ranked girls have ample time to practice, since so many live in Chicago.

While mostly confident, given her many previous wins, Louise lets an ounce of trepidation enter as she waits for the final 100-meter race.

If only I'd had more time to practice.

When she mentions this to her coach before the trials, he shrugs it off without a worry on his face.

"You're going to have more time to train for the Olympics," Coach Quaine tells her.

There's no hint of doubt in his voice, no thought that she won't succeed. Seeing Quaine's confidence fills her with the same belief that the Olympic games aren't some far-off dream two thousand miles away.

The day has already been full of drama. As more than five thousand people stand watching the first sets of heats in the 100 meters from the stands, a local favorite named Ethel Harrington fails to qualify when she stops running after 80 meters, mistaking the location of the finish line. Tidye runs a 12.4 in her heat, besting Babe Didrikson's 12.6. To the chagrin of the competitors, meet officials allow Harrington to compete in the finals even though she failed to qualify. Louise knows if this happened to her—if she hadn't finished the race—no one would argue on her behalf to allow her to run in the finals. No one except for Coach Quaine.

Babe Didrikson continues to capture the crowd's attention. Every time Louise sees her, Babe is running, jumping, posing for a photograph. Before the races, the Texan announces to the 250 competitors, "Ah'm gonna lick you single-handed," and that's exactly what she proceeds to do. She not only beats all the other girls on the track that day, but she also hurdles over the rules for competition. A "three-event rule" has been set in place in order to allay any concerns about the health and safety of women competing in track and field. The Rules of the Amateur Union in Force state on January 1, 1932, that "no woman shall be allowed to compete in more than three events in one day, of which three events not more than two shall be track events." On this day, however, Babe competes in eight events, despite the resistance she receives from Fred Steers, the manager of the Olympic team and the chairman for the AAU women's track and field committee. Steers informs Babe she needs to scratch certain events, but she ignores him and participates in them when her name gets called. Several times an event is put on hold in order for Babe to finish her other race, leaving the other girls to stand waiting in the heat.

With the meet beginning at 2:00 p.m., the afternoon blisters on, the cinder track radiating like a stove. A block of ice appearing to weigh more than one hundred pounds is delivered on the side of the field, and all the girls take turns sitting on it. Louise notices some cracks and holes on the track due to the heat and all the day's activities.

The 100-meter race is the crowd favorite. The six qualifying competitors are Wilhelmina von Bremen, Elizabeth Wilde, Louise Stokes, Tidye Pickett, and Mary Carew, plus Ethel Harrington, who receives special permission to compete in the lineup. Initially, when the officials allow Ethel Harrington to compete in the six slots for the finals in the 100, Tidye loses her spot and is moved to seventh position. Fortunately, she has an ally pleading her case to be on the team. The *Chicago Defender* describes the dilemma afterward:

"Miss Pickett will have to thank George T. Donoghue, member of the South Park commission and one of the judges, for her success. . . . Miss Pickett became seventh and was thus automatically out of it. Then Mr. Donoghue stepped up and fought for Tidye's place in the finals in view of the charity being shown the other girl. Mr. Donoghue, white, is to be congratulated for his fairness in the Race girl's behalf."

The drama before the 100 meters foreshadows more controversy. For now, the race is all that matters on this sweltering day.

The gun fires. The close pack sprints and Ethel pulls out ahead slightly. Ten yards from the finish line, she stops running, apparently thinking she's already crossed it. Ethel doesn't finish the race and is disqualified. Louise, Mary Carew from Medford Girls Club, and Tidye are a three-way tie at 12.5, a satisfying finish, since the top six runners make the Olympic team. Carew is a familiar competitor Louise has grown used to running against. She isn't as familiar with the other black sprinter from Chicago, Tidye Pickett. Wilhelmina and Elizabeth tie for second at 12.4 and Ethel wins at 12.3.

Louise discovers just after the day's races that she isn't going back home to Massachusetts. The team waves 'bye to a tearful Evelyn Furtsch, who did not make the team, watching her slide into the car with her coach and mother for the long drive back home to Tustin, California. Louise and the rest of the girls' Olympic team depart from Chicago via train to head west. Coach Quaine is ecstatic, shouting how she's earned the right to represent Uncle Sam in Los Angeles. It feels surreal to Louise, something she simply can't believe until she sets foot in California herself.

The buzz of that day centers solely on Babe, who wins six of the eight events she entered. She doesn't usually compete in the discus throw, so her fourth-place finish isn't a surprise. Yet losing her heat in the 100 meters by a step might sting, despite her taking home six gold medals along with breaking four world records and single-handedly earning more points than the second-place team at the stadium. One reporter calls Babe's performance "the most amazing series of performances ever accomplished by any individual, male or female, in track and field history."

Lost to the Paramount newsreel and the major papers, whose headlines are obsessed with the nineteen-year-old Texan hurricane, is the story of two younger girls; eighteen-year-old Louise and seventeen-year-old Tidye. In the same quiet and respectful manner they have carried with them up to this moment, Louise and Tidye suddenly enter the history books by being the first two African American women to be heading to the Olympics. The *Chicago Defender*, taking a special interest in these particular athletes, knows the significance and states, "The prejudiced South would not have permitted these two stars to enter a race with their white sisters."

· · ·

Across the country in a stadium in Stanford, California, Ralph Metcalfe blasts off the starting line, putting himself ahead of the other runners to begin the 100-meter final. These Olympic trials are held on the same day as the women's trials, on July 16. Metcalfe entered Stanford Stadium after sweeping every race he'd entered at the Central Collegiates, the Drake Relays, and the NCAA and the AAU championships. The unusual fast beginning proves to be a false start for Metcalfe, so the runners have to get set once again. His second start was stand strong.

Running against him was the formidable Eddie Tolan, another black runner, who looked nothing like the powerful Metcalfe. As one of only two black athletes from the University of Michigan, Tolan is seven inches shorter and thirty-five pounds lighter than Metcalfe. He runs with his left knee wrapped in a bandage to protect it from a knee-ligament injury he received while playing football, one that ended his football career and left him with a visible limp. The thick eyeglasses he taped to his head in the races make him look more like a mad scientist than an Olympic runner. Metcalfe knows Tolan is fast, however; there is a reason the students at his high school in Detroit called him "The Midnight Express."

Eddie Tolan set a record in 1929 in the 100-yard dash along with tying the record in the 100-meter dash. From 1929 to 1931, Tolan won the NCAA championship in the 200- and 220-yard dashes along with the AAU championships in the 100- and the 220-yard races. That streak ended when Metcalfe stepped onto the scene and shook the ground Tolan and everybody else ran on.

Before the race, Metcalfe catches Tolan chewing gum as he always does. This habit helps to calm his nerves, and it happened by accident. One day during a workout, Tolan forgot to throw the piece in his mouth away and sprinted with it, realizing he chewed to the pace of his running. After learning about this, his coach told the runner to keep chomping on the gum during races and to chew faster to help him accelerate.

The gum-chewing doesn't stop "the Black Panther of Marquette" as one paper dubs Metcalfe, or "the Marquette Meteor" as another calls him. While Tolan leads most of the race, Metcalfe passes him with 20 meters left and wins the 100-meter event by more than two feet. He does the same with the 200 meters, catching up by the midpoint and then fighting a strong wind to once again edge out Tolan by a couple of lengths.

The stage is now set for Metcalfe and Tolan to continue to battle over the title of the world's fastest man. They will line up against one another in just two weeks on an international stage at the 1932 Los Angeles Olympics.

IN A COUNTRY *full of the unemployed and the hungry, with the grim and gaunt faces of men and women standing in long food lines waiting for bread and soup, and with the wealthy and the politicians failing to see the urgency and take action, people need hope. President Hoover offers little, stating the "economic depression cannot be cured by legislative action or executive pronouncement."*

Western Bonus Army lays siege to U.S. Capitol, spending the night on plaza lawns in protest for delay of cash-payment redemption of their service certificates from WWI. July 13, 1932.

In the midst of a failing campaign to be reelected, President Hoover faces off with veterans of World War I who camp in front of the White House. In the summer of 1928, twenty thousand veterans and family members flock to the capital to try to force Hoover to grant an early payment for a war bonus they are to receive in 1945. On July 28, only two days before the Olympic opening ceremonies in Los Angeles, with the president demanding an evacuation and the veterans refusing, Hoover commands Army Chief of Staff and Major General Douglas MacArthur to lead six hundred United States troops into Washington to clear the area. Tear gas is used on a crowd that includes wives and children. The night ends with the veterans' encampment, aptly named the "Hooverville Slums," set ablaze.

In the summer of 1932, with no shred of optimism coming out of Washington, D.C., the city of Los Angeles offers some light in a very dark time. The decision to move ahead with the games despite the crumbling strength of the country is summed up in The Games of the Xth Olympiad Los Angeles 1932 Official Report:

"In the years 1930 and 1931, when the ugly head of depression loomed

Titus Alexander congratulating the African American male members of the 1932 U.S. Olympic Track & Field Team. L to R: Cornelius Johnson, Ed Gordon, Ralph Metcalfe, and Eddie Tolan.

up before the eyes of all, Los Angeles could have retrenched in her broad programme of preparations, without neglecting any of her specific Olympic obligations. It was determined, however, that preparations should continue as scheduled, to the end that everything should be as nearly perfect as possible for the celebration of the Games, even though general participation of the nations was doubtful and liberal patronage by a financially depressed public hardly to be expected."

As eyes turn to watch what unfolds in the upcoming Olympics, six black athletes have an opportunity to instill a new kind of hope in the hearts of millions across the country. Ralph Metcalfe, Tidye Pickett, and Louise Stokes, along with Eddie Tolan, Cornelius Johnson, and Ed Gordon, enter the Los Angeles Coliseum ready to change the image of the American Olympic athlete and inspire an African American community that desperately needs some confidence amid the joblessness and hopelessness.

CHAPTER EIGHT

TOGETHER YET ALONE
1932

Feeling the steady motion of the fast-moving train as it crosses the Mississippi, Tidye Pickett imagines the notes of the trumpet and Louis Armstrong singing in her mind.

"Up the lazy river, how happy we will be . . ."

Tidye and the fifteen other girls on the Olympic track team glide over the steel railway tracks of the Union Pacific, a route that begins in Chicago and cuts through Cedar Rapids, Omaha, and North Platte until arriving for an overnight stay in Denver. They have now reached Clinton, Iowa, and the mighty Mississippi, crossing it on the 460-foot-long Clinton Rail Bridge. Thick, towering steel beams swallow them for a few seconds as their Pullman car rattles over the truss bridge. All the girls look out at the old man river, many seeing it for the first time.

The packed streets, sidewalks, stores, and schools in Chicago seem swept away like dust floating behind her. Mile after mile, Tidye looks out the window of the sleeper car and marvels at the world outside. She has seen pictures and heard stories about heading west to California and the vast plains between Chicago and Los Angeles, but her imagination has been no match for the grandeur of the landscape God has made. The smooth, gently sloping terrain covered with grass and fields stretches out to infinity.

"I wonder if the bed above us ever pops open," Louise, who sits next to her on the comfortable sofa seat, asks as she glances at the closed berth above them.

From the first time Tidye and Louise set foot in Chicago's Union Station and see the train decorated with a red, white, and blue banner that read U.S. OLYMPIC TEAM, they feel like movie stars and millionaires riding across the country in a Pullman car, lounging on plush seats that turn into beds at night. They have already decided that Louise will sleep in the upper berth while Tidye takes the lower one.

A sudden door opening and a flurry of steps rushing down the aisle cause all the girls to pause and look. Babe Didrikson whisks by in her sweat suit, acting as if she isn't in a train passing seats full of passengers. She has already done this once before, jogging in order to keep training. The girls know it's more for show than anything else. Babe ambles through the whole train, causing the same sort of commotion and sensation she provokes at track meets. For spectators, it's as entertaining as watching a movie in a theater, yet for her teammates, Babe's actions have become tiresome.

Jean Shiley is one of those teammates, a twenty-year-old from the Philadelphia suburb of Havertown who competes in the high jump. Shiley went to the 1928 Olympics, coming in fourth in the high jump event even though she hadn't expected to be competitive. After the Depression hit and her family lost everything like so many others, she left her home in Pennsylvania to go to the Olympic trials in Chicago carrying only five dollars. Shiley found a ride to Chicago, being able to eventually exchange the train ticket she'd been given for money to bring home presents from the Olympics. Once Shiley earns a place on the team and heads to Los Angeles, the girls elect her to be the captain of the team, much to Babe's displeasure.

Shiley is honest about Babe's behavior on the train years later. "She had no social graces whatsoever. She constantly wanted to be on center stage. It was impossible to know her because she was always chattering, talking, bragging . . . she ran around with her medals from Evanston, saying, 'I'm the greatest, no one's better than me, Babe Didrikson.'"

Tidye watches as Babe exits their sleeper car and enters another. She knows the Texan doesn't like her, and has felt that way from the very first time Babe saw her on the track. At least Louise is accompanying her on the trip. The other teammates seem nice and friendly as well. On their faces, many share the same expression as Tidye: a combination of surprise, shock, and sheer elation to be there. Sitting across from them is Evelyne Hall, the hurdler from Chicago whom she already knows. Evelyne is twenty-two years old and married, yet she is shy. Evelyne was a premature baby and suffered from pneumonia, scarlet fever, and scoliosis before spending a year in a body cast at twelve. In many ways, Evelyne is the opposite of Babe Didrikson. Mary Carew, whom Louise knows from her hometown in Massachusetts, is a young, naïve high school girl just like the two of them. There is Elizabeth Wilde from Kansas City, who arrived to the trials with only an overnight bag and no expectations. She travels with the same clothes and bag to Los Angeles.

As the train rattles on, Tidye shifts in her seat. She is grateful, knowing she barely made the team, and also knowing she wouldn't have been able to afford this trip if it weren't for a grant from a wealthy doctor. She is also thankful that Louise is there to ease her mind to some degree as they sit next to each other, talking, playing cards, and staring out at the scenery. Tidye finds a lot in common with Louise, the girl from up north.

*   *   *

The two young ladies have never looked more elegant. As Tidye and Louise get ready in their hotel room for a special dinner being held in the Olympic team's honor, they compliment each other on their dresses. Both are excited to attend the banquet in this opulent hotel.

For one night, the girls on the American Olympic team are treated like diplomats and movie stars at the famous Brown Palace Hotel in Denver, Colorado. Opening in 1892, the triangular red stone edifice has been built in an Italian Renaissance style. Upon entering the grand lobby off Broadway Street, guests look up to see the opulent atrium of the hotel, one of the first to use this style of design. From the moment the Brown Palace Hotel opens, it welcomes presidents, royalty, famous figures, and the elite of the world. And now, on Tuesday evening, July 19, it hosts the young women competing for the United States at the upcoming Olympics.

Those welcoming doors opening off Broadway Street remain shut for Tidye and Louise. Instead of walking into the grand lobby, the two young women are told they can't enter the hotel this way. As Babe and the coaches make a grand spectacle in their arrival at the hotel, the black women are forced to come in through the back.

The *Denver Post* sponsors the visit for the team as they stop in Colorado for two days and one night. A highlight is a banquet in the Grand Ballroom held in their honor. The ballroom on the eighth floor features a two-story ceiling and impeccable views of the surrounding Rocky Mountains.

Tidye and Louise never enter the ballroom. Before heading down to the dinner, they are told they can't eat with the rest of the team. They are directed to their special seating, a floor away. There is nothing they can do.

As Fred Steers, the team manager, and George Vreeland, the Olympic team coach, mingle and introduce the ladies of the Olympic team to the banquet's VIP guests, two remain unnoticeably absent. History barely registers Tidye and Louise's visit to the historic hotel. While the rest of the team is treated to a posh, white-tablecloth banquet in their honor, Tidye and Louise receive their dinner on a makeshift table of a hotel floor few know exists.

Since many of the guests staying at the hotel are affluent and accustomed to traveling with a maid, nurse, or servants, their "help" is allowed to stay tucked away in the attic of the hotel, the same attic Tidye and Louise now find themselves in, separated from their team's celebration. Neither the coach nor members of the team venture to Tidye and Louise's living quarters.

Louise and Tidye never had a chance to see the elegant ballroom. The only African Americans permitted to enter it are those working as waiters. There is no complaint from either girl, however. This is the world they know, and though Malden and Chicago are far better than places further south, treatment and traditions such as this are common all over the country. Even for Olympians.

Unaware of what is happening in Denver, The NAACP expresses concern for all the black athletes, especially the female athletes, and sends a telegram to Avery Brundage, the head of the American Olympic Committee, requesting fair treatment for Tidye and Louise. Brundage, however, does not respond.

The morning after the girls arrive, they go straight to a morning workout at the Denver University stadium. At least they're allowed to be chauffeured in brand-new Hudson-Essex Pacemakers. Later they put on exhibition events at Merchant Park. Tidye and Louise realize the impact altitude has on the team. The girls, as they're called in every new article, participate in interviews by the newspaper and radio station along with having their picture taken at every turn. While one interviewer speaks with a group of the girls, Babe notices she isn't participating, so she makes a commotion and gets their attention by playing her harmonica. Louise and Tidye remain mostly quiet, staying close by their coaches. The *Denver Post* lists each athlete's name with a description: students, two teachers, two stenographers, a bookkeeper, a housewife, and Babe, who was noted as the "Ace of the Squad." For the team photo, Louise stands with her arms crossed behind her back, with Fred Steers slightly in front of her. Tidye crouches directly below Louise, giving a focused, somber stare at the camera.

Years later, in 1984, Tidye will say, "There were a few athletes and team officials who did not hide their bigotry." One of those will be the biggest name on this team.

• • •

Cold water rips Tidye awake, running down her neck and her back, which are settled into the pillow and cushions of the lower berth on the sleeper train. She jerks out of the blanket and stands up, the water sprinkling her arms and legs while ice cubes drop to the floor. Tidye pats her head to see why it's so wet. She isn't sure at first if this is a dream or a nightmare until she sees the outline of Babe Didrikson standing only a few feet away in the walkway. Her hand clutches an empty pitcher.

It's late at night as the train pushes closer to the West Coast. They left Denver on July 20 and plan to reach Los Angeles by the twenty-third. Babe's antics around the team and especially on the train have only intensified. She thinks it's amusing to pull pillows out of the girls' beds while they sleep or throw them at her teammates. Tidye saw her putting ice down one of the girl's backs. This pales in comparison to the endless bluster coming from the Texan. Like the time they stopped at a station in Albuquerque, New Mexico. Babe exited the train and quickly discovered a Western Union bike not being used. She hopped on and began to pedal all around the station while screaming out, "Did you ever hear of Babe Didrikson? If you haven't you will!"

Hearing Babe proclaim her upcoming victories in the Olympics is one thing, and getting into a pillow fight with Gloria Russell another, but this is different. This isn't just Babe being silly; this act is malicious and deliberate.

As Louise climbs out of the upper bunk to see what is happening, Tidye begins to yell at Babe. Always a competitor, Didrikson doesn't back down, hurling back harsh words. Some of the other girls stir while the pocket of anger fills the Pullman car for a few moments.

Tidye doesn't believe for a second this is simple good-natured horseplay. Babe doesn't like anybody who threatens her in any way, but she seems to have a particular attitude toward the only two African Americans on the team, whether by ignoring them or by deliberately dousing them and their beds with a pitcher of water.

History confirms that Babe carries some of the racist beliefs held by many at the time. Claims would surface of Babe using the N word and belittling African Americans. One of her teachers is quoted later in life as saying Babe "really did hate blacks in those days. I think she went out of her way to antagonize them and, truly, to hurt them."

The tough, brutish Babe doesn't intimidate the girl from Chicago who barely weighs one hundred pounds. Tidye stands her ground and refuses to be bullied, telling Babe to stop it and to stay away from them.

More than fifty years later, after history records the efforts of Babe Didrikson with books, articles, photographs, and documentaries, Tidye makes one simple comment about the incident to a reporter:

"That big girl from Texas, Babe Didrikson, who won so many medals, just plain didn't like me, didn't want me on the team . . . it was prejudice, pure and simple."

• • •

Waves of people, estimated at around 105,000, fill the Olympic Stadium as the American team proceeds from the west end rounding up the Parade of Nations and marching around the track. The United States brings 400 men and 74 women to the competition. In total there are 1,334, representing thirty-seven nations. Thanks to the

Great Depression, the number competing in the 1932 Olympics is considerably less than the 2,883 representing forty-six countries in Amsterdam's 1928 Olympics.

In rows of four, the American men stride confidently in their white pants and matching comfortable short-sleeved cotton shirts. Louise and her teammates walk in long white dresses and shirts under red vests. The bell-shaped hat feels unfamiliar and awkward on her head, but that is nothing compared to how hot and uncomfortable the stockings and her tight, white buck shoes feel.

They have been in Los Angeles for seven days after their train eventually pulled into the Union Pacific station on the morning of July 23. The group photograph taken in front of the station just before they board the buses to their destination seems to reveal what Louise and Tidye are thinking. Dressed in a white, short-sleeved dress and matching cap, Louise stares at the photographers with a look of disbelief. Tidye, in a colorfully patterned dress, kneels in the first row with other girls, her face pointed down, her soul perhaps still reeling from the train ride. The two girls are proud to be cracking open a door that has been shut for a very long time. The *Pittsburgh Courier* proudly prints Tidye's picture, proclaiming, when Tidye runs the girls' relay, "The Chicago school girl will be the first colored girl ever to wear the star-spangled shield of U.S. in the world games."

For the first time in Olympic history, athletes live together in a special area known as the Olympic Village, a tradition that continues to this day. The newly built Village offers 550 portable houses, each built to accommodate four athletes in a pair of rooms. The Olympic Village also includes five dining halls and amenities such as a post office, a hospital, and a movie theater.

Only men are welcomed into the Olympic Village, however.

The women participating in the games stay at the Chapman Park Hotel on Wilshire Boulevard, ideally situated near the training grounds as well as many shops and theaters. Three American girls share a beautifully decorated large suite, consisting of a kitchen, a bathroom, and a large bedroom with desks and chairs. The official report for the 1932 Olympics would give a very complimentary overview of the accommodations:

"In the beautiful private garden adjoining the hotel, tea was served each afternoon until the day of the Opening Ceremony. After that time the Olympic guests were away at the various afternoon competitions. Meals were served in a large, beautifully decorated dining room. A general menu, prepared in American style, was served to all, and in addition, special dishes were prepared upon request for any of the groups. Pure distilled water was served in the dining rooms and was available on all the floors."

Evelyn Furtsch's father receives a phone call from Los Angeles Athletic Club board member Aileen Allen telling him to rush Evelyn to the Chapman because a room and a spot on the team have been

Los Angeles, looking north at the intersection of Hill Street and 7th Street, decorated for the Summer Games of the Xth Olympiad, 1932.

arranged for Evelyn. The week is busy with training, press interviews, and requests for photographs and autographs. Big-name Hollywood stars are seen interacting with some of the athletes. Mary Pickford and Douglas Fairbanks, Sr., visit the women's track team during dinner at Coconut Grove, wishing them good luck. Of course, in the center of it all was Babe, with her publicity-hungry manager and agent who makes the trip to support Babe, wooing all the reporters by treating them to dinners and filling their papers with all sorts of stories about Didrikson. Babe herself keeps one thing consistent; she is always quoted giving the same grand claim time and time again.

"I came out to beat everybody in sight and that's just what I'm going to do. Sure, I can do anything."

Standing in the Los Angeles Memorial Coliseum that temporarily changed its title to Olympic Stadium, Louise feels glad that all the fanfare leading up to the games is over. Tidye enjoys seeing the

1932 USA Women's track team publicity photo in opening ceremony uniforms. Los Angeles, July 1932. Standing, L to R: Evelyne Hall, Simone Schaller, Gloria Russell, Wilhelmina von Bremen, Ruth Osborn, Babe Didrikson, Evelyn Furtsch, Mary Carew, Jean Shiley, Louise Stokes. Seated: Tidye Pickett, Ethel Harrington, Elizabeth Wilde, Nan Gindele, Lillian Copeland, Annette Rogers, Margaret Jenkins.

costumes from around the world and trying to learn words in different languages. Soon they will be competing. With everyone lined up in order, the loudspeakers blast through the stadium.

"Ladies and gentlemen. We direct your attention to the tribune of honor."

Just below the press section in one part of the stadium are members of the Olympic committee standing with their elegantly dressed wives and surrounded by leaders and dignitaries from all over the world. As the horns blare, Louise looks over at the first mechanical scoreboard to be used in the Olympics and the quote displayed on it.

"The important thing in the Olympic Games is not winning, but taking part. The essential thing is not conquering, but fighting well."

These are uttered by the founder of the Modern Olympic Games, Baron Pierre de Coubertin, the same man who once stated "As to the admission of women to the Games, I remain strongly against it."

President Herbert Hoover chooses not to attend the games, in part because of the rioting taking place in Washington after World War I veterans camp out and demand their bonuses. In Hoover's place stands Vice President Charles Curtis, who proclaims "open the Olympic Games of Los Angeles, celebrating the Xth Olympiad of the Modern Era" to the crowd of more than one hundred thousand in the stadium at Exposition Park.

While standing, Louise notices Jean Shiley, their team captain, slipping off her shoes, so she follows her example and does the same. All the girls have been complaining about the cramped, ill-fitting shoes they'd been given. Now they can easily slip them off. Louise joins the other athletes from thirty-seven nations in raising her right hand and declaring the Olympic oath.

"We swear that we will take part in the Olympic Games in loyal competition, respecting the regulations which govern them and desirous of participating in them in the true spirit of sportsmanship for the honor of our country and for the glory of sport."

There is not a cloud in the sky. A warm breeze drifts by Louise,

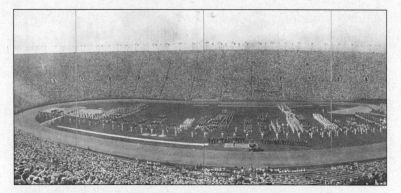

The 1932 Olympic Games opening ceremony in Los Angeles.

the sort summoned by the Pacific Ocean and quite unfamiliar to a teenager from the Boston area. As the flags adorning the stadium applaud in their motion, two thousand doves are released toward the heavens. They cluster and careen for a few seconds before scattering to the open freedom that awaits beyond the stadium. The Olympic flame bursts alive, followed by the singing of the national anthem by a one-thousand-person chorus accompanied by a two-thousand-piece orchestra.

The official report sums up the goal of the 1932 Los Angeles Olympics with an inspiring testament:

"It is the Olympic Games breathing a spirit capable of overcoming barriers of race, creed and color, spanning the centuries from 776 B. C. with an all-pervading spirit of sportsmanship and good will."

Not all barriers of race, creed, and color are overcome at these Olympics, however.

• • •

On the day of the opening ceremonies, the *Chicago Defender* announces the possible injustice with a headline that reads "Tidye Pickett May Lose Olympic Spot." Reporting that a "bit of back room

1932 USA Women's track team publicity photo. Los Angeles, July 1932.

treachery" is occurring against the African American racers, starting first by replacing Jimmy Johnson on the 400-meter relay team even though he qualified. Metcalfe, of course, is running so well that replacing him would be "downright suicide for the meet." Yet Russ Cowen from the *Defender* writes "Lily-whiteism, a thing more pronounced than anything else around here on the eve of the Olympic Games, threatened to oust Tidye Pickett and Louise Stokes from participation and put in their stead two girls who did not qualify."

Tidye and Louise assume they will be competing in the 400-meter relay in these Olympic Games. Their qualifying times assure them this will be the case. Yet days before the race, the *Chicago Defender* reports that team officials decide one of the girls who qualified behind Louise and one who didn't qualify at all will, in fact, be running instead of Tidye and Louise. "The injustice of this move is being placarded by track followers out here but to no avail, for unless

Avery Brundage rules otherwise Misses Pickett and Stokes will not run on the team."

Discovering the obvious racism at an event self-described as "overcoming barriers of race, creed and color," the NAACP sends a telegram to Jean Shiley. The message demands that Tidye and Louise receive fair treatment and compete in either 100 meters or the relay. Shiley is surprised the telegram comes to her, so she takes it to the team's coach, George Vreeland.

"We have to do something about this," Shiley tells him. "I think that we ought to give everybody a fair trial."

The coach attempts to do this. The seven girls in contention to be on the relay team race in trials against each other in the days before the games begin, having their times and starts and hand-offs with the batons all scrutinized. As the race approaches, all Tidye and Louise and the rest of the girls can do is wait to see what Vreeland and the other officials on the team decide.

―――――――――――

WHILE THE WORLD *watches the athletes competing in Los Angeles at the 1932 Summer Olympics, the Germans wait to see the results of their election on July 31. As their country suffers through the Great Depression with millions unemployed and searching for relief, Adolf Hitler plays on their desperation with an unrelenting political campaign blitzing the Germans with propaganda. The message isn't simply that Hitler is a competent leader. It defines him as Germany's savior.*

Joseph Goebbels, the Nazi Party propaganda director, leads this campaign by promoting thousands of Nazi rallies each day throughout Germany and publishing millions of pamphlets, newspapers, and posters. With the slogan "the Führer over Germany," Hitler visits twenty cities in six days to effectively deliver his message. Altogether he will give more than two hundred speeches in 1932.

On July 31, the eve of the election, Goebbels gives one more speech, in Munich, Germany. The propaganda needs to be concise and clear, and to call upon the Germans' emotions.

"Our finances have collapsed, the economy is in ruins, the factory chimneys have stopped smoking and the furnaces are cold. Seven million unemployed are on the streets, the middle class is ruined, the specter of civil war is about, farmers are driven off the land, the people are divided by class and occupation."

After a series of struggles and shifting political moves starting in 1928 when Hitler received only 2.6 percent of the national vote, the Nazis stun the German Republic in 1930 by capturing 107 seats in their parliament, with Hitler considered by many to be a revered hero of the country. Two years later, Hitler runs for the presidency against Paul von Hindenburg, the German president running for a third term. While Hitler fails to win the presidency, he realizes the 13 million votes cast for him verses the 19 million electing Hindenburg make him truly a force the republic will have to reckon with.

Strategic propaganda is the driving force that pushes the leader of the National Socialist German Workers (Nazi) Party into power. While in prison for the Beer Hall Putsch revolt, Hitler crafted his beliefs around indoctrination and publicity in Mein Kampf: "By shrewd and constant application of propaganda, heaven can be presented to the people as hell and, vice versa, the wretchedest existence as a paradise." Those closest to him know his propensity for deception, with one of his finance ministers writing that Hitler "was so thoroughly untruthful that he could no longer recognize the difference between lies and truth." These lies and half-truths matched with Hitler's oratory gifts are fueled and used by propaganda communicated not only through art, books, and theater but in new ways such as radio, records, and film.

There is another way Hitler, Goebbels, and the Nazis will implement this propaganda. Athletics. They will have four years before unleashing this on the world.

CHAPTER NINE

DEFEAT

1932

THE OLYMPIC STADIUM pulses like a heartbeat, with the crowd roaring to life to cheer the athletes on the field. Sixteen-year-old Mack Robinson feels the energy and excitement and knows this is what he wants. Not to be a spectator in the stadium he snuck into, but to be on the track warming up like the sprinters he's here to watch, feeling the adrenaline soaring through his body as it builds up to sprinting 200 meters.

The stadium is only half an hour away by car from his house on 121 Pepper Street, so getting here is easy. He is wide-eyed watching Ed Gordon win a gold medal in the long jump, but this is different. The runners on the track have his undivided attention.

Ralph Metcalfe and Eddie Tolan are his heroes.

As he waits for the race to begin, Mack thinks about another one of his heroes. His mother remains an example to him, not just of how to work hard to support a family but also of how to carry herself. Mallie Robinson has made it clear to both her family and her neighbors that she isn't intimidated by any of the white folks nearby who don't want them in the neighborhood. She is led by her devotion to God; his mother always looks at everything through the lenses of her faith.

"God is watching everything you do," she tells Mack and his siblings. "So make sure you're doing the right things."

Mack knows it takes doing the right things to end up at a place like this, competing in the Olympics. He's been having success at his track meets at school, being cheered on by everybody, including his admiring young brother, Jack. He's not only been winning in the 200 meters and 220 yards, but also been beating others in the broad jump.

Watching his heroes at these Olympic Games, Mack is inspired to commit himself to rigorous training. Four years from now, he will be twenty years old and in peak shape to be able to compete against runners like Metcalfe and Tolan.

• • •

The favored runner in the 100-meter race crouches in the center lane, ready for the gun to sound again. The first time one of the runners got off before the shot, resulting in a false start. Ralph Metcalfe knows even though he is expected to win, he needs to have a fast start. Takayoshi Toshioka, the first Japanese athlete to qualify for an Olympic sprint final, is known for his quick starts. The other fastest man in the world, Eddie Tolan, is running on the far left lane of the track. When the crack of the pistol finally rings out, Toshioka bursts ahead of the pack to lead it for 40 meters, then starts to fade as Tolan moves ahead with Metcalfe gaining. With only 20 meters to spare, Metcalfe catches up to Tolan and bolts down the lane, blasting through the tape at the end with Tolan right there with him.

Spectators and officials wonder if it's a dead heat. Metcalfe is so assured of the victory that he poses for the cameras right afterward, brandishing a big, winning grin. News reporters begin to write up Metcalfe's victory, yet he isn't announced as the winner. For an excruciating few moments, while judges study the photos, everybody must wait.

The electro-photographic timer used for the race guides the judges to their determination. Eddie Tolan, crossing the finish line with his body straight verses the lunging Metcalfe, is proclaimed the winner.

For a single second, Metcalfe's body grows as stiff as cement, his heart and soul refusing to accept this reality, his flawless physique slumping in defeat. Metcalfe snaps out of it, doing what he knows to be the right thing. He heads over to embrace and congratulate his exuberant competitor.

The photographs Metcalfe will eventually see after the race tell a different story, one he will always believe the rest of his life.

"I've never been convinced I was defeated," Metcalfe says years later in an interview. "I think it should have been a tie race because the timers gave me the same time they awarded to Eddie Tolan. I congratulated him and he congratulated me."

Metcalfe is flashed around the world as the winner, since it's visible to everyone that he breaks the tape. The judges, however, deem that Tolan's entire body crosses the finish line first. At the moment, Metcalfe still holds out hope for a gold medal.

At least there's still the 200, he tells himself.

Metcalfe learns later the judges are thinking the very same thing when deciding the victor for the 100-meter race.

"I had been told later on that the officials thought that I would be a certainty of winning the 200 meters because they thought I was strong in the 200 meters and they gave it (the 100 meters) to Eddie Tolan because they said it was his last Olympics and that I would win the 200 meters."

Metcalfe knows something is wrong with the 200-meter race the moment he lines up in lane 2 to await the start. He's far too close to Eddie Tolan's starting point in lane 1. When Tolan catches up to him far too early, Metcalfe does something he's never done before or since: he tightens up. The smooth strides Metcalfe is so accustomed to winning with suddenly become short and choppy. As Tolan wins the gold, Metcalfe is left with a bronze medal. Finishing so far behind in third place proves his initial concerns.

I started in lane 2 from the relay marker.

This means Metcalfe ran three yards more than any of the other sprinters.

"It was no question that I spotted the field at least eight or nine feet," Metcalfe said later in his life. "I did not know that. If I'd known I was running a handicapped race, I would have run it entirely different."

Perhaps if the German runner, Arthur Jonath, had come in second instead of fourth place, there would have been an international controversy, yet all three medals are awarded to Americans, with George Simpson placing second. While positioned on the victory stand next to Tolan, who is several inches higher, Metcalfe briefly stands with his hands on his hips, a look of frustration and confusion on a face typically photographed with a confident smile. But

Ralph Metcalfe (silver medal) and Eddie Tolan (gold medal) on the medal stand for the 100 meters at the 1932 Olympics in LA.

Ralph knows the value of conducting himself with respect both on and off the track, so all he can do is accept the results and be gracious in defeat.

Everything about the Los Angeles Olympics has been a hurdle for Metcalfe to overcome, especially having to pay his way by serving as a waiter in the dining car on the Santa Fe Railroad. Yet he has grown close to Tolan over the course of the experience.

Metcalfe's professionalism and his mannerly posture are noted by the public and the press as much as his muscular frame and menacing speed. A sportswriter for the *Los Angeles Times*, Braven Dyer, writes, "There may be better sprinters in the world, but I doubt it. There may be better sportsmen in the world, but I doubt it."

. . .

Near the end of the games, two girls find themselves together, yet together they stand alone. Over a week since feeling the soaring sense of pride and accomplishment at having arrived at these Olympic Games and achieved something out of their dreams, Louise Stokes and Tidye Pickett stand watching the race from the sidelines, harboring crushed souls.

Tidye and Louise are surprised, like so many others, that Metcalfe loses in both the 100 and the 200. They witness the results of Babe Didrikson's efforts, seeing her set a new world record in the javelin throw, barely edging out Evelyne Hall in the 100-meter hurdles in a race tighter than the 200-meter final, and then losing the high jump to Jean Shiley after her last jump is ruled to be a foul, much to her anger and dismay. Babe finishes the Olympics with two gold medals and a silver along with three world and Olympic records.

All of this builds up to the women's 4x100-meter relay, which Louise and Tidye have been training for ever since coming to California. There are no heats for the relay but only the final race on August 7. While both have posted stellar times in the previous year and in the timed trials for the American women's team, Louise and

Tidye receive the news on morning of the relay heats that they will not be on the relay team. Coach Vreeland chose Mary Carew and Evelyn Furtsch to run instead of Tidye and Louise.

All they can do is stand and watch from the grandstands.

They watch sweet Mary Carew start the 400-meter relay and not get flagged for jumping as she does so many times. The American girls run in the preferable middle lane, and Carew remains ahead when giving the baton to Evelyn Furtsch. Then comes Annette Rogers and finally comes Billie von Bremen.

The American women win by a large margin of three yards, not only capturing gold but breaking an Olympic record in the process.

Tidye and Louise celebrate with their teammates. They watch the foursome hugging and jumping up and down and kissing one another. Yet regardless of any sort of celebration and feeling of victory, elation, and pride, the two girls also feel a deep sense of loss, a realization that they could be watching themselves in another life where the best man or woman *could* actually win, where the choices could be made by coaches who held no biases.

Carew is chosen to be the lone woman on the victory podium, to stand there with her teammates on the ground in front of her, while the thousands filling the stadium stand at attention and listen to the national anthem and see the flapping American flag being raised. Mary Carew said years later that "that was the greatest accomplishment in my entire life." She learns that gold medal winners are suddenly placed in a very select club, and the four women are invited to radio shows all over the country, to the world's fair, and to events and celebrations, being put in the spotlight and celebrated with each one.

Louise knows she should have been chosen. She had beaten Carew before in several races in New England. Just like Tidye, Louise can't say anything.

Years later, she opened up about what happened at the 1932 Olympics.

"A pretty fast stunt was pulled," Louise says. "The only thing that would have helped us was to have a man stand up for us as well as going to all the meetings. This is what happened when we didn't have anyone to support us."

Tidye and Louise take a bit of solace in the fact they at least have each other.

• • •

"Girls Get Great Trip, Though Barred from the Olympics."

So the headline reads in the August 13, 1932, issue of *Afro-American*. Louise's long, lean figure while running and Tidye's piercing eyes and pretty profile are pictured in the article that proclaims "it was demonstrated here once again on Sunday that American Negro Olympic participants must convince that they are absolute winners before they start when the first and only two colored girls ever to qualify for an Olympic team were unceremoniously discarded and replaced by two white girls."

Tidye doesn't disagree with the headline or the statement. As with so many things in this life that are out of her control, she simply has to accept them and move on. These are the realities for black folks, she thinks.

On Tidye's trip back home to Chicago, this time traveling by herself, another Louis Armstrong tune plays in her head. She wishes she could turn on the radio and listen to the soothing melody.

"Though fortune may forsake me, sweet dreams will ever take me home."

PART TWO

"HE JUMPS TO *his feet, there he is. Shakes my hand. Like an old friend. And those big blue eyes. Like stars. He is glad to see me. I am in heaven. That man has got everything to be a king. A born tribune. The coming dictator.*"

Joseph Goebbels writes this in his diary when he first meets Adolf Hitler, his idol, face-to-face in November 1925. While Hitler always seems to have a plan perpetuated by hate and venom, well worded and delivered to the masses with a glorious wrath, he soon has an accomplice in Goebbels. A man who doesn't mind speaking in the accompanying spotlight while other times lurking in the shadows, Dr. Josef Goebbels helps sculpt and shape Hitler's rhetoric into a movement that forever changes the moral character of a nation.

Born in 1897 as the middle child of a family living in the industrial town of Rheydt, fifteen miles from Düsseldorf, Goebbels nearly dies in his early childhood from pneumonia, and when he is four years old develops the bone marrow disease osteomyelitis. The disease causes his right foot to shift inward while stunting its growth. After an operation at age ten fails to correct the condition, his foot remains paralyzed for life. Goebbels writes in his diaries, "From that moment, my youth held little joy for me. I had to look after myself, and could no longer join in the other children's games. I became lonely and solitary. My former friends had no affection for me."

Full of shame for his deformity, Goebbels becomes a lonely and bitter figure, despising not only others but God himself for making him a cripple. His isolated condition uncovers a love for reading and an understanding for the power of knowledge. While his intelligence begins to give him a cocky and contemptuous attitude toward his peers, he is still "driven by an exceptional craving for recognition from others," a drive that becomes inflamed later in his life.

Due to his clubfoot, Goebbels is unable to serve Germany in World

War I. After earning a doctorate in German philosophy from the University of Heidelberg in 1922, he pursues his sole ambition of becoming a writer, eventually penning poetry, newspaper articles, and a novel. A year into his unfruitful writing career, Goebbels grows despondent and is forced to work at a bank in Cologne, a low-paying job he deems to be full of greed and materialism, traits opposing his nationalistic viewpoint.

Years of bitterness and resentment for the rest of the world are only magnified during this period, including a hatred for Jews honed to monstrous heights once Hitler recognizes Goebbels's superior abilities to communicate. As a banker in 1923, he witnesses the Jewish banking methods and despairs that they are ruining Germany and its people. Add to that the failure of his budding writing career and the rejection of his material, primarily by newspapers and magazines owned and operated by two prominent Jewish families.

In 1924, Goebbels becomes impressed by Hitler's fervent belief and determination in the proper place of the true Germans. His diary from July gives a call and command to his countrymen, one he eventually carries out with oratory skills only dwarfed by his coming messiah:

"We need a firm hand in Germany. Let's put an end to all the experiments and empty words, and start getting down to serious work. Throw out the Jews, who refuse to become real Germans. Give them a good beating too. Germany is yearning for an individual, a man—as the earth yearns for rain in the summer. Only our reserves of strength, enthusiasm and utter commitment can save us now. Can only a miracle—and nothing less—save us?"

For Goebbels, Adolf Hitler is that miracle. Goebbels, still in his twenties, understands the message in Mein Kampf when he reads "propaganda tries to force a doctrine on the whole people. . . . Propaganda works on the general public from the standpoint of an idea and makes them ripe for the victory of this idea."

After seeing Hitler in the summer of 1925 at the Gaue leaders' conference in Weimar, he writes, "Now I know that the man who leads was a born leader. I'm ready to sacrifice everything for him." Meeting and spending time with Hitler only intensifies Goebbels's enthusiasm and passion. "I can accept this firebrand as my leader. I bow to his superiority; I acknowledge his political genius!" he writes on April 13, 1926. Then two months later, he calls Hitler a dear comrade. "You can't help liking him as a person. And he has a stupendous mind. As a speaker he has constructed a wonderful harmony of gesture, facial expression and spoken word. The born motivator! With him, we can conquer the world. Give him his head, and he will shake the corrupt Republic to its foundations."

With Goebbels by his side Hitler soon does shake the foundation of the republic. Hitler quickly recognizes Goebbels's gifts as an orator, with an articulate and rich voice that could boom and vary in tone and expression. While following Hitler as the appointed Nazi Party leader for Berlin, Goebbels studies and masters the art of propaganda, viewing it from all possible points. In 1928, he describes seeing the film Ten Days That Shook the World and writes, "So that's what revolution is. We can learn a lot from these Bolsheviks, most of all from their use of propaganda. But the film is too explicitly propagandistic. Less would have been more effective." Describing the Nazis' message to the people in 1930, he states that "our election propaganda has been exemplary" and "we now just stay the course."

Propaganda becomes central to Goebbels's task in the Nazi Party and as Hitler's right-hand-man. Hitler later makes a statement that many attribute to Goebbels:

"The most brilliant propagandist technique will yield no success unless one fundamental principle is borne in mind constantly, it must confine itself to a few points and repeat them over and over."

This is a passage from Mein Kampf that Goebbels read and adopted as a mantra in his political and professional life. In 1933, the trajectory for Goebbels, Hitler, the Germans, and the entire world is changed the moment Hitler officially comes to power.

After a series of resignations and refusals of support within the German government, along with Hitler's refusal to accept anything other than becoming the chancellor, Hindenburg proceeds to confirm the future

Führer to the only position he would take. The fate of Germany and the world is sealed. As the New York Times *later writes, "The Reichstag was dissolved and in the campaign that ensued the Nazis unleashed a flood of propaganda eclipsing anything that had gone before." As chancellor, Hitler has the strength of the government behind him, and soon the Nazis will be unstoppable in their efforts to take over Germany.*

CHAPTER TEN

DO THE LITTLE THINGS WELL

1933

"THE RABBIT." THAT'S the nickname they gave Ralph Metcalfe back in high school, and it's the only nickname he wants to stick. All the other monikers and titles the papers now give him refer to the color of his skin. It's a practice he's come to resent. Yet in 1933, he will have to learn to live with many assorted nicknames as he continues to make headlines throughout the year. For a short while after the 1932 Olympics in Los Angeles, Metcalfe lets doubt and discouragement seep into his life. Yet he soon finds himself wanting to move on, continue running, and winning again. He sets his sights on the 1936 Olympics.

Marquette University greets Ralph Metcalfe like a hero home from war when he arrives back on campus to celebrate the "international honor he brought his school" with his stunning performance at Madison Square Garden in New York. On February 25, 1933, Metcalfe equals the world record in the 60-meter dash, beating the media's professed sprint king, Emmett Toppino of New Orleans. It's a spotlight that slowly overshadows his Olympic upset.

Metcalfe is hailed a hero, but the *Manitowoc Herald-Times* also proclaims him as the "negro speed king."

A feature on Metcalfe a week later calls him a "sable catapult."

It's not enough to break the world record for the 60-yard dash by running a time of 6 and $\frac{1}{10}$ seconds on March 11. He is described as the "sensational negro sprinter" by the *Philadelphia Inquirer*, and the "colored dash star" by the *Lansing State Journal*.

A journalist from the *Kingston Daily Freeman* becomes creative and calls Metcalfe "ebon-hued."

The press never forgets his color or his size, with the *Cincinnati Enquirer* giving him the title of the "husky Marquette sprinter."

He becomes a comic-book superhero when the *Ogden Standard-Examiner* calls him the "negro flash."

With each victory chipping away the bricks of regret from his Olympic experience, Metcalfe reads about his two-time gold medal competitor, Eddie Tolan, in the news. He hears of Tolan's endeavors after the smoke from the Los Angeles fireworks clears. In November 1932, Tolan turns in his amateur card for racing and instead begins working as a vaudeville actor, appearing on the stage with a unit directed by Bill Robinson, a famous African American tap dancer and actor. The papers explain that Tolan is the sole provider for his mother and siblings in Detroit, and that he plans to earn enough money to allow him to continue his studies in the field of medicine.

By January 1933, Tolan tells reporters, "I don't think anything could induce me to run again." Living in Detroit, Tolan begins working as a file clerk in a county office. His dreams of becoming a physician start to fade. The realities of life during the Depression and the lack of opportunities for African Americans and for retired athletes force the competitor to accept that simply getting by may be his best path forward.

Metcalfe knows that no amount of records, wins, or medals will give him a free pass in life. One has to work hard for every single thing received, especially for a man or woman of color. In a speech he will give years later at a Black Athletes Hall of Fame event, Metcalfe states that each victory seen and every record broken represents "the sweetness of winning the battle, of knowing that in spite of the racism and the prejudice, a black person can still be a champion."

Indeed, for Metcalfe, being black and a champion seems to share the same meaning in the national press.

On March 22, 1933, he sets a new Canadian record in the 60-yard dash, and the *Shamokin Daily News* from Shamokin, Pennsylvania, makes sure readers know he is a "giant negro." The *Press and Sun-Bulletin* from Binghamton, New York, will be a bit more creative, listing Metcalfe as the "dusky Marquette University flier." The *Salt Lake Tribune* goes for a more general description with "the colored midwestern runner."

A few days later, the Associated Press proclaims him as "Marquette University's negro speedster" in his win in the 60-meter race at the Central AAU meet. Two days after that, he equals another world record in the 60 yard, and he becomes "Marquette University's ebony flyer" in the *Journal and Courier*.

He is "the rangy Marquette negro" one week and the "sable cyclone" the next.

Then the "Negro dash artist."

Next up is the "Flying ebony."

By the end of April 1933, the monikers have yet to cease. The *Emporia Gazette* will deem him a "crack colored sprinter."

"Marquette's colored dashman" is what the *Daily Tribune* says.

"Marquette's dark comet," the *Manitowoc Herald-Times* tries to one-up three days later.

After beating rising track and field star Jesse Owens in Chicago, Metcalfe becomes the "midnight express" in the *New Castle News*. A photo showing Metcalfe and Owens posing along with sprinter James Johnson from that event has a caption stating "Three Aces of Spades Star in AAU Games."

Perhaps the best will be saved for that July, right before Metcalfe heads overseas to Europe to compete with fellow American athletes. The *Brooklyn Daily Eagle* calls Metcalfe the "Black Diamond Express from Marquette and present king of American Sprinters."

Metcalfe and six other American track and field stars set sail on the SS *Deutschland* for Europe on Wednesday, July 5. They spend the summer competing in fourteen various meets in Germany, France, Hungary, Sweden, Poland, and Czechoslovakia. Six are major events while the others are local competitions. Metcalfe is dumbfounded by the crowds' reaction to him, applauding him at every single opportunity they could. He arrives back in the States more than two months later, having won all twenty-three races he enters and carrying back more medals than any of his other talented teammates.

Metcalfe knows that his being black has nothing to do with his speed. He will know it for the rest of his life. Yet he also knows that every award and recognition he receives represents something more—the possibility of black excellence and black pride.

Ralph Metcalfe prepares for an NCAA meet at UCLA. Los Angeles, 1934.

By the summer of 1933, Ralph Metcalfe has seared his name onto the world records for eight events, either tying or beating the times:

> 40 yards—4.3 (world record holder)
> 60 yards—6.1 (world record holder)
> 60 meters—6.7 (world record holder)
> 70 yards—7.7 (tied world record)
> 100 yards—9.4 (tied world record)
> 100 meters—10.2 (world record holder)
> 200 meters—20.3 (world record holder)
> 220 yards—20.4 (world record holder)

The title "fastest human" gives him satisfaction for what it signifies. A whole community of people watches him not only compete but win, and keep winning. He plants seeds and fuels the flames of hope deep inside that maybe they can do the same.

• • •

Enrolling at the private Catholic Marquette University isn't a decision based solely on finances and the scholarship they offer. Metcalfe's interest in and appreciation for the Catholic Church began when he was in high school, so attending classes and spending time on the Marquette campus only confirms his interests and conclusions about the Catholic faith. A Jesuit priest doesn't lead to Metcalfe's conversion; instead, a fellow track teammate encourages him to take the next step in his faith. Metcalfe explores this with Reverend John P. Markoe, the director of the men's Sodality at Marquette. Markoe shares with Metcalfe the beliefs and practices of the Catholic Church, leading to his Confirmation day on December 8, 1932. He then joins the Church of St. Benedict the Moor, a colored mission just off the university campus.

Metcalfe receives counseling from Father Grace, the dean of liberal arts. Initially Metcalfe decided to major in physical education, planning to have a career as a coach upon graduation. Yet Father Grace, noting Metcalfe's good grades and classwork, encourages him to think of another path. He advises him to pursue a career in either law or medicine.

"Ralph has the brains and the ability to make good in a profession, and I believe that a person of his race would have more opportunities in law or medicine than in teaching work," Father Grace says.

With that counsel, Metcalfe shifts his plans and begins taking the prelegal course at Marquette.

Later, the all-star athlete shares how his faith has carried him, surely assisting to ease the pain of the unfair experience in the Olympics.

"Catholicity has opened my eyes," Metcalfe wrote. "It has brought me new happiness. It has consoled me and heartened me. I rely on prayer in my athletic and class efforts, as much as I do in my physical and mental abilities. And my plea to heaven at the moment is that I may ever remain faithful to the Church."

Faith on and off the track will carry him far.

$$\bullet \quad \bullet \quad \bullet$$

There is one thing that Metcalfe has faith in that not many others do, and that is his ability to play football alongside his career as a sprinter. Everybody knows Coach Jennings doesn't want Metcalfe to play football, even though it is the sprinter's favorite sport. Injuring his legs would be all too easy during a game, and the future hall-of-fame track coach knows it. Truthfully, nobody at Marquette wants Metcalfe to play. His greatness can be displayed on hard cinder rather than soft grass. However, after hearing about Coach Jennings's notable resistance to his star's ever setting foot onto a football field, one of Marquette's assistant football coaches has an idea for a glorious prank.

The assistant coach's nickname is Tarzan, and John Taylor exemplifies it. He earned it while attending Ohio State as a freshman, and then later when he played for the Chicago Bears, where rumors stated he started the Bears-Packers rivalry after punching one of the Green Bay players in the mouth. The first part of Tarzan's prank is to share a little information with a news reporter, telling him, "Don't print this, but Metcalfe is going out for football next season." The reporter, of course, prints the leak, just as Taylor knew he would. Taylor buys numerous copies of the newspaper when it publishes and puts them on Coach Jennings's desk, acting as though he is concerned about Metcalfe.

One afternoon while Coach Jennings stands in the middle of the field during a practice, Metcalfe runs out toward him wearing a football uniform and carrying a ball. The Marquette football team races over to tackle him, pretending to pile on top of him. When the players finally get up off the ground, Metcalfe stands and begins limping toward Jennings with a look of dismay on the runner's face. Of course, Coach Jennings becomes incensed at the football players, yelling and afraid for Metcalfe's legs, until he sees everybody laughing—including Metcalfe.

The track giant never puts on the football uniform again, yet Metcalfe will still cheer on the sidelines during games.

* * *

"The little things count."

The attentive faces of high school boys and girls all watch Metcalfe as he stands and addresses them at the front of the assembly hall in Sumner High School in St. Louis. The school prides itself in being the first black high school west of the Mississippi River. Located in the thriving African American neighborhood of Ville just northwest of St. Louis, the impressive three-story Georgian Colonial Revival building sits on Cottage Avenue. Ville has grown due to the segregation of the city, and the black community includes a hospital and a hotel.

Sumner High opened in 1875, becoming the first high school opened for African Americans west of the Mississippi. Named after Massachusetts senator Charles Sumner, a Harvard-trained lawyer and avowed abolitionist who fought to end slavery, Sumner becomes notable for its excellence among African American high schools in the country. Some of its students come from outside the city, with boys and girls moving to live with relatives just for the opportunity to enroll at the school. Future attendees include Tina Turner, Arthur Ashe, and Chuck Berry, who gives his first public performance at the high school.

With Thanksgiving only a week away, Metcalfe visits Sumner and other local black schools, sharing his story with hundreds of teenagers. He has already visited Vashon High School, which opened in 1927 to accommodate the overcrowding at Sumner. The students treat him like a celebrity, but by now Metcalfe is accustomed to the fanfare. This sort of notoriety is becoming far too normal for the kid from Chicago. Metcalfe was lionized even in Japan after breaking a record in Manchuria.

His fame and achievements still don't mean Metcalfe is above doing the little things he speaks to the students about. He shares his childhood aspirations of becoming a quarterback and not the sprinting superstar he is today, and how he once entertained the hope of playing football for Marquette before realizing this might jeopardize his track career.

"A fellow must be thinking about his team and his school," Metcalfe tells the students. "You've got to do more than make a reputation for yourself. Your coaches discover what you can do best and encourage you to concentrate on that."

That is why Metcalfe remains on the sidelines for Marquette football games, serving as the water boy for the team. He is proud to be able to participate in this capacity and tells the assembly so.

"They had no one who could get water to the football players on the field as quickly as I. To relieve the players before they are burnt out is an important job. I was asked to do that."

None of the kids watching him appear bored while he speaks. No boys are cutting up and no girls chatting. The students hang on to his every word.

"I would rather be the best water boy in the land than a mediocre football player with no career on the track," Metcalfe says. "By being water boy, I serve the team and the school and I preserve myself to represent the school on the track. More than that, I represent my race."

That is what he did in Europe while racing against their best in between meeting the prince of Sweden or the captivating French singer Josephine Baker. Or, just as he's doing now, speaking to the young men and women who look up to him for the same fact that made crowds in Europe cheer for him and other places exclude him from walking into their premises.

"Do the little things as well as the big things," Metcalfe says, finishing his talk.

After he sits down to a sea of applause from the inspired students, the school choir stands and sings the appropriate song, "Water Boy." Metcalfe's face lights up with the confident, charming smile that's been photographed and admired for the past couple of years. A fitting way for 1933 to close, listening to the boys and girls proudly sing the old folk song.

> *There ain't no sweat boy*
> *That's on a this mountain*
> *That run like mine boy*
> *That run like mine*

THE WORLD WATCHES *Adolf Hitler, and he knows this. One of Hitler's first actions in his new role as the Reich chancellor of Germany is to create* the Reich Ministry of Public Enlightenment and Propaganda on March 14, 1933. There is only one man who can head such a key Nazi organization. Joseph Goebbels enters this position with an intent to "act as a firebrand" for the Nazi Party.

Goebbels works tirelessly from 1933 and on to promote the message of Hitler and the Nazis. His plan is to "work on people until they accept our influence, until they begin to grasp in terms of ideas that what is taking place in Germany does not just have to be accepted but that they can accept it."

One area he focuses on heavily is the film industry. Having always been a fan of cinema, Goebbels makes plans to grow the industry while also maintaining Nazi control over its members, creating a Nazi film department that excluded any Jewish men and women. He persuades a talented filmmaker he admires, Leni Riefenstahl, to produce a film about Hitler. Riefenstahl's first propaganda film for the Nazis, The Victory of Faith, consists of footage taken at the annual Nazi rally at Nuremberg that year. After the premiere of the film is considered a success, with Hitler moved by its portrayal, Goebbels imagines the spectacular potential that filming the Olympics can bring to the Nazi propaganda machine.

In April 1933, Goebbels is already thinking ahead. "German sport has only one task: to strengthen the character of the German people, imbuing it with the fighting spirit and steadfast camaraderie necessary in the struggle for its existence."

Initially, Hitler and his party do not have much of an interest in the upcoming '36 Olympic Games, with a Nazi newspaper, Der Stürmer, calling them "an infamous festival dominated by Jews" and Hitler himself once stating they were "an invention of Jews and Freemasons." That changes later in 1933, however, as Hitler realizes the opportunity Germany has on a world stage if they hosted the games. Hitler holds his first official meeting with the head of the German Olympic Committee, Dr. Theodor Lewald, to express his support for the upcoming games. In October 1933, Hitler and Dr. Lewald will visit the Olympic Stadium in Berlin to look in on the renovations taking place.

The plans are to increase the seating in the Olympic Stadium initially built in 1913 for the 1916 Olympics. After seeing the work in progress, Hitler immediately concocts another plan: The old stadium needs to be torn down, with a larger structure capable of seating one hundred thousand people replacing it. He wants the rest of the world to stand in awe of the new Germany he is creating.

Hitler relays his commitment to hosting the Olympics in a speech at the end of 1933:

"Today I have granted my final approval for the commencement and completion of the structures on the stadium grounds. With this, Germany is being given a sports arena the likes of which are to be found nowhere in the world. The fact that the completion of the planned large-scale construction works is creating many thousands of man-days is something which fills me with particular joy. However, buildings alone are not sufficient to guarantee that German sports are accorded a position in the international competitions which corresponds to the world prestige of our nation. Much more significant is the unified, committed will of the nation to choose the best competitors out of all Germany's Gaue and to train and steel them so that we may pass the forthcoming competition with honors. A no less important task is the sustained and lasting attention to physical exercise in the entire German Volk as one of the most important cultural assets of the National Socialist State. We will make of this a permanent basis for the spirit of the New Germany in the physical strength of its Volk."

Lurking and lingering in the background stands Goebbels, knowing full well the message the New Germany sends to the rest of the world. At the Nuremberg Rally in 1933, the same one filmed by Leni Riefenstahl, Goebbels continues to proclaim edicts on the philosophy of the Nazi propaganda.

"World propaganda against us will be answered with world propaganda for us. . . . The truth about Germany will get through to the other nations, also in respect to the racial question. We have done what is necessary, and therefore fulfilled our duty. We do not need to fear the world's judgment. The world is cordially invited to send its journalists and representatives to Germany so that they can see for themselves the courage and

Hitler congratulates filmmaker Leni Riefenstahl at the premiere of *Victory of Faith*. Berlin, Germany, 1934.

determination of the government and people to remove the last remnants of the war and the November revolt, and to introduce a balance of power that will guarantee Germany a secure existence, honor, and its daily bread. No one who sees this nation at work can have doubts about its future. The more foreigners visit us, the more friends young Germany will win."

CHAPTER ELEVEN

LOOKING AHEAD
1934

THE BUS STOPS in the parking lot of Burlingame High School. Archie Williams looks out the window and can't help his amusement. Even though he graduated from University High in Oakland a year ago and currently attends San Mateo Junior College, the only facility they have for sports is this beat-up gym in an old high school at the center of town. The baseball team practices down at the much superior city park, while Archie and the track team travel five miles away to Burlingame every afternoon from 3:00 to 5:00 p.m. to practice. Waiting for them back at San Mateo are cold showers, courtesy of the baseball players using all the hot water.

Harry Osborne, one of Archie's best friends, suggested going to junior college in the first place. Archie had never been a good student in high school. He was more interested in playing with the other kids at his grandma Fannie Walls' Home for Children, so college was an afterthought. No one in his family had ever gone to college. Once he and his friends graduated high school, they faced what the rest of the country faced in 1933: a bleak future with few options. That fall and winter, Archie and Harry spent time goofing off while caddying at a golf course and not making much money. One day, Harry had a crazy thought.

"Let's go back to school."

"Go back to school?" Archie said with a chuckle. "What the hell are you talking about?"

"Come on—let's go to J.C.," Harry said. "It won't cost anything. We can go for nothing. Or let's go to San Mateo."

"Way down there?"

San Mateo is over an hour's drive from Oakland, across the bay and south of San Francisco.

"Yeah, let's go and check it out," Harry told him.

When they eventually visit the junior college, they find a widow living nearby who rents out a small building in her backyard. Archie and Harry call it the shack. They can have a place to sleep along with two meals a day for only five dollars a week, about the amount of money they make caddying. They decide to go ahead and go for it.

"So, what the hell are you going to be?" Archie asks Harry before they enroll in the junior college.

"I'm going to be a dentist."

Archie decides to one-up his friend. "Well, I'm going to be an engineer."

They both laugh about their half-joking aspirations. Archie knows going back to school is a good thing. He will be bettering himself and not sitting around the house and getting into trouble. When he first decides which classes to take, Archie tells his counselors how he always wanted to attend the University of California, reminiscing about his view of Cal's Sather Tower from his home as child. The counselors pinpoint the classes he should take. Archie signs up for courses he has never heard of, such as trigonometry, in which he earns an A. After his first year at San Mateo, taking analytical geometry, physics, and surveying, Archie thinks to himself

This little stuff is nothing. Perhaps being an engineer wasn't such a far-fetched idea in the first place.

Heading out to practice on the field, Archie doesn't dream about being a star athlete as he did in high school. His classes and his goal of getting into Cal are far more important than competing on the cinder track. Yet his coach, Tex Byrd, keeps encouraging him, complimenting him often on his form and speed.

"I think you have the material that it takes to make a college team like Berkeley," Coach Byrd says.

"Well, you're the coach," Archie tells him. "I'll do what you tell me to do and we'll see how it works out."

At this particular afternoon practice, Coach Byrd comes up to Archie before his first jog around the track.

"I want you to try to run something different today," the coach says.

"What's that?"

So far, Archie has been running and competing in the 220-meter race, and he doesn't know what any of the guys he is racing against look like, since all he can see during each race is the back of their heads.

"I want you to try the 440 today," Coach Byrd says. "I think it's a good fit for you. For your temperament and your stride."

After warming up, Archie runs the distance while being timed by his coach. He clocks just under 52 seconds, which the coach tells him isn't bad.

"If you can get it below 50, you'll be able to make a team like Cal," Coach Byrd says.

After the bus ride back to San Mateo and taking yet another cold shower, Archie and his buddies walk over to Cal University and sneak up to the athletics field on the campus. They often climb under the fence around the old track and watch the guys on the track team run.

Archie longs to attend this school the following year despite being only a sophomore. He knows he can run and he believes, as Coach Byrd said, that he might be able to get onto Cal's track team. But more than that, he wants a degree from the school. That is the goal and the plan. Archie enjoys challenges, and this is certainly one worth trying.

Watching the sprinters on the track move with grace and precision, Archie envisions himself among them. Even if he doesn't get in, or if he doesn't graduate, Archie knows one thing.

At least I can say I tried.

• • •

Louise Stokes smiles as she opens the small pink-gold compact and looks at the mirror and makeup inside, which so far have gone untouched. They are a gift from Janet Gaynor, the attractive and charming movie star she met at a luncheon held at the Ambassador Hotel a year and a half ago before the Olympic Games began. Gaynor spoke with her and had been very friendly. She gave Louise the compact, which will forever remind her of those bittersweet '32 games, where memories of traveling to California and meeting all sorts of new friends remain in stark contrast to being excluded from hotel rooms and being pulled from the races.

On this Tuesday evening in April, the athletes at Harlem's Mercury Athletic Club are holding a dinner for Louise. To all of the African American boys and girls in the room, she is a hero. It doesn't matter to them that she never ran in the Los Angeles Olympics. Louise, a black girl from Malden, Massachusetts, actually *made* the team and really *traveled* all the way to the sunshine state.

Since last Saturday she has been in Brooklyn, where she competed in the Women's National Indoor Track Championships at the Second Naval Battalion Armory. Louise was disappointed in her third-place finish in the 50 meters, crediting her performance to a poor start and to the fact that she has never run on this indoor track. Her friend Tidye, whom she has kept in touch with by writing letters, also competed. Hampered by a bad foot, Tidye placed fourth in the hurdles. Many other familiar faces are there as well, such as Evelyne Hall and Annette Rogers, two of the sprinters from the '32 Olympic team.

The buzz around the championships has concerned the unlikely comeback for Betty Robinson, the 100-meter-dash gold medalist at the 1928 Olympics. A horrific plane crash in 1931 resulted in Robinson's breaking her leg and derailing her amazing career. For her first race back, she competes in a relay for the Lincoln Park team from Chicago. Robinson's team, the same one Tidye Pickett runs for, wins the title and brings the trophy back to Illinois.

A few days after that track meet, Louise wears a long dress and heels at the Mercury Athletic Club. She can't help wondering if this gala is anything like the one she and Tidye missed in Denver on the way to Los Angeles. Perhaps this is a gift from God to compensate for the mistreatment in Colorado. If they had gone to the banquet, Tidye and Louise would have been dwarfed by the giant personality of Babe Didrikson, who is nowhere to be found on either a track or a field these days. Louise has heard stories about Didrikson doing everything from performing on the stage to competing with a traveling basketball team to playing baseball and golf. Frankly, it is not easy to miss the incorrigible Texan star.

"What's next for you, Louise?" a reporter asks her this evening.

"I want to compete in the championships in San Francisco," Louise says. "Then maybe go to London to compete against some of their runners."

"What about the Olympics?" someone asks.

"I'm planning on training for the Olympics once I'm back home in Malden. After that I think that will be enough running for me."

"What do you think of New York?" another reporter chimes in.

"I like it very much," Louise says. "I'm just not used to parties and dances and all that. I'd prefer being home listening to the radio."

Before the night is over, Louise thanks her fellow athletes in the room and promises that she will come back to New York to run in the Mercury Athletic Club's first annual track and field meet in May.

━━━━━━━━━━━━

IN 1933, THE *same year Ralph Metcalfe becomes known as the fastest man alive, the lynchings of African Americans peaks, with twenty-eight African Americans murdered across the country. The lives of black Americans are riddled with fear, violence, and poverty as the Great Depression crushes the unemployment rate to 50 percent among African Americans.*

Some of those lynched are beaten and tortured before being taken to their execution. Many are hanged, while some are shot or burned alive. The lynchings force the president of the United States to openly address the situation to the rest of the country that December. The year 1934 opens with the promise of an antilynching bill introduced in the Senate on January 11. Previous antilynching bills have failed to pass the Senate. If passed, the legislation will result in a five-year jail term for any state officers found negligent in a lynching along with a thousand-dollar fine to the county.

"This new generation, for example, is not content with preachings against that vile form of collective murder—lynch law—which has broken out in our midst anew," President Franklin D. Roosevelt says in a radio address. "We know that it is murder, and a deliberate and definite disobedience of the Commandment, 'Thou shalt not kill.' We do not excuse those in high places or in low who condone lynch law."

Lynch law is witnessed for the first time at the start of the new year at the county jail in Hazard, Kentucky, which can't keep the prisoner, Rex Scott, in and the unruly mob out. The mob has grown to more than three hundred men, circling the jail and sending in thirty leaders of the group, all of them wearing masks. They force the jailer to open Scott's cell, then they drive him out of town. On Wednesday, January 24, the first lynching of 1934 takes only an hour from the time the armed men seize the young black man to the moment they hang him from a beech tree in a graveyard. Scott is twenty years old and charged with "slugging" a miner named Alex Johnson. Johnson is in critical condition in the hospital, only to die two hours after Scott is lynched.

While the Hazard county jailer is eventually removed from his position, the lynchings across the country continue. First Lady Eleanor Roosevelt joins forces with the NAACP and its leader, Walter White, as they work on legislation to end the lynchings. Mrs. Roosevelt arranges a meeting with Walter White and President Roosevelt at the White House to discuss the widespread murders. The meeting over tea begins amicably yet ends with an exasperated FDR clearly stating his position.

"If I come out for the antilynching bill now, they will block every bill I ask Congress to pass to keep America from collapsing," FDR says. "I just can't take the risk."

Congressmen Robert F. Wagner and Edward Costigan agree to draft a bill that punishes the crime of lynching. However, when Roosevelt refuses to speak out in favor of the Costigan-Wagner bill, Congress soundly defeats it.

While clearly against the antilynching bill, FDR is gathering intelligence from both Germany and America on the growing debate over par-

Howard University students picket, wearing nooses around their necks in protest of the National Crime Conference in Washington, D.C., when the leaders of the conference refuse to discuss lynching as a national crime. 1934.

ticipating in the 1936 Olympics. Hitler's immorality fuels more members of the Olympic Committee and the Amateur Athletic Union to encourage a boycott of the Berlin Olympics. While many of the athletes are very aware of the controversy, some know little of the conditions of African Americans and Jews in the upcoming host country. For most of them, Berlin is the furthest thought from their minds and the Nazis are simply specters written about in the newspapers.

CHAPTER TWELVE

THE WORLD'S FASTEST MAN
1934

STAGGERING ONTO THE train, Jimmy LuValle forces his legs to move a little more before sitting and resting the muscles. His thighs and calves ache, his feet are calloused and throbbing. As the railway car begins to move, LuValle closes his eyes but still feels in motion. Somehow, he hasn't stopped from the moment he set foot on the track at Berkeley earlier that day.

There was the 100, a burst of pure and raw speed. Then the 220, a sprint with steady strides and a vicious finish. And, of course, the quarter-mile, the event he is becoming known for. Yet LuValle also throws the javelin, takes off in the broad jump, runs a leg in the relay, and participates in the hurdles. In that last event, LuValle loses a shoe and then tumbles over one of the hurdles, landing hard on the cinder. It's happened before, so he takes it in stride. It is just one of the many events he entered in the meet.

Their team needs any help it can get in racking up the points. Nobody comes to UCLA to run track. Like LuValle, most attend because it's close to home and very cheap. He pays only thirty-five

James LuValle training on the track at UCLA.

dollars per semester to attend the college. Naturally, all the athletes compete in multiple events. Many leave slowly limping.

People are noticing LuValle, now far from the college freshman still trying to decide whether it's best to stay off the field due to his past hospitalization. The *Los Angeles Times* call him the "Brain Wonder" and the "Westwood Whirlwind." His school records in the 220-yard dash and the quarter-mile turn heads and produce talk. Still, it doesn't affect him. His primary concern at school is his studies. He has no grand ambitions for running and where it might take him. For now, he is just having fun, or at least trying to have fun without passing out from participating in every event out there.

As the train car rocks back and forth bound toward his home,

James LuValle with UCLA teammates Vejar, Lott, and Miller after setting a relay record.

LuValle thinks about the upcoming track meet where he'll be running against the speedy Al Blackman in both the 440 and the 220. Blackman has a terrific start and sprints the first 300 yards, yet LuValle can finish better. It will be a close match, and the 220 will be close as well. LuValle is slightly worried, not because of his competitor but because of his new running shoes. The tight ones replacing the torn old shoes he retired today desperately need breaking in. They suffocate his feet and feel too tight for competing. The thought of putting them on only makes him more tired.

• • •

On a perfect July day in Toronto, Canada, with temperatures in the seventies, Tidye Pickett lines herself up with the sand pit, then begins to sprint down the runway. She rushes and doesn't hesitate a second as her foot lands on the takeoff board and propels the rest of her body forward. Gliding through the air, she lands in the sand, then instantly pops up to see her spot. The officials measure her jump at 18 feet 1½ inches.

Tidye doesn't just take first place in the running broad jump, she also breaks a Canadian record by four inches. It is the start of a big day for the nineteen-year-old.

Traveling more than five hundred miles from Chicago, Tidye and her Highland Park Athletic Club team compete in front of twelve thousand at Toronto's centennial track and field games. Tidye arrives eager to brush off a disappointing track season last year. She's spent months training with her coach, John Brooks, adding hurdles to her events.

After the broad jump, Tidye races in the 60-meter dash, finishing a yard ahead of her teammate, Doris Anderson, to win with a time of 7.2 seconds. This doesn't surprise her; in her last indoor meet for the season, Tidye managed to set a world mark for the 40-yard dash. The 80-meter hurdles are more of a question mark for her, since she's still so new to the event.

She starts strong and remembers what John Brooks has taught her. Her coach knows something about finding track and field success. He had been a strong favorite to make the 1932 Olympic team in the broad jump. Earlier that year, Brooks had been called a one-man track team by the *Chicago Tribune* after his jump of 24 feet 8⅜ inches won at the Drake relays in May. Along with the broad jump event, Brooks also excelled at the 220-yard low hurdles. During the same season, at the University of Chicago, he also won the 70-yard hurdles, the 100 yards, the 220 yards, and the 440 yards. There was some pressure placed on Brooks from the papers, especially with statements like "already Brooks is being compared to Binga Dismond, Chicago's greatest Negro athlete, who for years shared the world record for the quarter mile." His Coach Ned Merriam told the papers that Brooks would clear 25 feet in the broad jump this year, and with continued competitions he would get closer to the world record.

Coach Merriam would be right when Brooks jumped 25 feet 23¼ inches at an NCAA championship meet. Yet on the day in

John Brooks long-jumping at the Drake Relays.

1932 when his little Chicago protégé, Tidye Pickett, ended up making the Olympic team, Brooks just missed it after a fourth-place finish with a jump of only 24 feet 10⅝ inches.

After Coach Brooks began to show her how to jump over hurdles, Tidye almost won her first hurdles race by a couple of inches. Perhaps if she hadn't been competing in other events as well, she would have been fresh enough to win. *The Defender* summed up her debut as a hurdler in 1933:

"Miss Pickett's performance was very impressive not only because the winner is the holder of the American record but also because Miss Picket had run a heat, semifinal, and final in the 50-meter dash and a heat in the hurdles all within a half-hour."

Now in these Toronto Games, everything in the race goes well until Tidye slips over the last hurdle. As she runs to the finish line, her Canadian competitor gets there in front of her. Once again, she's come in second in the 80-meter hurdles. The winner is Roxy

Atkins, a local star surely propelled to victory by the twelve thousand Canadians watching.

The biggest satisfaction and surprise on this day is Tidye's last event, when she helps her teammates set another Canadian record, this time in the 440-yard relay. It's late afternoon when Tidye starts the relay for her Chicago team. The first runner needs to be a fast and reliable starter, and that's Tidye. They finish with a 48.6 mark.

The relay victory and record are the most meaningful for Tidye. She is able to be a part of a team, to help them start out strong and never fall behind. She is also able to do something her coaches didn't allow Louise or her to do in those '32 Olympics: Step out onto the track and show others what she was capable of.

All she needs to do is master those hurdles and she will be a formidable force in the event.

* * *

With his junior year nearing its close, Mack Robinson's heart, which worried doctors and prompted Muir Tech to have his mother sign a waiver, is still holding out fine. Often referred to as the Torrance Tempest, Robinson's high school team captures the state titles at Edwards Stadium in Berkley, with Robinson winning the 100-yard dash. He knows he will be able to run even faster and jump farther in his senior year.

Mack remains moved and inspired by meeting one of his heroes last fall in '32. Ralph Metcalfe, fresh off winning two medals in the Los Angeles Olympics, visited the Robinsons' home church one Sunday morning to speak to the congregation. The seventeen-year-old Mack greeted the debonair athlete after the service was over. "I ran up and tugged at him—hero worshipping," Mack stated years later, telling Metcalfe, "I can run too!" Metcalfe grinned and gave him a pat on the back, encouraging him to keep going.

Robinson can't imagine that one day, he'll be competing with Metcalfe.

. . .

The white Marquette University uniform doesn't fit as snugly as it did at the start of the season. Metcalfe can see the frayed edges of the uniform and feels a little bittersweet. It is the final time he will wear the Marquette Golden Eagle uniform. It is also his last meet in Marquette Stadium.

In 1934, Ralph transfers to the law school, since two years of college work have been a prerequisite for enrolling at the law school since the early 1920s. Although Metcalfe is an excellent student, he apparently finds his studies at the law school quite challenging. He passes on a few critical meets to study while sprinter Jesse Owens would take the wins. Eventually he transfers back to the undergraduate college for his final season and final meets.

Today is his last meet as captain. The last time he'll sprint between the white lines to see the white men in white shoes, white pants, white shirts, and white hats standing near the finish line to carefully watch and time the winner. Their eyes and watches will be set hopefully on the captain of the Golden Eagles. On this clear, hot June day he plans to leave the Milwaukee home crowd with something special.

In this final season, Metcalfe has had to nurse a bleeding muscle in his right leg, forcing him to sit out of a handful of the meets until returning on April 28 at the Drake Relays in Des Moines, Iowa. He wins the 100-yard dash for the third year in a row at the meet, even though his leg is not yet fully healed.

Now, in this final race as a Golden Eagle, running against him in the 100 meters is Jesse Owens. It is not the first time they've competed against each other. Over a year ago, in 1933, Metcalfe beat the young rising star from Cleveland. After the race, the two competitors congratulated each other.

"I thought I had you beat," Owens told Metcalfe.

The elder statesmen gave Jesse a playful grin. "Maybe that's what beat you, Jesse."

Those words motivate Owens as much as the 1932 Olympic silver medal motivates Metcalfe.

All legends have a starting point, and for Jesse Owens, his begins in his sophomore year in 1931 at Cleveland's East Technical High School. At the state championships that year, he finishes fourth in the 100-yard dash, second in the 200, and wins the broad jump. His jump breaks the Class A record with a leap of 22 feet 3⅞ inches, a mark that had been standing since 1923.

In their 1933 race, Metcalfe has enough speed to beat the young and friendly-faced sprinter by a foot. In the 200 meters, Metcalfe isn't challenged, winning by more than five yards. Then, just to remind everybody of his status as the "world's fastest man," Metcalfe anchors the 4x100-meter relay, receiving the baton while they're in second place but rocketing ahead to win.

Jesse Owens will always admire and respect Metcalfe, saying later in life, "When I write that Ralph Metcalfe was the greatest sprinter of his day, I'm sure most of you will draw a blank. But he was—the best. Me included."

This time Metcalfe has to work a little harder to beat Owens. Once again, as he passes the men in white and clocks an impressive time, Metcalfe becomes the first runner since the 1890s to win two events at these championships for a third year in a row.

His time for the day in 1934 is 10.4 seconds, a tiny fraction above another memorable time—*10.38 seconds,* the time both he and Eddie Tolan made in Los Angeles. The time he tied or won the Olympic race yet received second place.

Metcalfe's time is coming. These two victories at these AAU championships are another step toward his goal. These next two years until the 1936 Olympics remain crucial.

He is already thinking ahead toward defeating all of his rivals in Germany.

ON THE VERY *same night Metcalfe makes history at Marquette Stadium, Hitler will do the same. The Nazi leader has no desire to race or compete. His idea of competition is to defeat his enemies or to make sure they can never line up against him in the first place.*

Since helping to create the private army known as Storm Troopers or the SA (Sturm Abteilung), Hitler sees this paramilitary formation grow to nearly three million men by 1934. Ernst Röhm, the head of the SA, is a close ally and friend to Hitler, but many of the German leaders, including Hitler, worry the SA has grown too big and too dangerous, especially with its fanatical desire to eliminate all the traditional elites holding power in Germany. Hitler and the Nazis realize those national elites are necessary to bring the country together in order to work toward starting a war. By the spring of 1934, Röhm no longer believes in such Nazi leaders as Josef Goebbels.

Over the course of several days, Hitler and the Nazis eliminate key political rivals by killing leaders of the SA, an event known as the "Night of the Long Knives" or "Operation Hummingbird." The primary targets include Röhm as well as Gustav Ritter von Kahr, the man who defeated Hitler at the Beer Hall Putsch in 1923.

After planting rumors of an imminent SA takeover, Hitler orders his elite soldiers to seize and murder multiple SA leaders. These soldiers are the Schutzstaffel, a group Hitler formed in 1925 to act as his personal bodyguards. They are most widely known as the SS. In 1929, the SS were expanded when Heinrich Himmler became the head of the Schutzstaffel. On the "Night of the Long Knives," Hitler states that fifty-eight men are killed with another nineteen shot after trying to escape. The exact number of those murdered is never known, though it is estimated to be between 150 and 200. More than 1,000 individuals are taken into custody.

The Germans aren't mortified to hear about the cold, calculated killings, but rather relieved. The SA had been an oppressive force in the country, and the people wanted an end to the bloodshed and violence brought on by the Storm Troopers. With many of the SA leaders gone, the rest of the Storm Troopers readily submit, with any troublemakers or those deemed "degenerates" purged immediately.

Never again will another party pose any sort of threat to Hitler. Against the odds throughout many years, Hitler has risen to be the supreme ruler and savior of Germany, with the desire to continue his conquests in the rest of the world. Before that, however, Germany will have to convince the rest of the world that it is unified and that it is indeed a New Germany.

The 1936 Olympics offer Hitler an opportunity to do just that. It gives the Nazis a chance to showcase the prowess of the Aryan master race before the rest of the world.

CHAPTER THIRTEEN

THE NAZIS TAKE CONTROL

1934

WITH EACH RUNG of power Hitler and the Nazis climb, American voices begin to shout their concern about participating in the Berlin Olympics. They look at the Nazis' troubling policies and programs, such as the "Aryans only" policy implemented in April 1933, one that collectively ends the careers of many of the country's top athletes. Helene Mayer, considered the most gifted female fencer in the world and resembling the Aryan prototype with her blond hair and her height, is kicked off the Offenbach Fencing Club and banned from any competition in the Berlin Olympics because her father is Jewish. Some athletes find solace in competing for other countries, yet many remain banished from the pages of history altogether. The possibility of the United States refusing to attend the 1936 games looms large, as Hitler and Nazi officials answer concerns issued from both the International Olympic Committee and the public.

Initially, the American Olympic Committee president, Avery Brundage, joins with those raising doubts about America's involvement with the Berlin Olympics after Hitler becomes the chancellor in 1933. Brundage questions situations such as that of Dr. Daniel Prenn, one of the world's best tennis players, ousted from the German Davis Cup team simply because he is Jewish. "My personal, but unofficial opinion is that the Games will not be held in any country where there will be interference with the fundamental Olympic theory of equality of all races," Brundage says in 1933. "The Olympic protocol provides there shall be no restriction of competition because of class, color, or creed." Brundage stands by the Amateur Athletic Union's decision to turn down the invitation to compete in Berlin unless they are assured Jewish athletes can compete. However, who Brundage is devoted to soon becomes apparent.

Brundage isn't as offended by Hitler and his anti-Semitism as he is at the idea of the Olympic ideal being tarnished. As an athlete and self-made millionaire, having amassed his wealth in the Chicago construction industry, Brundage sees the value of competition and is known to believe that revolutionaries are not bred on the playing field. According to him, sports and politics do not overlap.

"Where amateur sport with its high ideals flourishes, there civilization advances," Brundage said as he welcomed the British track team at the international track meet four years earlier. It is the same event Ralph Metcalfe ran in, the same one at which he, Eddie Tolan, and other black athletes would not be allowed to room with their white counterparts.

As doubt looms over the Germans' commitment to Olympic protocols banning racial discrimination, Brundage asks IOC president Comte Henri de Baillet-Latour for advice on the situation. Baillet-Latour later writes, "I am not personally fond of Jews and of the Jewish influence, but I will not have them molested in any way."

After the IOC declares that Germany complies with all the laws regulating the games, especially in regards to excluding any individuals, Brundage is chosen to personally visit Berlin to inspect what is happening. He is told to make a decision on the spot whether to accept or reject Germany's invitation to attend their Olympics.

For six days, the Germans show Brundage around. They smile and allow him to study the sports facilities and athletes in Berlin. Brundage meets two of the best athletes on the German team, high jumper Gretel Bergmann and the ice hockey player Rudi Ball, both Jewish athletes. While the deputy Reich sports leader, Arno Breitmeyer, remains at his side, dressed in his full SS uniform, including the high cavalry boots, Brundage meets and speaks with Jewish leaders at the Kaiserhof Hotel. He comes to believe the conditions are fine, seeming to understand the situation with his Nazi hosts when explaining to them about the men's club he is a part of in Chicago that bars Jews.

Reports surfaced only a year earlier about the anti-Semitism raging through Germany like a wildfire. Jews are taken off the streets in broad daylight, beaten, thrown into jail, and tortured. Prominent Jews lose their jobs, everyone from judges to band members. For more than a decade, Hitler has been preaching about the ills of the Jewish population, six hundred thousand of whom reside in Germany.

None of that seems to matter when Brundage goes on to state the Germans promised "there would be no discrimination against Jews. You can't ask for more than that and I think the guarantee will be fulfilled." Viewing no outward acts of aggression or racism toward the Jews, Brundage gives his full-fledged support for the games to continue as planned, stating the Olympics are "an international event and must be kept free from outside interference or entanglements, racial, religious or political."

The American Olympic Committee accepts Germany's official invitation to the Olympics with a following resolution:

"In light of the report of Mr. Brundage and the attitude and assurances of representatives of the German government, we accept the invitation of the German Olympic Committee to the 1936

SA picket in front of Jewish businesses, 1933.

Olympic Games. The German Government has very generously provided for Jewish representation on its Olympic Team."

In neither Brundage's report nor the AOC's resolution is there any mention of treatment and discrimination against black athletes. The politics of the games still don't affect the prejudices that are simply part of them.

• • •

Between 1933 and 1936, two groups are largely responsible for the rising opposition to Germany's hosting the coming Eleventh Olympiad. First, there are the legalists who doubt Germany's promise to follow the Olympic protocol and not discriminate against any Olympic athletes for any reason including race or religion. Second there are the moralists who refuse to continue to legitimize Hitler and his Nazi Party and deem awarding the Olympics to them unconscionable.

Brundage disagrees with the legalists and ignores the moralists. Others will have to accept the AOC president's assertion that the

Olympic Games are not meant to engage in political matters but to rise above them. He states in the *New York Times*, "Frankly, I don't think we have any business meddling in this question. We are a sports group, organized and pledged to promote clean competition and sportsmanship. When we let politics, racial questions, religious or social disputes creep into our actions, we're in for trouble, and plenty of it."

Some take Brundage's mind-set a step further, viewing the Jewish opposition to the games as unnecessary grumbling. "My own view is that we are pandering too much to the Jews!" Evan Hunter, secretary of the British Olympic Association, writes to Brundage after his visit to Germany. The president of the International Amateur Athletic Foundation, J. Sigfrid Edstrom, states his views on the matter to Brundage: "The Jews have taken a too prominent position in certain branches of life and have—as the Jews very often do when they get in the majority—misused their positions."

By 1934, the Nazis forbid Jews from accessing health insurance and ban them from the labor front. Their holidays are removed from the German calendar. Yet those public decrees overshadow private and more ghastly dealings, such as the growing concentration camp at Dachau. The camp opens in March 1933 to handle the massive overflow of men and women rounded up and imprisoned without trial because of their opposition to Hitler. An article a year later, in the *New Republic*, lists its conditions for the one thousand seven hundred prisoners placed there by the Germans:

"The prisoners are divided into three classifications, each treated differently. . . . The third class is composed of leading Communists and all the Jews. This class performs the hardest work on the smallest rations . . . are beaten more than the other prisoners, and nearly all of the murders are perpetrated on members of this class. Within the last-mentioned class, the Jews are segregated, because no Aryan is allowed to share sleeping accommodations with a Jew."

The article shows the seeds of evil sprouting in Dachau:

"The Nazis appeared one night to take over control. Their leader made a speech to his followers, of which the following quotations are of interest: 'Always remember that no human beings are here, only swine.'—'Whoever does not wish to see blood may go home immediately.'—'No one who does harm to a prisoner need fear reprimand.'—'The more you shoot, the fewer we must feed.'"

America and the rest of the world don't recognize the festering evil growing in Germany. Brundage, focused solely on the glory of the coming games and what they will mean, simply refuses to accept the glimmers of facts related to the Nazi Party. He declares the following:

"Certain Jews must understand that they cannot use these games as a weapon in their boycott against the Nazis."

• • •

Work proceeds that year on the sprawling new Olympic sports complex five miles west of Berlin. It rests on the same site once intended for the canceled 1916 games. With Germany's full resources

Hitler inspects a replica of the Olympiastadion.

behind the Olympic preparations, "Reichssportfeld" is trumpeted as the greatest sports facility in the world. The grounds and structures include an amphitheater used for events such as boxing. The lawn, Maifield, will feature gymnastics and equestrian events, and an aquatics center, Olympiapark Schwimmstadion Berlin, is fashioned for swimming and diving. Of course, the most spectacular gem in all of the Reichssportfeld is the Olympiastadion, a stadium built of natural stone with 110,000 seats. The Olympiastadion will be the world's largest stadium and will feature a viewing area specifically built for Hitler and selected Nazi officials.

With Hitler's order that costs are of no concern, the Olympic Village can hold more than four thousand of the athletes in 140 houses constructed by the Wehrmacht. Each house is themed after a German city and features designs and decorations symbolic of that city. Among the features of the Olympic Village are a movie theater, a shopping area, places to exercise, swim, and hike, a state-of-the-art hospital, a postal office, and an abundance of dining halls.

The Olympic Stadium is only a short walking distance away from the Olympic Village. Officers from the German army will be assigned to each visiting team to serve their needs during the Olympics. Buses and cars are provided to the teams to assist them in any travel they desire.

The games will establish the goal stated by Hitler's master of propaganda, Josef Goebbels: "Our first task in this ministry will be to win the whole people for the new state. We want to replace liberal thinking with a sense of community that includes the whole people."

Construction of the new stadium costs more than expected—thirty times the initial estimate. Despite the cost, Hitler remains undaunted in his quest to display his country to the world. He can display the wealth and power of Germany while also demonstrating that the Germans are warm, caring, joyful hosts. In doing this, Hitler will reveal the Aryan race to be superior to any other inferior race, or so he believes.

IN 1934, FAR *across the ocean, the flickers of optimism and change are ignited throughout America as young black men and women makes strides in their own right.* Zora Neale Hurston's first novel, Jonah's Gourd Vine, *is published, and Aaron Douglas's mural* Songs of the Towers *will be commissioned by the Works Progress Administration (WPA) for the Harlem branch of the New York City Public Library. Both Hurston and Douglas are major figures to emerge from the Harlem Renaissance, though even the brightest lights can't eliminate the darkness still suffocating many parts of the Depression-ravaged nation, in places like Jackson County, Florida, where racism and segregation remain poisonous.*

On a brisk October eve in 1934 another mob of armed white men congregate and search for a suspect in the shadows of midnight in Greenwood, Florida. The man they have already tried and convicted and now hunt for is a young African American named Claude Neal. Neal is only twenty-three years old, works on a farm, and can't read or write. Neal has a wife and a three-year-old daughter. He is guilty of raping and killing a twenty-year-old white woman named Lola Cannady. Guilty, of course, in the eyes of the men and women who want justice for Lola.

After Lola's body and beaten-in head are found in the woods, Neal is discovered shortly thereafter with bloody clothes stashed in the wash and a torn shred of his shirt at the crime scene. The evidence against him looks convincing, so after Jackson County sheriff W. Flake Chambliss arrests Neal for murder, the desire for justice can only last so long. The sheriff has Neal moved to several different jails in order to keep him from being taken by the furious public wanting revenge. By doing so he manages to buy some time for his prisoner. Neal is driven more than 150 miles from Greenwood to Brewster, Alabama, where he makes a full confession. News of his admitting to raping and killing Lola Cannady blazes through the public like a wildfire. More than a hundred men drive the long distance to force the deputy to release Neal. They bind their prisoner and then bring him back to the Florida town where he is to be executed.

Newspapers all across the country pick up the story about the planned lynching by a furious mob. "Mob Takes Negro From Ala. Jail: Believe He Will Be Turned Over to Father of the Girl He Killed" is the headline on October 26 for the Marshall Evening Chronicle in Marshall, Michigan. The Dothan Eagle in Dothan, Alabama, runs one stating "Florida Mob to Burn Negro At Stake." The Clovis News-Journal, as far away as Clovis, New Mexico, reports on the mob taking Neal, quoting them as saying, "We'll tear your jail up and let all the prisoners out, if you don't turn him over to us."

Neal never makes it to Lola's parents alive, however. The six men who take Neal, the leaders of the lynching party calling themselves the "Committee of Six," decide the several thousand people waiting to see Neal's death are too big a group, so they drag the young black man into the woods near the Chattahoochee River. There they torture and mutilate Neal, savagely murdering him before bringing his naked body back to the Cannady home, where it is further stabbed and struck by men, women, and children. What is left of Neal's corpse hangs from an oak tree on the lawn of the courthouse. Postcards are printed showing off the photo of Neal's hanging body. Some townspeople reportedly take souvenirs to remember the event: fingers and toes that have been cut off.

Soon more newspapers report the horrific aftermath of the lynching. No one is ever to be charged in the death of Claude Neal. Eventually it is reported that Neal and Lola were lovers. Suddenly this display of cruelty and abomination seems too much for many Americans. Thousands protest by writing to President Roosevelt and crying for justice. While his wife is motivated to do more, and eventually acts upon these emotions for years to come, Roosevelt doesn't want to act with the midterm elections approaching, knowing the Southern Democrats are critical to his win.

CHAPTER FOURTEEN

ANYONE IS BEATABLE

1935

METCALFE KNOWS WHAT it means to be regarded as the fastest man in the world. For him, it has always meant more than just that. For him and Eddie Tolan and Jesse Owens, they are not just the superstars of track. "They represent black pride. They represent the great pain of battling overwhelming odds to accomplish a goal."

Despite the racism that still remains rampant in the country, Metcalfe and others are showing that black people can still be champions. And every year that arrives comes with another new competitor staking the claim as the best. The young, rising star name Ben Johnson is one of them.

As a freshman from Columbia University, Johnson first races Metcalfe in 1934 and beats him. His five-foot-seven-inch height and weight of less than 150 pounds make Johnson resemble a high school kid, yet his speed earns him a nickname, not unlike the one given to Metcalfe. Johnson is "the Columbia Comet."

At the AAU championship in March 1935, Metcalfe once again finds himself racing against Johnson. On this night at the indoor championship at Madison Square Garden, Johnson doesn't just defeat Metcalfe and Jesse Owens in front of sixteen thousand spectators. He ties Owens's impressive world record of 6.6 seconds in the 60-meter dash.

Undaunted, Jesse Owens shatters the indoor record for the broad jump not once but twice, landing on 25 feet 9 inches. Eulace Peacock broke Owens's record in 1934, so now it belongs to the Ohio star.

Metcalfe loses the title of "world's fastest man," though the title does not mean much to him. He believes it should be "world's fastest man tonight." The saying is simply a bragging right, just as the medals are reminders of past victories. They don't signal an athlete's worth or impact.

Metcalfe knows the long, hard struggle all of them have as black athletes. Now another black superstar has emerged, and yet again there is a champion for many to root for.

God has a plan for everything.

This is something he believes. His faith is as strong as his athletic prowess, and in 1935, he'll certainly need both.

• • •

His faith was tested earlier, at the start of the year, when a fire breaks out in Metcalfe's home on Forty-second street in Milwaukee, Wisconsin. Firemen arrive to extinguish the flames wreaking havoc in part of his home, but the damage proves to be very costly. Everything he owns is permanently saturated with smoke, but fortunately he owns few things to begin with. His most cherished belongings are inside a trunk that is rescued.

When Metcalfe finally opens his trunk, he discovers nothing inside. Every single cup, badge, medal, and trophy has been stolen.

Police say they will investigate, but none of Metcalfe's memorabilia of his winnings are ever recovered.

His 1932 Olympic medals are forever gone.

There's a reason for everything, he reminds himself.

• • •

"Love many and trust few. Always paddle your own canoe."

Louise glances at the familiar quotation on the dog-eared page of her autograph book from the 1932 Olympics. Heartfelt messages scribbled in pen and pencil are randomly etched throughout. Some people simply signed their name, while others wrote words of encouragement like the old faithful "Never give up." One of her favorites came from an athlete named Smitty.

"If at first you don't succeed, don't give up, but change your speed."

On a warm April morning while she readies herself for the day, Louise considers how she did just that: changed her speed. Her own times in recent races are indeed getting faster. Yet the concentration on running has resulted in low grades and lots of absences from school.

Laziness isn't the reason; there's not a single thing about Louise synonymous with the word. She attacked her senior year as she did every race, deciding to take a heavy load of English, math, history, stenography, and art, assuming she would graduate with all her other classmates. The glee club interested her, so she joined, along with playing on the basketball team and singing in the choir at Eastern Avenue Baptist Church.

It ends up being too much.

Her senior school year closes with Louise getting C's and D's in several subjects. She will need to go back after the track season to finish the remaining classes. For now, Louise decides to focus on running instead. Coach Quaine believes she can win a gold medal in the upcoming Olympics, and he wants it as much as Louise does. With the intense training and heavy workload at home, Louise decides not to return to school.

Her parents aren't happy and fight with her over the decision, but ultimately the choice is left to Louise. She is twenty years old—a grown woman now—and knows where her heart and abilities are leading her.

Louise Stokes taking her Malden High School homeroom photo.
Malden, Massachusetts.

Did I make the right decision? Louise asks herself after hearing the latest speculation in the news about the Olympics. There are ominous reports of the Nazis in Germany and the occasional rumbling of boycotting or backing out of the Olympics next year. Now those rumblings are becoming louder and more frequent.

Will the U.S. even compete in the upcoming Olympics?

All anyone can do is change their speed. The Olympics—if they do happen—are just over a year away. It is time to move to a new pace and to find solace in the possibilities of what might come.

. . .

"TYDIE STARTS RECORD BREAKING RELAY."

Despite having gone to the 1932 Olympics and finding her name in the papers many times already, Tidye still can't get publications to spell her name correctly. Even her hometown newspaper, the *Chicago Defender*, misspells it in April when they publish a photo of her along with the other three members of her relay team.

"Chicago's park system relay team invaded Canada last week for two track meets and succeeded in not only winning both, but setting a pair of world's records. One of the records went to Tydie Pickett when she snapped one-tenth of a second off the 40-yard hurdles. Miss Pickett is shown just as she started the relay team off on its record-setting relay."

In the photo, "Tydie" appears to be slightly separated from the three white girls, with just enough distance to have her stand out. Whether that was intentional or not, the young track star has already grown accustomed to sticking out among her fellow competitors. Winning can do that.

Another photo features her a month later. The diminutive young woman, with bright and friendly eyes and a natural smile, poses and proudly displays several medals and trophies she has won in the last few years. The *Chicago Defender* states that Tidye will "very likely compete in the coming world's events to be held in Germany in 1936."

. . .

They flew me across the country just so I could finish in fourth place.

The captain of the UCLA Bruin track team left June 12 by plane to compete in the annual invitational meet at Princeton University. James LuValle sets the pace, as he always does. However, he doesn't realize how much the flight has taken out of him. He is the favorite to win the race, but Eddie O'Brien, a sophomore from Syracuse, finishes with a blast in the final 80 yards, winning the race with a time of 47.3 seconds.

LuValle never wanted to go east to run, content with staying near school and focusing on his studies, yet running times between 47 and 47.5 earned him an invitation. Earlier in the year, the AAU tried to force him to run in the indoor meets taking place on the East Coast, warning they would make him ineligible if he didn't participate. Yet with his heavy fall class load along with his job on campus, LuValle still considers running fun, but just a pastime, one certainly not worth the time and effort of traveling several thousand miles. After the threat by the AAU, LuValle decides to tell the president of the university, Dr. Robert Cordon Sproul.

"We'll see about that," the president tells him.

After Dr. Sproul makes one phone call, LuValle never hears anything again about his needing to go out east.

With his heavy course load in the fall, LuValle can ease up a bit in the spring in order to facilitate traveling and competing in meets. As he works in the chemistry department after school, the team coaches stay later to practice with him after the rest of the track team goes home. The deal is for LuValle to get there as fast as he can, which is seldom before four-thirty or five. It is impossible for him to be on the track when his teammates arrive at two or three in the afternoon.

"The main thing was I was trying to get an education in the sciences," LuValle will say about those days. "I had a combined major in chemistry, physics, and math. It kept me busy."

• • •

Metcalfe wipes the sweat off the side of his face as he glances over at Jesse Owens on the side of the track. The sun seems to be stepping on top of them, smothering and suffocating the athletes at the University of Nebraska's Memorial Stadium. It is Independence Day, and more than fifteen thousand spectators have chosen to watch the festivities on the track before the day disappears and fireworks light up the sky. The 100-meter final has arrived, and Metcalfe feels ready to regain his position as the fastest man alive, though he has to do it against a runner who just made history two months ago.

On May 25, 1935, at the Big Ten Track and Field Championships at Ferry Field in Ann Arbor, Michigan, the unthinkable happened. Jesse Owens, an Ohio State sophomore who will go on to be referred to many times as a son of a sharecropper and a grandson of a slave, won the 100-yard, the broad jump, the 220-yard, and the 220 low hurdles events in 45 minutes. Owens tied a world record with the 100-yard and broke world records in the three others with his performance.

With the rise of track stars like Jesse Owens and Ben Johnson, Metcalfe finds it easy for both competitors and reporters to forget about him or simply assume he is the old man on the track. Yet some have not forgotten. His Marquette track coach writes an article for the papers with a bold headline stating, "He's Greatest Athlete of Modern Times." Metcalfe is honored to hear the praise. "His consistency and amazing power, together with his good sportsmanship, mark him as one of the greatest runners the country ever produced." Coach Jennings lists his many accomplishments and records, numbers that Metcalfe either forgot or never knew. Like winning eighty-nine of his ninety-six races while he was at Marquette.

"Metcalfe is a true champion, and I think you'll hear more of him by the time the 1936 Olympic Games roll around," Jennings says at the end of the article. Metcalfe certainly hopes and plans on that being true.

Digging his cleats into the carved-out hollow he'd dug for his start in lane 3, Metcalfe kneels in position. Owens positions himself in lane 4 right next to Metcalfe. The first few seconds are everything for the slow starter. Especially now with a lightning bolt like Owens who starts fast and ends faster.

The shot goes off and the runners break out of the starting line, only to hear a second shot for a false start. With his massive chest sucking in air, Metcalfe strides back on the track, adrenaline coursing through him. Another shot is followed by a second quick crack. There are eleven false starts in all. The starter eventually comes up to the runners and gives them a friendly bit of encouragement to get their act together.

Metcalfe wants the twelfth try to be lucky, and he gets off to a good start, just behind Owens. Soon he runs side by side with the younger sprinter at the 40-meter mark, then plows ahead of Owens, knowing he is going to beat him today. Yet Metcalfe sees a figure on his right staying with him, starting to move ahead of him, and it isn't Owens. It is another sophomore, Eulace Peacock from Temple.

No time is left to keep surging, it's over, and Metcalfe and Owens have both been beaten. The conversation revolves around the older and younger greats competing to see who is the quickest, but it turns out they are both beaten by someone younger. Peacock's time is an incredible 10.2, breaking the world record.

Peacock isn't completely unknown, since he broke the world record in the 100-meter race the previous year in a meet in Oslo, Norway. Owens matched this on his monumental day in Michigan in May when he also set three other records. Peacock is only twenty but still has not been a factor in races so far in '35. Not until today. Peacock not only beats Owens in the 100 meters, but he also outperforms him in the broad jump, winning with a 26.3-foot leap.

Like Owens, Eulace Peacock was born in Alabama, a year after him, and moved with his parents to New Jersey. As a star on his high school football team, Peacock arrived at Temple University excited to play for "Pop" Warner, who was lured from Stanford to coach. Yet after everybody witnesses Peacock's breathtaking speeds, the school decided that he needed to drop football and instead focus on track, a decision that he hates.

Days after this win, Peacock once again beats Owens in a race, one that Metcalfe doesn't run. "Jesse Owens Bows Again To Eulace Peacock" reads the headline in the *Wisconsin State Journal*. Newspapers love to create drama, high stakes, and hyperbole. Only recently, Metcalfe read an article with an Olympic coach saying he would never beat Jesse Owens again, nor would anybody else. Yet Owens *is* beatable.

Jesse Owens and Eulace Peacock shake hands at the Penn Relays, Philadelphia, Pennsylvania.

Anybody can be beat. It just depends on the day, the moment, and the speed.

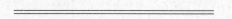

LONG, FLOWING FLAGS *of red, black, and white adorn the Ufa Picture Palace in Berlin on March 28, 1935. A fleet of Mercedes-Benz 770s lines the street in front of the theater, with a fence barricading the spectators on the other side. The opulence sparkles under the spotlights, but this is no ordinary movie premiere.*

A year earlier, Hitler asked the talented filmmaker Leni Riefenstahl to once again film the annual rally in Nuremberg, but this time she is allowed to do so without any interference from the Nazi propaganda offices. This means she doesn't have to come under the scrutiny of Josef Goebbels, who in turn regards the entire film with indifference. The Germans' reaction to her film, The Triumph of the Will, *however, is much more enthusiastic.*

After the official guests, including Hitler, arrive at the spectacularly decorated theater, renovated by Hitler's architect of choice, Albert Speer, they are treated to a cinematic treasure. The drama on the screen begins with the opening crawl:

20 years after the outbreak of the World War

16 years after the beginning of German suffering

19 months after the beginning of the German rebirth

Adolf Hitler flew again to Nuremberg to review the columns of his faithful followers

The results of Riefenstahl's work are also highly influential, with The Triumph of the Will *becoming the Nazis' most popular propaganda film. Much of the success is due to the director's artistic flair, not only with her careful use of cameras but also in how she edits the footage in postproduction. Her technique of employing cameras in motion on rails is revolutionary. Riefenstahl learned from her work on the first Nuremberg rally she filmed, and this time she has a bigger budget and more time to prepare. Hitler and his Nazi Party have never looked so spectacular, foreshadowing the coming glory expected in the Berlin Olympics.*

Hitler is thrilled with the results, smiling and presenting the director with a bouquet of lilacs after the viewing. Several months later, August of that year, Hitler asks her to film the upcoming Berlin Olympics.

As Hitler and Goebbels continue developing their propaganda ma-

Adolf Hitler, Rudolph Hess, Julius Streicher, and NSDAP officials at the 1935 Nuremberg Rally.

chine, they also continue to successfully implement their Nazi ideology. New laws are announced at the 1935 rally in Nuremberg, laws that give the United States and the rest of the world more cause to reject the invitation by the Germans to compete in the upcoming Olympic Games.

CHAPTER FIFTEEN

THE BOYCOTT DEBATE

1935

FROM JULY TO December, across America both north and south, hardly a day goes by without discussion and debate over the boycott of the upcoming Olympics. Most of the conversation centers on the Nazis' views and treatment of the Jewish population, with very little focus on the discrimination against African Americans.

A leading proponent of the American boycott of the Olympics is Jeremiah T. Mahoney, a former judge in the Supreme Court of New York State. He was friends with Avery Brundage for many years, once writing "how fortunate the AAU is to have you (for the second time) as its President." After Judge Mahoney is elected AAU president in 1935, he soon opposes Brundage's stance regarding the Berlin games. In July, he is outspoken about such views to the press.

"While I can't attempt to speak for the entire Amateur Athletic Union, I can speak for myself," President Mahoney declares. "If these renewed reports of religious persecution in Germany are substantiated, I can unqualifiedly state how my vote will be cast. It will be dead against an American team competing in any country that does not recognize equality of races and faiths."

Mahoney concedes that the decision is not his to make, however.

"There is the American Olympic Committee yet to be considered. Will I attempt to bring this issue to a head? That's something for the 1935 convention to determine. It will be held in December and, by that time, we ought to know what we are about."

Avery Brundage answers publicly, stating, "I haven't heard of anything to indicate discrimination against athletes of any race or religion since last year when there were reports that Jewish athletes might not be permitted to represent Germany in the games. The question was answered by assurances from German political and sports figures that there would be no racial, religious or political interference of any kind."

Mahoney remains unconvinced. "I regret to say that irrefutable proof seems to exist that the discrimination in Germany against Jewish athletes has been continued in such a manner as to justify a definite and positive decision by America that she will not participate in the Olympic games in Berlin unless conditions are radically changed at once." Stating that discrimination has been proven beyond a shadow of a doubt, the president of the AAU continues to say, "The Nazi government has stupidly directed action against German Jewish athletes in an un-American, unsportsmanlike, uncharitable, and un-Olympianlike manner."

In the spring of 1935, Mahoney writes a letter to the president of the German Olympic Committee, Dr. Theodor Lewald, declaring the country is guilty of "monstrous incidents of racism, brutality, and genocide." He titles the letter, "Germany Has Violated the Olympic Code." Yet the statements still fall on many deaf ears in the sports community.

The athletes vying to compete in Berlin aren't immune to the questions but rather are encouraged to engage in the dialogue. When asked about his stance on the situation, Ralph Metcalfe gives his honest opinion. "I have made several exhibition appearances in Germany and surely found no antagonism. Recent reported affronts to those of my faith should bring these current matters to a head and I hope for an amicable settlement of the difficulties."

Some of the athletes won't publicly state their views, while others have not yet decided themselves what to make of the boycott. In the August 24 edition of the *New York Amsterdam News,* an open letter is written to these silent athletes in the middle of the boycott begging them to refuse to participate in the Berlin Olympics. They specifically name Jesse Owens, Eulace Peacock, Ralph Metcalfe, Cornelius Johnson, Willis Ward, James LuValle, and Ben Johnson in their letter.

"You have challenged and vanquished the myths of racial superiority and inferiority," the *Amsterdam News* states, remarking on the way they've shown courage with their achievements and how they now have a great opportunity before them. "Yours is the opportunity to strike a blow which may hasten its inevitable end. As members of a minority group whose persecution the Nazis have encouraged, as citizens of a country in which all liberty has not yet been destroyed, as leaders in a field which encourages the removal of all barriers of race, creed and color, you cannot afford to give moral and financial support to a philosophy which seeks the ultimate destruction of all you have fought for."

Another publication, the *Cleveland Gazette,* shares the sentiment, stating, "Refusal to participate would do untold good in helping Germany and the world to realize that racial bigotry must be opposed in its every manifestation."

The position that the black community took on the boycott was rarely covered by the white press, therefore the black press spoke up for themselves. However, there was never a unified front on this issue, with some black newspapers encouraging a boycott while many pushed for participation in the Olympic games. For the latter, the sentiment came from a *Baltimore Afro-American* reporter who said that the Olympic Games offered a chance to raise up the "despised darker races and lower the prestige of the proud and arrogant Nordic."

. . .

Avery Brundage's defiance grows as 1935 passes. He states in October that "the Olympic Games belong to the athletes and not the politicians." As the chairman of the American Olympic Committee, who some could have argued had a political mind-set and bent himself, Brundage says those who demand an Olympic boycott "haven't been closer to Berlin than Manhattan Island." Yet the case is made by some that Brundage is a bit too cozy and comfortable with Hitler and the Nazis. Columnist Heywood Broun writes in the *Reading Times* that "Brundage has been in Germany and comes back to report that all conditions are lovely. Might it not be a good idea for Mr. Brundage to get a little closer to America and a little further away from the Nazi host who showed him a good time?"

All one needs to do is watch and listen to rhetoric and announcements made one month earlier at the annual Nuremberg Rally for the Nazis. Laws are announced on September 15 that revoke the citizenship of German Jews, along with prohibiting a non-Jewish German from either marrying a Jew or having sexual relations with one. Jewish households can no longer have German maids under the age of forty-five as well. Hitler's justification is this creates "a level ground on which the German people may find a tolerable relation with the Jewish people." Like every move Hitler makes toward the systematic and government-controlled extermination of a group he has called "parasites," the Nuremberg Laws are simply another step to the Holocaust.

The Nazis' definition of a Jewish man or woman doesn't arise from their beliefs, but rather from whether they have three or four Jewish grandparents. Even if the grandparents no longer practice Judaism and are converts, they are still considered Jews. By November

1935, the Nuremberg Laws broaden to prohibit marriage or sexual relations between Germans and any people who could produce "racially suspect" children. The minister of the interior defines "any people" to be blacks, Gypsies, or their offspring.

Judge Jeremiah T. Mahoney demands the president of the German Olympic Committee, Dr. Theodor Lewald, resign his office. "I am convinced, and do not see how you can deny, that the German Jews are being excluded from the possibility of participating in the Olympic Games merely because they are Jews. That not only are they not encouraged to participate in the Olympics, but that the conditions under which they exist make it impossible for them to do so." He goes on to say, "I believe that participation in the games under the Swastika implies the tacit approval of all that the Swastika symbolizes. I believe that for America to participate in the Olympics in Germany means giving American moral and financial support to the Nazi regime which is opposed to all that Americans hold dearest."

Brundage remains as obstinate and combative as Mahoney, writing a pro-German letter to Hans von Tschammel und Osten, the Reichssportführer or "Reich sports leader," who has been a member of the Nazi Party since 1922. "The sordidness of the attacks against me and the lowly methods in the futile efforts pursued to black American participation have caused me to become more resolute than ever and I shall fight grimly to the very end."

Fighting to the very end is exactly what Brundage does. The boycott debate comes to an end at the 1935 AAU convention in New York City, held from December 6 to 8. Around two hundred delegates meet at the Commodore Hotel to end the bitter struggle. Brundage arrives saying the battle was won two years earlier, yet he also stresses that an open fight on the convention floor "might very easily wreck the structure of the AAU." Mahoney, however, says that "there is a preponderance of sentiment in favor of a boycott of the Olympic Games." A boycott decision by the AAU means that representatives will promptly seek to have its organization withdraw from the Berlin games.

"If the result means my death, I care not," Mahoney says in his passionate twenty-minute speech to the delegates before their vote. "There is more at stake here than Olympic ideals. It's humanity itself. It is one of the most momentous questions ever presented to an athletic organization . . . the Nazis want to make us a tail to the Hitler kite. They want Hitler to be able to boast to the world press that this country participated in the Olympic Games with the full approval of the United States and in full accord with Nazi principles."

Brundage argues every side he can, asking where the money is coming in to pay for the boycott movement. "I've heard it said that $1,000,000 will be spent to keep our athletes free from competing at Berlin. Since when did money enter into the Olympics and amateur

Avery Brundage (left) convinces delegates to vote for participation in the Berlin Olympic Games, New York, December 1935.

athletics? What would our founders think if they knew this?" He also reminds the delegates that the other sports leaders in the world have approved of participation, asking, "Are they to be insulted?"

The slight margin of victory would go to Brundage and the pro-Olympic movement as the AAU votes 58 to 56 against a resolution to investigate German Olympic conditions one more time.

The decision is final. America will participate in the 1936 Olympics.

. . .

Before the vote happens, future Olympic prospects Jesse Owens, Ralph Metcalfe, Eulace Peacock, Ben Johnson, and Cornelius Johnson write in December of 1935 to Avery Brundage expressing their favor for participating in the Berlin Olympics. "I have no reason to believe I would be mistreated in any way if I were successful in qualifying for the 1936 U.S. Olympic team," Metcalfe says, adding he "felt that no political situation should alter plans for the coming games in Berlin." They don't realize that official Nazi newspapers such as the *Völkischer* are writing that blacks should be excluded from the games for fear of the "sacred grandeur of the Olympiad" not being upheld.

Walter White of the NAACP responds with a letter to Jesse Owens on December 4, 1935. "I fully realize how great a sacrifice it will be for you to give up the trip to Europe and to forgo the acclaim which your athletic prowess will unquestionably bring you," White writes. "I realize equally well how hypocritical it is for certain Americans to point the finger of scorn at any other country for racial or other kind of bigotry. On the other hand, it is my firm conviction that the issue of participation in the 1936 Olympics, if held in Germany under the present regime, transcends all other issues. Participation by American athletes, and especially those of our own race which has suffered more than any other from American race hatred, would, I firmly believe, do irreparable harm."

In ending the letter, White tells Owens, "I am sure that your stand will be applauded by many people in all parts of the world, as your participation under the present situation in Germany would alienate many high-minded people who are awakening to the dangers of intolerance wherever it raises its head."

As the boycott debate finally comes to a head, the role of the African American athlete within the sports world is still open to question. The *Philadelphia Tribune* writes, "The A.A.U. shouts against the cruelties of other nations and the brutalities in foreign climes, but conveniently forgets the things that sit on its own doorstep." One example of this is showcased after Jesse Owens is deemed ineligible to be a finalist for the 1935 Sullivan Award for the nation's most outstanding amateur athlete. Three world records and a tied world record in one meet still haven't allowed him to escape segregation from the sports world. The AAU initially charges him with allegedly receiving money that year, yet gives him his amateur status back after he is absolved of any wrongdoing, a decision that comes after the Sullivan Award has been awarded to someone else.

In the middle of December, at the end of a combative year full of discourse and diatribes from all sides, a "scorching" letter is sent to the *New York World Telegram* from a writer named Charles A. Smythwick Jr., summing up the true dichotomy between the pride found in the Olympics and the prejudice found in America:

"But one wonders if, by chance, the next Olympiad were to take place in, let us say Atlanta, Ga., or almost any of the states below the Mason and Dixon line, would 'the powers that be' remove signs in the railroad stations reading, 'White on This Side,' 'Colored on That Side'?" Smythwick Jr. wonders. Would hotels open up their doors to all people despite their race? Could anyone arriving to the games sit in any train or bus seat they wanted to? Would towns remove signs saying they wouldn't serve Negroes?

Smythwick Jr. continues his point, writing, "Our great leaders cry out in stentorian voices that the German government has enacted discriminatory laws and permits acts of violence against a minority race. Have they forgotten that discrimination against the Negro in the South is sanctioned by law? Have they ever heard of Jim Crow?

"This is to be remembered by all charitable Americans: 'Clean thine own house before thou cleanest thy neighbor's.'"

TWENTY-FIVE CENTS. THAT'S *all the money John Woodruff carries with him. The loose coins sit in his pants pocket as the tall, lanky young man rides in a car belonging to the sheriff of Connellsville, Pennsylvania. Woodruff isn't driving, of course; the sheriff has graciously volunteered to chauffeur him an hour away to the University of Pittsburgh, where Woodruff will begin taking classes in just a few days. He doesn't know how else he could have gotten himself to the campus.*

If only Mom could see me now.

John Woodruff thinks about his mother and wonders if she watches him from Heaven. If so, it means she would have seen him graduate from high school that May, a feat no one else in their family ever managed, much less getting a scholarship to go to a big college. There is no way Woodruff could have managed to attend a university without a scholarship. And there is absolutely no miracle in this world that could have given him any other scholarship than one for running. Woodruff is forever grateful for Coach Larew and everything he has taught him on the track, and his Pitt coach Carl Olson for helping him get there.

Born on July 5, 1915, in Connellsville, a small town cuddled in the mountains of steelmaking country, John never knows all his eleven siblings. He is the second to the youngest, and some died in infancy from cases of the measles, whooping cough, pneumonia, and scarlet fever. One brother was killed hunting at the age of sixteen. Perhaps those diseases tried to close in around him, too, but John is born with a talent of stepping outside of the pack.

The Woodruffs are poor, especially with such a large family. Silas Woodruff, his father, is twenty-two years old when he marries nineteen-year-old Sarah, John's mother. His father is the son of Virginia slaves and employed by the H.C. Frick Coke Company, making a living digging coal and working with the coke ovens. Sarah does laundry for wealthy families in town. When it comes to John, the only thing his parents are concerned about is making sure the truant officer at his school never has to contact them about his missing classes.

John is born near the peak of Connellsville's profitable coal and coke boom, which begins in the 1840s. By 1920, the population of Connellsville grows to 13,804. It is said that, at one time, the city is home to more millionaires per capita than any other place in the country. At an early age John dreams beyond working in coal factories. He is smart enough to know the best thing he can do is to get an education and maybe one day go to college. Yet higher education remains a fantasy for many in Connellsville, even more so if you are black.

During his junior year in high school, Woodruff is forced to quit the football team in order to concentrate on chores and homework. One of the assistant coaches, Joseph "Pop" Larew, who also coaches the track team, asks him about trying out for the sport. Woodruff decides to go out for the track team in the spring of 1934. His mother agrees to the decision, since it allows him to get home earlier than he had while playing football.

In his first official competition, Woodruff competes in the 880-yard dash and the mile and wins them both, yet he also knows his times can be improved. He has a long way to go before becoming a strong runner. The first mile he runs is 4 minutes 44 seconds, compared to the world-record mile time of 4:06.8 set by American Glenn Cunningham the same year. Each race Woodruff runs showed him making progress. On and off the field, his coach is there to support him.

"If you keep doing well and improving your times, you might be able to get a scholarship to college," Larew tells him.

Unable to find employment or enlist in the navy, the idea of going away to college seems too incredible for Woodruff to imagine. Nobody in his *family has ever completed high school, he tells himself. So how can a poor black kid from the coal-mining town of Connellsville make his way onto some college campus?*

Now that Woodruff has answered that question, he knows he's been given a great opportunity and he plans to do something with it. Woodruff knows he was the best athlete in his high school, a knowledge not based on superiority or arrogance but on simple facts. Now he has to prove he is one of the best in college.

CHAPTER SIXTEEN

BAPTISM BY FIRE
1935

COACH BRUTUS HAMILTON, head of the track team at the University of California, has never heard of Archie Williams. The coach is a legend, an athlete who competed in both the '20 and '24 Olympics, earning a silver medal in the decathlon in the former. During his high school years at Missouri State High, Brutus swept victories in the broad jump, high jump, pole vault, and shot put at the championships, carrying his abilities to the University of Missouri. Not only did he excel in track and field, but he played on an All-American football team and a winning basketball team for an athletic club. Brutus tried his hand at baseball, having a tryout with the New York Yankees. Archie knows that whatever sport the coach might have played, Brutus would have been up for it.

How can Archie announce himself to someone like this? Archie is just another guy who wanted to go to Cal, someone who learned to get good grades in high school and who did pretty well academically in junior college. His own guidance counselor is unimpressed with Williams, trying to steer him from his dreams of becoming an engineer.

"What do you want to be?" Kelsey Van Every asks Archie.

"I want to be a mechanical engineer."

Van Every's face shows the disbelief. "Look—are you crazy? Why don't you become a preacher? Or how about a real estate man?"

"What do you mean?" Archie asks.

"You're not going to find a job," the counselor tells him. "If you want to go to college, pick out a career you can actually have."

Archie finds a summer job cutting weeds around the Kensington reservoir for a water company. He enjoys seeing how water is cleaned through the filtering plants. Archie imagines how nice it would be to work at a place like this, so he speaks to the personnel guy at the water company, but the man says the same thing. He doesn't think it is possible for a black man to be hired as an engineer. There simply aren't any African American engineers that can be found.

Archie remains undaunted talking to the water company employees and his counselor alike. "Please sign me up for that."

Archie becomes a committed Cal student, confirming those dreams he held as a kid eyeing Campanile from his porch. Since tuition is only twenty-six dollars a semester and he can save costs by living at home, he doesn't need to get a sports scholarship. Archie knows he is fast, but the priority in college is graduating, not running. Many of the guys he ran with at San Mateo Junior College went to Stanford, and though Coach Tex Byrd tried to get him enrolled in the school, he had no luck. Stanford has a lot of fine athletes at its school, but it doesn't have any black athletes. The only African Americans that are at Stanford wash dishes in the frat houses.

But no Stanford guy's ever beat me. Not yet.

Coach Byrd, a Stanford man himself, admits the truth himself.

"Archie, if you were white, I could get you into Stanford just like that. Get you a scholarship."

Archie Williams prepares for his morning class schedule.

It doesn't matter. Archie is a born Cal man, and he wants to prove Stanford wrong. His competitive nature kicks into gear after that first meeting with Kelsey Van Every, and while his grades won't be straight A's, he collects a few of them along with B's, keeping his grades high enough to never be in jeopardy of being dropped from the track team due to slipping grades. He knows he will have to be the one driving himself. Nobody is pushing any black student to graduate, and they sure aren't helping with job placements.

"I was a nobody," Archie says later in life. "Nobody recruited me . . . and I didn't care because I was going to play in the physics lab."

The track season arrives in spring, but Archie follows some of the guys he knows from his junior college and tries out for fall track. After making it, he begins to turn heads when he starts to win. Especially Coach Brutus's. The coach takes to working with him and extends the kind of coaching Archie has never received before. This includes taking an interest in Archie not only as a runner but as a young man. He learns about Archie's life and family and makes sure to stay informed of his grades. Coach Brutus knows the athletes are there to get an education as well as compete in sports, and he often becomes irate with the players when they are flunking off the team or simply not taking their coursework seriously enough.

Archie discovers the difference between athletes in junior college and athletes at a big university. Junior college lies somewhere between high school and college, somewhere at the halfway mark. Every now and then at the junior college he'd run against an exceptional athlete, but not often. Everything becomes tougher when he arrives at Cal: the courses, the competitors, the entire college experience. The coach calls it a baptism by fire, being thrown into the mix with the tough guys. And this was only in fall track. The actual spring season approaches, and that's when the temperature really gets turned up.

. . .

"Blue moon, you saw me standing alone," Ralph Metcalfe sings to the crowd in a Chicago club. As soon as Metcalfe blows a smooth note through his trumpet, his band jamming behind him, a familiar ache is lit. His trick muscle is back at it again, flaring up an invisible spark in the lower part of his leg. It doesn't affect his performance; he only picks up the trumpet at select moments of the show. Metcalfe hides his grimace as he belts out a few notes then resumes directing the guys in the band.

With the year nearing its end, Metcalfe hopes and prays that 1936 will be brighter and full of joy instead of sorrow. Lucy, his younger sister, died in September after battling an illness for just five short weeks. A big brother should never have to see his baby sister buried. Then there was the terrible accident just after Thanksgiving when Metcalfe had been driving and a man stepped right out in front of him. He knew how to control his body and react quicker than most anybody else, yet Metcalfe's car wasn't as cooperative, so when he swerved to avoid the pedestrian, the fender still struck the man, who would die a couple of weeks later. The authorities exonerated Metcalfe from any responsibility.

Playing with his band, the Creole Flashes, is an outlet for Metcalfe. His college track career has come to an end, therefore he is no longer training and competing as much as he has in the past. He studies law at Marquette along with working, and is elected class president that fall. Life becomes so busy he is forced to decline an offer to race in Europe earlier that August.

With all the discussion and arguments surrounding the boycott of the Olympics in the next year, Metcalfe is simply relieved an official decision has finally been made. He has always been in favor of going and has said so publicly in a few careful words. Personally, he thinks it would be crazy for him and all of the other athletes who are at the peak of their careers (some more so than him) to simply not go.

Metcalfe just wants to go over to Europe and dust all of those Germans who think they are better than everybody else.

THE WORLD WITNESSES *Adolf Hitler assemble his chess pieces of destruction across Europe. This is illustrated just weeks before the premiere of* The Triumph of the Will, *as German military forces march into the Rhineland and effectively violate the peace treaty that put an end to World War I, the Treaty of Versailles. The treaty punished Germany for its actions in the war, diminishing its military and demilitarizing forces in the Rhineland residing in the west along the Rhine River. Occupying the Rhineland also violates the agreements set by the Locarno Pact, in which the countries of Germany, France, Belgium, Great Britain, and Italy all guaranteed peace in Western Europe.*

In 1935, France and the Soviet Union create the Franco-Soviet Treaty of

Mutual Assistance, designed to encircle Nazi Germany and reduce its threat to central Europe. Hitler cites this treaty in a speech to the Reichstag on March 7, stating it violates the terms of the Locarno Pact. As he denounces the Versailles Treaty, Hitler claims complete innocence and peaceful measures with his military moves in the Rhineland, saying, "The German people is not interested in having the French people suffer, and vice versa," while also declaring his continued detestation of the Soviets. "I love my people and I know it can be fortunate only when life, according to its nature and its way, is possible for it. I will not have the gruesome Communist international dictatorship of hate descend upon the German people, which cannot only weep but can also laugh heartily through its life."

Eleven days later, Hitler takes this one step further, declaring an immediate military conscription in effect in Germany. "There is a cry of war today as if there had never been a World War or a Versailles Treaty," the proclamation states. With Goebbels acting as his mouthpiece to read this proclamation to the German people, Hitler's announcement forms an army composed of a dozen corps made up of thirty-six divisions.

The New York Times *features a headline that bears the ominous truth: "With Yearly Class of 300,000, Hitler May Soon Command Biggest Army In All of Europe." It goes on to state, "Hitler proclaimed to the German people yesterday that the Third Reich seeks only peace. That was what Wilhelm II used to say. He said it so often he came to believe it. Yet he also thought his army could defeat everything in sight."*

PART THREE

JOE LOUIS IS *in trouble, and everyone watching knows it. So far, they've been waiting for the knockout blow by Louis, but in the fourth round of this match with Max Schmeling of Germany, the champion suddenly seems vulnerable. The black community watches in utter disbelief as their hero is backed up and takes a flurry of hits before Schmeling nails a right hook that propels Louis to the mat.*

A year earlier, Ernest Hemingway writes Joe Louis is "too good to be true, and absolutely true . . . the most beautiful fighting machine that I have ever seen," after seeing the boxer decimate the former world heavyweight champion Max Baer and knock him out in the fourth round. Almost a hundred thousand spectators watch the fight on September 24, 1935, in Yankee Stadium.

Joe Louis is the son of a sharecropper who moved with his mother and stepfather to Detroit, Michigan, when he was ten. Encouraged to get into boxing, Louis wins fifty of fifty-four matches along with the national light heavyweight title as an amateur. He declares himself a pro in '34. The following year, Louis will win two notable bouts, one against "The Ambling Alp" from Italy, Primo Carnera, and the other against Max Baer.

By the time Louis boxes Schmeling less than two months before the Olympics in Germany, it is a foregone conclusion that Louis will defeat the thirty-year-old former champion. In Harlem, the lack of ticket sales can be attributed to the belief that Schmeling doesn't stand a chance of beating Louis.

"The fight won't go over three rounds," Joe tells his managers.

With a 27-0 record and a number-one ranking, Louis, in many ways, embodies the fate of the entire African American population. His wins are theirs, and so, too, will be his losses.

"The Brown Bomber," as he is called, never recovers from his knockdown. Schmeling lands another blistering punch in the fifth round with his

powerful right hand, and for the rest of the match, Louis fights in a daze, unable to respond to the German's unrelenting blows. Eventually Louis will go down in the twelfth, shaking his head and trying to lift himself off the canvas but unable to.

The defeat at the hands of a German boxer doubted by his own country shocks the black community. Maya Angelou writes about this fight, saying, "My race groaned. It was our people falling. It was another lynching, yet another Black man hanging on a tree." Reports of young black men looting in Chicago and New York follow, including a distraught young girl in Harlem attempting to poison herself. Some black newspapers question whether Louis is drugged during the fight. Arthur P. Davis, a literary scholar and university teacher, writes, "We all feel that the race has somehow lost prestige in this upsetting defeat. A foolish reaction? Of course; but it is one that American living inevitably forces upon us."

Bill Gibson of the The Afro American will say, "Joe was overconfident in a big way and he was consequently unprepared. His defeat is the most valuable lesson that he has learned thus far. He should be improved at least one hundred per cent as a result of it." Louis takes full responsibility, stating, "I have no alibi for losing. Max can sure hit and I took plenty of beating out there. Sure, I want to fight him again."

After having been mostly reticent about the upcoming fight, Hitler and the Nazis immediately use it for more propaganda. Joseph Goebbels congratulates Schmeling, saying, "I know you fought for Germany, your victory was a German victory." The Nazi weekly journal Das Schwarze Korps (The Black Corps) comments: "Schmeling's victory was not only sport. It was a question of prestige for our race."

For Hitler and his Aryan race theory, the Louis-Schmeling fight serves as a delicious appetizer to the upcoming Olympics. It also confirms in his mind the superiority of his race, one that he intends to shine in Berlin.

CHAPTER SEVENTEEN

TRIAL AND ERROR

1936

ONCE AGAIN, AN unlikely emerging star rises out of nowhere to shine at the women's Olympic trials for the 1936 Olympics. First there was Babe Didrikson back in '32, and now there's a tall, lanky girl from Fulton, Missouri, named Helen Stephens. Louise Stokes recalls first seeing her the previous September at the national championship meet at Ohio Field at New York University. In front of several hundred people on a cold and blustery day, Louise wins the 50-meter dash with a time one-tenth off her American record. Stephens easily beats all other runners in the 100- and 200-meter races, setting a world record in the former.

Entering these national championships on July 4, which also serve as the official Olympic trials, Helen Stephens remains the competitor to watch. Dee Boeckmann, the coach of the team, tells the *Providence Journal* this is "the fastest field of women athletes ever to grace our women's championship. Indeed, I term this group the fastest field of women track stars ever assembled anywhere." Coach Boeckmann explains that the top three finishers in all six events will qualify for the Olympic team. There will also be extras picked for the 400-meter relay based on their performance in the 100 meter. They will leave tomorrow, Sunday, to go with the coach to New York, where they will stay at the Lincoln Hotel until sailing out with the rest of the Olympic team on July 15 to go to Berlin.

Louise is happy to find the trials in her backyard at Providence, Rhode Island. Brown Stadium at Brown University is more than an hour away from Malden. Family and friends are among the four thousand spectators in the stands on this perfect day watching the women competing.

Babe is no longer competing in track and field, having chosen golf as her sport a year ago and continuing to find success as a competitor. Many familiar faces are here in Brown Stadium. Tidye is there, of course, racing in the 80-meter hurdles. Annette Rogers from the Illinois Catholic Women's Club, who won a gold medal with the 4x100 relay team at the '32 Olympics, competes once again in the 100 meter and the high jump. Two of the hurdlers who made the '32 team, Simone Schaller and Evelyne Hall, also line up against Tidye to see who will be going to Berlin. Ethel Harrington, who failed to qualify for the '32 team but was allowed a spot on it, will be racing against Louise in the 100 meter.

Like many of the young women, Louise remains unsure how she'll be able to afford the expenses to Germany if she does indeed make the team. She puts those concerns out of her mind for the moment as she lines up for the first heat, winning it with a time of 12.2 seconds. The favorite, Helen Stephens, wins it with an 11.7.

After winning her semifinal race with another 12.2, Louise falters in the final, falling behind five other runners. Harriet Bland, the third-place runner who makes the team, finishes the 100 meter with a 12.3, a time Louise could easily beat. Once again, Helen Stephens wins easily with an 11.7.

For the moment, Louise finds her Olympic dreams in jeopardy. She can't help thinking of the previous Olympic Games, and how

Tidye Pickett competes at the 1936 U.S. Women's Track Trials, Providence, Rhode Island, 1936.

she and Tidye were left off the relay team. She fears this will happen to her once again in these trials.

• • •

Tidye glides over the first six hurdles in her 80-meter event, but her leg clips the seventh hurdle, causing her to land awkwardly and bruise her ankle. She manages to get over the last hurdle and finish the semifinal in second place. The question now remains whether she'll be able to run in the finals.

She's not surprised to see Evelyne Hall in the finals. Earlier that year at the Central AAU meet at Stagg Field in Chicago, Hall beat her in the hurdles and took first place. John Brooks remains her coach, and he calms her nerves by reminding her that she is one of the fastest sprinters out there, and she's been racing in the hurdles for long enough to know what she needs to do, even with an ankle injury.

Forgetting the pain of her ankle and the pressure of the race,

Tidye takes second in the hurdles right behind Anne O'Brien. Surprisingly, Evelyne Hall takes fourth place.

Hall will be one of those athletes unable to go to Berlin due to the cost. "Because finances were next to nothing for women's track and field, the girls who made the team wired home for about a thousand dollars that they'd need in order to go," Hall will say. "It was easier for the girls who were from small towns. I tried to get money from the Parks department but I didn't get it."

Evelyne Hall was referring to her hometown of Chicago, the same city Tidye is from. Fortunately, Tidye ends up being one of the women whose fare to Berlin is paid for.

• • •

The young sprinter from Malden, Massachusetts, thinks of all the good people back home who have helped her get this far. The

Tidye Pickett and Louise Stokes make the 1936 U.S. Track Team. Providence, Rhode Island, 1936.

members of her church and the people in the community who have done anything they can to raise money for her in the event that she makes the team. Friends and neighbors and coaches in surrounding cities help with fundraisers and by donating things like stockings and food. Whatever way they can make a contribution, even if it is just a little pocket change.

For several days, Louise waits to see if her past performances on the track, along with her winning the preliminary heat in the Olympic trials, are enough to get her to the Olympics. When she hears the news that she's earned a place on the team, Louise feels a great sense of relief for all those people who are supporting her and her family. They believe in her and now they get to see her going to Berlin. There is more money to raise, but Louise remains confident that she will be able to get on that ship with her friend Tidye.

LINING UP TO *see the barriers stretching halfway down the track, Fritz Pollard, Jr., prepares for the start of the 110-yard high hurdles. If he could choose, this event would not be his first choice. Fritz grew up wanting to compete in the decathlon, but African Americans are not allowed to participate. His second-favorite event is the pole vault, and Fritz became good at it when he competed in Chicago Park District meets. Yet he has never been able to do the pole vault outside Illinois. Thus he is left with events such as the 100-meter sprint, which he found to be boring. Just three years earlier, Fritz raced and beat Jesse Owens in the 100-meter in high school, but never liked the run. Therefore he chose to run in the hurdles, having learned his technique from his father.*

It had to be the high hurdles, however; the low hurdles are too easy. The high hurdles carry an extra measure of difficulty, starting with the hurdles themselves. Heavy, bulky, and in the shape of an inverted T, the hurdles are more difficult to run over then the L-shaped hurdles that will soon be invented. Hitting one of the hurdles either slows you down or sends you tumbling. The timing of the steps in between hurdles has to be precise, otherwise the entire race will be thrown off. The form has to be perfect, and there are only 110 yards to work with, so naturally a runner has to be lightning fast.

Fritz Jr. glances over to where his parents sit. It is easy to spot his father. It always has been. The confident Fritz Sr. doesn't make him nervous, but rather instills that same level of confidence in himself.

Don't embarrass the Pollard name.

Fritz Jr. isn't just a son to a living legend; he is the only son, along with being the eldest, with three younger sisters. Between his father, his uncles, and the park right next door to their house, Fritz Jr. grows up fully integrated with sports. Now he is set to compete to make it on the 1936 Olympic team. Many have doubted his talent, but he has grown used to proving people wrong, especially bigoted grown-ups who have a problem believing a talented young black man can follow in his famous father's footsteps.

His grandparents, John and Amanda Pollard, have seven children, and as the Chicago Defender *states on October 9, 1937, they are "highly respected" and "enjoyed the distinction of being the only Race group in the entire Rogers Park community." Fritz Pollard Sr. attends Lane Tech High and excels in baseball, football, and track. Pollard Sr. has his own example to follow, since his father had been a champion boxer. Being only five-feet-nine and 165 pounds doesn't stop Pollard Sr. from making the Cook County All-Star team and then receiving a Rockefeller scholarship to go to Brown University. At the end of his first season in 1915, Pollard Sr. becomes the first black to play in the Rose Bowl. Much like what Louise Stokes and Tidye Pickett witness on their cross-country trip to California, Pollard initially is denied a room at the hotel where they were staying in Pasadena until a coach threatens to take the team elsewhere.*

After playing professional football in the American Professional Football Association (which later became the NFL), Pollard Sr. goes on to be the first African American to coach an NFL team. This lasts until 1926, when the National Football League unofficially segregates black players and coaches from the league, a ban that lasts two decades. Starting in 1933,

Pollard Sr. begins coaching the Brown Bombers, an all-black semipro team in New York.

The only drawback to being a member of the respectable Pollard family is having to live up to that last name. To his father, the name is everything, and Fritz Sr. tells him time and time again to never embarrass the family name.

When the gun finally goes off, twenty-one-year-old Fritz Jr. easily shoots up and bolts ahead of the other runners. Fritz Jr. plans to honor his family name in these Olympic tryouts.

Fritz Pollard Jr. arrives at a track meet.

CHAPTER EIGHTEEN

THE OLYMPIC "BLACK GANG"

1936

H OW'S YOUR COACH doing?" the guy from USC asks Archie.
"He's doing well."

Archie hears this a lot from athletes at the other schools. Everybody knows Brutus. He's a coach's coach, knowing how to get you to do your best without nitpicking everything and advising you on technique.

As he prepares for the trial heat for the 400 meters, Archie feels loose as a goose. They're competing at the National Collegiate Athletic Association meet at Stagg Field, Chicago. Just a week earlier, on a cold June day at the AAU regionals at Stanford, he ran a 46.3, his best time yet. So far, in his phenomenal sophomore year running for Cal, Archie has been doing everything right.

Most of this success can be credited to the instruction and insight from his coach, Brutus Hamilton. Archie admires Coach Brutus for both his athleticism and his intelligence. Brutus is a natural teacher, who loves literature and studies English.

The coach tells Archie to just do it, to just go out and run fast.

"Run faster than the others, and don't fall down, and don't run out of gas," Coach Brutus says.

Coach Brutus's main concern is the individual, not winning. Many times, Brutus encourages Archie to take a day or two off, sensing his exhaustion.

"I feel fine, Coach," Archie often responds.

"You heard me, take a day off. I don't want to see you out here for two days."

Coach Brutus never criticizes, yells, demeans, or complains. He always stays positive and always believes in an athlete's potential. Everything about him simply shares this belief:

You can be anything you want to be, and I can't do it for you. All I can do is point you in the right direction and give you a push, but you have to do it yourself.

Every week during that 1936 season in track, it seems as though Archie's feet are heading in the right direction and picking up speed, starting off by running the 400 meter in a time of 49.1 seconds, then improving race by race, from 48.8 to 48.6 then 48.2 and then below 48 and 47.

Now, at the start of this preliminary heat at the Chicago meet, Archie thinks of what his coach told him about elimination heats.

"Look, some of these guys want to save themselves in a race," Brutus said. "Every race that you run is a final. If you don't win, then it is final."

Archie approaches every single race as such, giving it all that he has. At the time, this is absolutely necessary for the 400.

"It's like a horse race," Archie would later say. "They had everybody start off, break from the pole. You have to run around the other guys. In fact, in those days they were pretty rough."

Starting off in this manner, the runners elbow and bounce off each other since there are no lanes. Archie moves ahead from the rest of the runners, and as he rounds the turn, feeling as good as he could, he's well ahead of everybody else. He sees Jack Weiershauser and another guy from USC who just finished their race. Both are watching him soar around the corner.

"Hey, Arch, slow down, you got it made," Jack says.

They're acting like he's got the race won, like he shouldn't worry since it's only a trial heat. Archie thinks about the team they're on.

University of Southern California.

I bet these guys are trying to make me run a lousy time, he thinks. He speeds up, perhaps simply to show up the guys on the sidelines. But near the end, he does ease up as he notices the cement sidewalk close to the edge of the finish line. The last thing he wants is to fall and injure himself.

When the officials call his time of 46.1 seconds, Archie only laughs and tells them they are crazy. The officials pull out the measuring tape as they always do and make sure it is official, and then they double-check their stopwatches in disbelief. They congratulate Archie on breaking the world record.

"I ain't going to argue with you," he tells them.

Suddenly running in the Olympics isn't just a wild thought. It's very much a reality for Archie. All he needs to do is focus on the next meet and on qualifying to make it to Berlin.

• • •

Back when Archie still attends junior college, he first sees James Lu-Valle running in the Fresno Relays and realizes he's good, especially when LuValle makes up 30 yards in a relay race. He knows that day that LuValle is his man. Considering they're the same size, Archie also knows he can learn a lot from him. He introduces himself and they become friends.

Much of the past year for LuValle has been spent in books and labs, allowing him to earn a Bachelor of Arts in Chemistry and to graduate Phi Beta Kappa. He is honored to receive the Jake Gimball Award for being designated the outstanding all-round senior. LuValle should have graduated in February, but he enrolled in an extra semester in order to take several courses he still desired to take. Now, he is debating what to do next. Much like Archie Williams, competing for the Olympics is a distant thought in his mind.

When he first entered UCLA, LuValle survived on a Regents' scholarship and his job in the chemistry lab. The school hasn't developed a master's program in chemistry yet; the program is just being introduced this year. Working as a research assistant, LuValle comes to know the professors intimately.

Now, entering the National AAU Championships at Princeton, LuValle knows of Archie's world record in the 400. This doesn't stop him from running all out and pressing into the finish line at the same time as Archie and another runner, USC's Harold Smallwood. The judges wait twenty minutes before rewarding the victory to Smallwood, announcing LuValle in second place and Williams a controversial third.

Archie admits his surprise. The time isn't fast at 47.7, so Archie figures he was either being dumb or was just exhausted. LuValle was always in the front during the race, so Archie could never get around and pass him.

In order for LuValle to afford the Olympic tryouts a couple of weeks after the Princeton Invitational, UCLA pays for him to stay at Princeton, a relatively inexpensive cost. Many of those running at the tryouts at Randall's Island in New York will reside at Princeton.

Considering the brutal conditions, LuValle said, "The Randall's Island meet should never have been held there." The high temperatures and the humidity affect everybody.

* * *

At the Olympic trials, the only relief from the unrelenting sun comes underneath the bleachers. Archie Williams sprawls out on the grass alongside Mack Robinson and Jimmy LuValle, listening to the packed crowd seated above him cheer the competitors as the voice of the announcer bellows through the loudspeakers. Randall's

Island Stadium on New York's East River still gleams from the fresh paint and unfaded wood after being finished only weeks earlier. Completed under the auspices of the Works Progress Administration, the twenty-two-thousand-seat stadium is opened by FDR and Robert Moses, on July 11, 1936, for the trials. Moses, a notorious urban planner and segregationist, vows no people of color should be in "white spaces." The unprecedented number of African American athletes at the track and field trials certainly breaks world records and bests the competition in front of the white crowds—in what is supposed to be an all-white space.

"They're dropping like flies," Archie tells his friends as they watch another runner limping behind the stands after failing to finish a race.

The sun and humidity pour over them, and no amount of water or shade can stop the temperature from squeezing every bit of energy out of each competitor. There are no do-overs for these

John Woodruff warms up on the track at Randall's Island at the U.S. Men's Track & Field Olympic Trials, New York, 1936.

races, not today. These are the Olympic trials. It is do or die. A lot of guys in this stadium aren't going to make it to Berlin, not even some considered favorites to go, such as George Verhoff, a high school kid from San Francisco, who broke the world record in the pole vault a week ago but doesn't survive the fierce competition. His stunning record is no help in these trials, and Verhoff won't end up making the team.

Life was all about being in the right place at the right time, and the Olympics exemplifies this. Some of the bigger names are being beaten by the heat and by their own bodies, while Johnny-come-latelies like Archie and Mack are suddenly making their names known.

You just have to have the goods on the right day, Archie thinks.

This Sunday is the second day of competition. Yesterday, on July 11, Archie ran a 46.7 time in his heat, having the leading time heading into the finals of the 400 meters today. LuValle was close with his time in the second heat of 47.3. The upcoming race is going to be all about want and grit with the seven runners.

"Looks like it's time to head back out to warm up," LuValle tells Archie.

LuValle speaks in his calm, matter-of-fact way. Archie stands and stretches, wiping the sweat off his neck. He feels antsy as he always does before a race, but he isn't scared or excited like some of the guys he has seen today. They carry expectations, hopes, and dreams with them. For Archie, this isn't some monumental, make-or-break event in his life. Just as Coach Brutus taught him, Archie simply needs to go out on the cinder track and show what he can do. What he *knows* he can do, despite the heat and the exhaustion.

Just get out there and run it.

• • •

The nervousness ritually creeps in before races, and LuValle always attempts to retreat from everyone and concentrate. Only moments ago, he had to run his father out of the dressing room simply to focus and have some quiet time to himself.

LuValle lines up for the 400-meter race, glancing over at Archie in the fifth lane, who looks eager to start. He is in the first lane, the lane where you can see everybody else staggered ahead of you. LuValle knows how to run this race and simply needs to trust his ability instead of watching the competitors in front of him. He knows the race will be fast, but speed is the theme of this trip.

New York is just too fast for James LuValle. Everyone he sees seems to be in too big a hurry to go somewhere, though he isn't sure where they exactly need to be. His trip to the city has been enjoyable; he is familiar with traveling, since he had done a lot of it with his father, an army man. He knows how to venture out and discover new places. Still, LuValle knows himself and when the rush is worth it.

I'm just a small-town boy in a big-time city.

After the gun goes off, LuValle never seems to gain his true stride. The sun has simply sapped his game. For a while, he nears the back of the pack, seemingly out of the race. After rounding the second turn, he runs in sixth place just as they all enter the straightaway. His experience and stamina take over, the speed he's been demonstrating the last few years kicking in automatically. By the time they reach the finish line, LuValle has gained ground and is threatening Archie and Smallwood.

His 46.9 is two-tenths of a second behind Smallwood, with Archie winning the race with a 46.6. Plans for attaining his master's degree will now have to be temporarily put on hold.

The three of them have earned a trip to Berlin.

• • •

To Mack Robinson, New York City feels as far away from California as Germany. Regardless of the times he's been posting, Pasadena Junior College wasn't about to pay his way to the Olympic trials in

Randall's Island Stadium, and he didn't have a dime to make the trip on his own. Fortunately, some generous local businessmen stepped in and raised the $150 for his train fare.

If only they had raised a little more to buy me a new pair of shoes along with the ticket.

He glances down at his spikes while he steps onto the track. They are the same ones he trained in, the same ones he ran with in college. Faded and battered, with the spikes worn down and barely effective, the shoes will have to do. Mack knows he needs to forget about any limitations he might have and simply run the race he knows he can run.

As he scans the crowd crammed into the stadium, a sea of white and blue stand out, with the men in their white linen suits and blue shirts, the women in bright, colorful pastel dresses. They have been vocal with cheering on the runners, especially any time Jesse Owens races. This is one of those times.

For the first time he can remember, the 200 meters is being run around a turn instead of staying in one straight path. This new format matches the structure at the coming Olympics. Mack lines up in lane 5 and blasts off to a fast start, knowing that Owens and Metcalfe are both inches behind him in lanes 2 and 4 respectively. He doesn't see Owens launching off to a poor start, but Mack is able to visualize the steady, sweeping Metcalfe going ahead of him as they reach the straight, leading the pack for the moment. Yet with 75 yards to go, Mack surges ahead of Metcalfe and races with confidence, only to finally be caught by Owens. He places second in the finals, earning the right to go to Berlin.

The surprise isn't seeing himself in the top three finishers. It's seeing who *isn't* there alongside him and Owens.

· · ·

Metcalfe stops at the side of the track and bends over, vomiting his breakfast and lunch on the grass. He can't swallow enough oxygen, since the air feels too thick to breathe. He stares back at the track and feels anger simmer inside.

I didn't train enough.

The cold spring and his trick muscle flaring up on him, the nights out with his band, his studies, and his job as an attendant at a mental home—all of these are contributing factors to his result in the 200 meters. Fourth place. Only two-tenths of a second separate his time from the others. The young Robinson kid and Packard inched ahead of him, while Owens won at 21 seconds flat, which doesn't come as a surprise, though this blistering day continues to be full of them.

Metcalfe thinks about the cut he endured as a young butcher slicing open fish. Life and death separated by an inch. Just like a tenth of a second. The slightest sliver of a mark, of a time. He knew it when he was young and he knew it with Tolan and he knows it now.

He can hear Coach Jennings telling him, "I told you to quit your

Jesse Owens and Ralph Metcalfe greet each other at the
U.S. Men's Track & Field Olympic Trials, New York, 1936.

job." The one that took forty-eight hours of his week. But Metcalfe felt he owed it to his family to continue to provide for them; he made that choice. Having only an hour to train every day, especially in a cold spring in Wisconsin, suddenly shows. As does the muscle he pulled during a meet earlier that spring.

I just won the 200-meter championship last week.

But only today matters, only right now.

· · ·

After setting a world record in the high jump, along with fellow jumper David Albritton, Cornelius "Corny" Johnson has some fun when the reporters ask him how he feels. He tries to wave them away, acting as if this is just another day at the track. Of course, jumping 6 feet 9-¾ inches isn't just another ordinary feat.

"Don't ask me how it feels to establish a world's record," Corny says. "I just saw what I had to do and did it. That's all."

It only takes him two jumps to set the record. The crowd is quiet as he launches over the bar, only to see Albritton follow moments later. There is no need to raise the bar to 6 feet 10 inches.

Corny wants to send a message of hope to Americans.

"Tell the folks that I'll be there doing my utmost and if anybody bests me in that high jump, they'll have to do more than jump ordinarily. I am tickled to be in this gang of fellows and feel that they will more than justify the records they have made here. And so it's on to Berlin for us and we hope you will be pleased with what we try to do."

Out of breath and with beating hearts, the new members of the American Olympic team echo similar thoughts with reporters.

"The boys are getting faster and faster every year," Ralph Metcalfe says. "I am glad I made this team because I may not be able to compete further after this year. My studies will take up most of my time. I have a degree from Marquette now, but I want to finish law and that will take plenty of time. I also have a leaning toward

Social Science and may turn to that. However, on my return from the Olympics, I will know definitely what I am going to do. I'll do my utmost in the games abroad and hope to make the same 'grade' on the track there that I did here."

James LuValle notes, "It's a great team we are sending over and I believe the boys will give a good account of themselves."

Archie states, "It is one of the finest groups I have been associated with."

The promising athletes who do not make the team seem more disappointed in not to being able to compete with their fellow athletes than with those abroad. "My greatest regret is that I am not going with this gang," Ben Johnson says. "They are the finest fellows I've ever met and my sincerest wish is that each and every one of them places no worse than he did in the tryouts." Ben was ill from the heat of the day on Saturday and didn't sleep any that night, so he has a poor showing on Sunday. Eulace Peacock also shares his regrets. "Naturally I am sorry I am not making this trip, since so many of my friends are going, but I wish them all the luck in the world and hope they bring back the championship in their events. They have the stuff."

***

WHEN THE DAY *is over, and the combined Olympic trials for the men's and women's events have all been decided, a total of sixteen black men and two black women make the team. Newspapers all over the country write about the influx of "Negroes" heading to Berlin, including the* Chicago Defender, *which prints the headline "The Olympic 'Black Gang' Sails For Germany."*

1 & 2:   *"Cornelius Johnson, of Compton, Calif., and David Albritton, of Ohio State, two long-legged Negroes, both set a new world's record of 6 feet, 9¾ inches in the running high-jump."*

3:    "Jesse Owens, the dusky Buckeye bullet of Ohio State, won his third event in the tryouts with a new world's record of 21 seconds for 200 meters around turn."

4.   "Jesse Owens . . . was pushed to a new record of 21 seconds flat by Mack Robinson, the Pasadena junior college negro boy."

5:    "John Brooks, former University of Chicago negro, cleared 25 feet, 3⅜ inches to finish second."

6 & 7:   "Archie Williams, the California flash, started the parade by winning No. 1 place in the 400 meters. Williams running in the fifth lane showed that he was a good judge of pace and when the field hit the back stretch he had a ten yard advantage. Jimmy Luvalle coming from fifth place in the stretch finished third behind Smallwood of U.S. to make the team and the trip. Smallwood and Luvalle closed with a rush, however Williams was strong enough to beat off their challenge."

8.   "Ralph Metcalfe, dusky Marquette flier, five-times nationals champion, and co-holder of the world record for the event, finished fifth and was eliminated in the 200 meter dash to the astonishment of all. He made the team by running second to Owens in the 100 meters."

9.   "A dusky high hurdler achieved Olympic passage for the first time in history as young Fritz Pollard, Jr., son of the former All-America half back at Brown University, ran second to the peerless 'Spec' Towns in the 110-meter final."

10.   "The 800-meter final, won by long-striding John Woodruff, 21-year-old University of Pittsburgh negro runner, produced the most shocking upsets."

11-15.   "Before 19,152 enthusiastic fans Wednesday night, at the Chicago amphitheatre, Jackie Wilson, 118 pounder from Cleveland; Howell King, Detroit welterweight; Jimmy Clark, Jamestown, N.Y. middleweight; and Arthur Oliver, Chicago *heavyweight, clinched berths on the Olympic squad. This is the first time in the history of the games that Negroes are to compete on an American boxing team." Willis Johnson, another boxer, also makes the journey to Berlin.*

16. *"John Terry, Titan Weight Lifting Association of New York City, earned the right to represent the U.S. in the Olympic Games at Berlin next month by placing second in the 132 pound class in weightlifting championships of the National AAU held at Princeton on July 4. Terry is not a newcomer to the weight lifting game, he has been a consistent performer in the sport for a number of years and has made an enviable record."*

17 & 18. *"Misses Tydie Pickett and Louise Stokes, both of whom won places on the 1932 Olympic team, will go to Germany for their second appearance in the world games as a result of their showing in the trials held in Providence, R.I."*

The Chicago Defender *sums up their thoughts regarding Hitler and his confidence: "Hitler and his Nazi compatriots were quite joyous in the welcome they gave Schmeling for having disposed of Joe Louis, the Brown Bomber. I wonder what they will think when they see these black speedsters defeating the best of the world at Berlin in August. Well, turn about is fair play, friend, Hitler!"*

CHAPTER NINETEEN

AN ALMOST COLOR-BLIND OCEAN

1936

LOUISE STOKES WATCHES the massive white flag slowly rise up the mast of the 705-foot-long luxury liner docked in Pier 60, the five interlocking circles displayed prominently on the flag as the wind waves it back and forth. The skyline of Manhattan serves as the backdrop to the ship that the liner is named after. Thousands line the docks around them, with bands playing and surrounding boats blasting their horns in celebration. The 334 athletes on the deck stand at attention to watch the Olympic flag raised and hear "The Star Spangled Banner." With her heart racing, the girl from Malden, Massachusetts, lets out a long breath of relief, knowing she almost didn't make it onboard today.

Leading up to her departure for Berlin, Louise was uncertain about raising the necessary funds for the trip. This isn't unusual; most of the athletes making the team have been scrambling to figure out how to pay the five hundred dollars each of them needs for the trip. Only days earlier, she took off from Malden on a train heading to New York, uncertain whether she would ultimately be heading to Berlin or back to Malden. Her pastor at Eastern Avenue Baptist

Church, Reverend W. H. Edwin Smith, helped to raise money for the railroad portion of her journey, but the big question was whether more money would come in.

This very day, she woke up uncertain if she'd make the trip. At the eleventh hour, her town came through for her, sending a waiver for the necessary amount. The mayor of Malden, John Devir, along with her own Coach Quaine, raised the money from folks in her town. They raised enough to send along $75 for expense money and to keep another $105 for her homecoming.

Louise wants to win for the people of Malden who sent her to Berlin. She wants to make sure the money waiting for her return is justified.

Her friend from Chicago stands next to her on the deck of the SS *Manhattan*. She can't help smiling at Tidye. Once again, they are the only two Negro women on the Olympic team.

The women's track team pose for publicity photos as the SS *Manhattan* departs for Germany, 1936. New York.

The ship's siren screams to announce they are underway. The tugboats begin to pull the liner away from the pier and down the Hudson River, all while the throngs of athletes, coaches, and media wave the miniature red, white, and blue flags they've been given. Louise Stokes feels lost in the crowd on the deck waving good-bye to crowds they pass on both the New York and New Jersey sides of the river. She grins at Tidye. Her friend gives her a knowing look, one that signals how they both feel.

Here we go again.

. . .

The photographer asks for another photo, telling them to smile, but Archie Williams won't oblige. He still feels stiff and far too decked out in the uniform they gave all the athletes after they made the

African American athletes pose on the SS *Manhattan*. L–R, standing: David Albritton, Cornelius Johnson, Tidye Pickett, Ralph Metcalfe, Mack Robinson, and Willis Johnson; kneeling: John Terry, John Brooks.

1936 African American Olympic track stars pose on the deck of SS *Manhattan*. L to R: James LuValle, Archie Williams, John Woodruff, Cornelius Johnson, and Mack Robinson.

team—a blue coat and pants with a tie matching the American flag and a straw hat. They are also given powder-white shoes that seem to glow beneath him. Standing there in front of the railing of the SS *Manhattan* as it begins to head down the harbor, Archie and his fellow black teammates link arms while posing. James LuValle stands on his right, while the tall kid from Pennsylvania, John Woodruff, poses on his left. Cornelius Johnson, the great high jumper, lines up next to Woodruff, then next to him comes the friendly-faced sprinter, Mack Robinson. If he didn't know, Archie might think they resembled a kind of traveling musical band.

In some way, Archie can't help feeling that he is part of some herd. Yet at the same time, they've all been given an instant amount of affluence, something none of them had before. They're put up at the Hotel Roosevelt after making the team, then given their uniforms and instructions and granted the good old VIP treatment. For the last five days before the boat left, they stay at the hotel and are allowed to eat anything they want. Archie couldn't wait to board the vessel, since the only boat he had ever set foot on was a Southern Pacific ferry boat going from Oakland to San Francisco. Seeing this huge ship with its chimneys, smokestacks, and horns blowing astounds him. A loud band plays while he and others boarded the ship.

Archie isn't surprised to find himself rooming with Jimmy LuValle or that they've put the black athletes together in the same staterooms. In fact, he doesn't really think much of it. Archie knows this is an opportunity to continue to create a bond with fellow athletes. There are three and four to each stateroom, and all of them start to go back and forth between the rooms.

On that first day of setting out to sea, Archie hears the news that Harold Smallwood has come down with some kind of illness. This is big for Archie and LuValle, considering that Smallwood won the AAU championship in the 400 meters, and came in second at the Olympic trials, right behind Archie and in front of LuValle. Archie hopes it isn't something serious.

Dinner that first night on the SS *Manhattan* is no different than the feasts they have enjoyed at the hotel. The menu consists of chicken soup, roast chicken, mashed potatoes, and peas, along with a dessert of ice cream and hard candy. Archie hears the tall crew of rowers from Washington are given additional vegetables for their diet.

Archie doesn't feel as if he is on a ship cruising at twenty knots. He also doesn't feel as if he is in his own country, where signs divide the room into "whites only" and "colored." They're all one big team consisting of 359 athletes. For once, the only colors that matter are red, white, and blue. He won't hear any derogatory talk from the Germans while he is there and will only learn about the German press labeling them as "black auxiliaries" later.

"I didn't hear about all that stuff until I got back home," Archie says years later. "I couldn't read German. I just heard people saying this and that, and I was aware of their super race, whatever, Aryan supremacy—but they didn't prove it to us!"

• • •

The world flips around like a child rolling down a hill. After being at sea for a couple of days, Tidye can't shake the woozy sensation. She's already thrown up every single thing in her stomach. Now she can only dry heave and feel the muscles in her stomach tighten while her stateroom never stops spinning.

Initially, Tidye participates in posing for reporters as they snap photos and film the athletes on the deck. The women on the track team are told to line up and run in place, so Tidye stands next to Louise and they jog for several minutes while wearing their knit short-sleeved shirts and long skirts. Tidye starts to feel a bit woozy, with the winds whipping her hair and the steady, circling motion of the waves starting to really affect her. She takes a second to capture

Louise Stokes and Tidye Pickett participate in exercises on deck.

the vast ocean with a camera she borrowed and is filmed by one of the many passengers with motion cameras as if she is taking a photo herself.

While the room rumbles around, Tidye closes her eyes and remembers the cross-country train trip to Los Angeles. She can't believe she had been a part of that, something that now feels like a decade ago. The pride she felt then has only magnified. There wasn't any fear in leaving her family in 1932, nor is there any now. Tidye knows she has the support of the people back home in Chicago. This sickness might be dragging her down, but she is going to fight it and manage.

I've been managing things my whole life.

Louise and the other athletes keep Tidye up-to-date on the events and happenings on the ship. There are so many festivities she can't be part of. She flashes back to being in that opulent hotel in Denver while traveling to the Los Angeles Olympics and not being able to participate in the banquet held for the women's team. This is different, however.

A lot of people are backing me. A lot of people are counting on me.

Tidye and Louise aren't completely on their own, either. Since they're staying in an extra-large cabin that is roomy enough to contain a card table, and since she's seasick and has to stay in bed, their room becomes the central gathering place for the black athletes. And Louise makes a few new friends on the deck of the ship.

Tidye feels proud to be part of this group of extraordinary individuals representing the United States. There are many people who kept her focused, telling her to ignore what she heard and experienced while people spoke about the boycott and Hitler. She did exactly that, always telling herself she was going to do a good job.

Once I get off this ship I'll feel better. I know it.

She only wishes she could train just a little, that she could do anything to try to keep in shape. Anything to help her with the upcoming race.

• • •

It's not as though the athletes have the whole ship to themselves. The regular passengers on the SS *Manhattan* still outnumber the Olympic team, so space is tight for the athletes to train. The tourist class and certain other sections of the ship are given times where they can work out. Wrestlers, rowers, basketball and baseball players are able to practice on the sun deck at designated times. Swimmers practice in the pool from 7:00 to 9:00 a.m. as well as 2:00 to 5:00 p.m. Boxers have a special ring on the aft promenade deck.

As the luxury liner cruises along, the young athletes revel in the endless entertainment, from bingo and casino night to the captain's ball and dancing. Plus, there is the endless smorgasbord of food, all day and night long.

The camaraderie among the athletes is infectious and natural. There are no racial matters when it comes to the black teammates and the others, including their fellow southerners. All have one goal

Louise Stokes and a teammate aboard the SS *Manhattan*.

Cornelius Johnson and Dave Albritton on the SS *Manhattan* deck.

in mind, and that is to maintain a gentlemanly conduct on and off the track, thus bringing respect to their country.

Cornelius Johnson enjoys playing checkers four hours daily on the trip, while two boxers, Howell King and Willis Johnson, outdance everyone on the ship. News is buzzed about daily, such as the story of the girl they find on board as a stowaway right after they leave New York. The young woman, who is a waitress, supposedly boarded the ship with a boyfriend, then fell asleep after a few drinks. She is confined to the brig. There is also talk about who will be coaching Jesse Owens, whether it is his own coach, Larry Snyder, or the Olympic coach, Lawson Robertson. Owens states publicly he will be coached by Snyder, of course, but the debate still rages.

The 400-meter star from the University of California, Harold

Smallwood, continues to recover from an attack of appendicitis he had right before setting out to sea. The officials monitor him to see whether he will be healthy enough to compete in the games. Meanwhile, the *Oakland Tribune* writes that "Uncle Sam's No. 1 hope in the springs and broad jump," Jesse Owens, has to shake off a head cold and laryngitis he picked up on the boat, vowing to get back to real work once they land in Berlin.

The athletes learn that team officials, after having studied the pictures of the tryouts, have assigned athletes to the 4 x100-meter relay team. Those include Sam Stoller of Cincinnati; Mack Robinson of Pasadena California Junior College; Foy Draper from the University of Southern California, and Eddie Glickman of Brooklyn. They begin practicing while on the ship.

The discussion of race remains in the minds of reporters. The *News-Press* in Fort Myers, Florida, contains a headline on July 30 reading, "Dark Battalion Best U.S. Bet," and an opening line stating, "There are 10 streaks of color, ranging in shade from deep coffee to the light brown tone of the boxer Joe Louis, in our Olympic track and field personnel this year." The writer calls these athletes "dark angels," then delves into the supposed science for "the negro's great strides in sprints and jumps." Claiming that anthropologists say it has to do with the anatomy of a black athlete, the writer quotes a trainer as saying that "athletic performance is 95 percent condition and there the 'under-privileged' negro, who isn't invited to campus cocktail parties, has it on the white boys." He also says black athletes aren't distance runners but "they have the stamina to run long races and a glandular makeup . . . so maybe they're just too lazy to run anything except dashes."

Of course, this newspaper reporter has surely not met someone like Johnny Woodruff, for whom the 800 meter is not a simple "dash." He just makes it look like one.

• • •

400-meters track stars Archie Williams and James LuValle pose for photos on the deck of the SS *Manhattan*.

In their stateroom, which smells like sweat and socks, Archie glances down and pinches his full belly.

"I think I've gained fifteen pounds," he tells LuValle, his roommate. "At least fifteen pounds."

"Coach wants me to fatten up," James says to Archie.

"If you don't gain weight on this trip, something's wrong with you," Archie says.

It seems as if all they are doing is eating or planning to eat or thinking about eating on this big New York ocean liner. There are three or four different dining halls open twenty-four hours. In the morning they wake up and can have croissants, sweet rolls, coffee, cocoa, and fruit juice. Around 9:00 a.m., the gong rings for breakfast, where you order off a menu. Steak and eggs and almost anything else. A coffee break arrives around ten in the morning, a massive lunch in the afternoon, and tea time a bit later. At dinner, they order once again off a menu. For those still awake later at night, they can pig out on anything available, all while doing almost zero exercising except for some push-ups, sit-ups, and jogging up and down the deck a bit.

It would be nice to train instead of having a week off, Archie thought.

Along with all of the time-consuming meals, they spend a lot of time playing card games on the trip, mainly with the other black athletes, such as Metcalfe, Robinson, and Woodruff. Then there are athletes like Tarzan, a Native American from the Narragansett Ashaway Reservation in Rhode Island, who enjoys spending time with all of them.

Tarzan Brown made the Olympic team after his surprising victory in the Boston marathon that year. Tarzan's running style resembles his name: He takes off as fast as he can and runs that way as far as he can, never pacing himself. In this year's marathon, he built up such a lead he was barely jogging near the end when the defending winner, Johnny A. Kelley, passed him at the foot of a long hill. As Kelley passed Tarzan, he gave him a contemptuous pat on the butt, expecting never to see the runner again. Yet Tarzan bolted up the hill and soared past an awestruck Kelley to become the youngest winner of the marathon.

"He ran the Boston marathon barefoot last year," LuValle says. "And he came in 13th place. This year he won it."

There are plenty of characters like Tarzan on the SS *Manhattan*. Guys like Jack Torrance, a funny, big old monster of a man at six foot eight and 250 pounds. He tells them all about being a deputy sheriff in Louisiana. Archie finds it ironic that a good ole boy from Louisiana is frolicking around with a bunch of black boys from different parts of the country. There is also Harold Cagle from Oklahoma, whom they all call "short stride." Cagle plays an old, beat-up guitar and sings for his teammates with little urging.

One day a few athletes run into the stateroom with the latest news: the good-looking swimmer Eleanor Holm Jarrett, who is a bit of a celebrity, has gotten into trouble after staying up late hanging out with the newspapermen and drinking too much. She has a husband and a popular nightclub act. She is a heavy favorite to win the 100-meter backstroke in Berlin, but this might change that fact. The outspoken woman once said she trained on "champagne and late hours." A female chaperone advises Eleanor to go to bed because it is after the 9:00 p.m. curfew. Eleanor, with champagne glass in hand, snappily replies, "Oh, is it really bedtime? Did you make the Olympic team or did I?" Avery Brundage summarily removes Eleanor from the team. James LuValle finds it unfair and considers joining the two hundred team members who petition Brundage to reverse the ban.

Archie and LuValle also keep up with the team gossip on Harold Smallwood. He has been moved into the infirmary, since his cabin on D deck is too warm and he has a raging temperature. The status of the 400-meter runner remains of obvious interest to the two, since they compete against him. Both want the runner to heal as quickly as possible. Smallwood would want the same for either of them.

After multiple reports surface that some Olympians are staying up late, drinking, and gambling, most notably Eleanor Holm Jarrett, the athletes are issued a list of dos and don'ts. These include forbidding them to gamble at poker and blackjack games, warning them against leaving their quarters unless fully clothed and to not indulge in overeating. Smoking and drinking are left up to the athletes, with Brundage saying he couldn't "go around wet nursing more than 300 persons for the eight-day voyage." Soon after this, he reports how things were going.

"The deportment and spirit of the team, with a few exceptions, have been admirable throughout the voyage," Avery Brundage tells the press while aboard the SS *Manhattan*. "Such disciplinary action as was felt necessary to take in one case produced gratifying results."

Avery points out that they are dealing with high-strung and anxious athletes who are coming out of very strenuous Olympic trials.

* * *

Ralph Metcalfe feels out of sorts, and it's not because of the steady rocking of the sea. It is a combination of everything—his lack of training and his trick muscle flaring up, not being able to sleep, and waking up too late. He feels sluggish and in need of some good workouts, though none can be had on the SS *Manhattan*. He knows his athletic peak has already arrived.

Tolan went to Australia last year and set a bunch of records.

Metcalfe thinks about his fierce competitor Eddie Tolan. After briefly leaving his job as a registrar of deeds in Detroit to go abroad, Tolan came back and resumed his work there. Eventually, every single athlete needs to let go. Age forces them to.

When is it time for me to let go?

Metcalfe knows he will always be able to do one thing, however: motivate others. He does so with his fellow athletes.

They all know him, of course. Besides Jesse Owens, Metcalfe is among the biggest names on the team. He is also among the oldest at twenty-six. Most of these guys are college students, only twenty-one and twenty-two years old. Metcalfe can tell that Owens, the young athlete from Ohio State, looks up to him like the others. Light-hearted teasing and storytelling among the group helps to pass the time. The nights are late, singing songs and playing games and simply conversing. Metcalfe has gotten to know a number of his fellow athletes over the years, but grouped together in Deck D with nowhere else to go, the camaraderie is a blessed thing to see.

Metcalfe doesn't joke around or play games as much as the other guys, though he loves to laugh at their antics. He never talks about the 1932 Olympics unless he is specifically asked about them, only saying, "That's the way it was, there's nothing I could do about it." He makes it clear to all of them, however, that he isn't coasting into

African American track teammates relax on the deck of the SS *Manhattan*. L to R: Cornelius Johnson, Ralph Metcalfe, Fritz Pollard, and John Woodruff.

these games like this ship. His goal is to win and to beat everybody, including Owens.

Before the ship arrives at Hamburg and they all finally set foot on solid ground, Metcalfe gathers as many as possible of the black athletes together so he can to talk to them and share some encouragement and wisdom. They all listen carefully to what he says. He has the history, the age, and the experience to back up every word.

"We all know where we're going and what this means," Metcalfe says to his fellow competitors.

There are those listening who are really just kids, guys like the good-natured Johnny Woodruff, who knows hardly anything about the political situation and the conversation about the boycott. There are the smart guys from California, Williams and LuValle, and the lightning-fast runner who beat him, Mack Robinson. And there are others, too, listening in—Corny, Brooks, and Pollard.

"It's a privilege to be representing the United States in these Olympics, especially *these* Olympics. And we all know there's been a lot of talk, a lot of words and rhetoric and vitriol thrown around."

Metcalfe speaks as a leader, a politician wanting to instill hope and inspiration. Owens stands there and has been in the center of the debate, perhaps more so than any other black athlete. He listens to Metcalfe just as the others do.

"All we should do is focus on our event. To think about our race, or our jump, our match. Represent yourselves and your school and country."

LOUISE STOKES ISN'T *the only one who nearly doesn't attend the Olympics because of the travel costs. Johnny Woodruff is another. The S.O.S, the newspaper of his hometown of Connellsville, makes a plea to the public just days before the ship leaves for Berlin.*

"Woodruff is a poor boy," the article reads. "He goes to Pitt on a scholarship and he works his way through school. Expected employment this summer must be forgone on account of the trip to Berlin and the boy is in New York waiting to sail Wednesday without any private funds at all." The article encourages readers to simply donate fifty cents for the cause. "THERE IS JUST 24 HOURS to collect this fund, whatever it might total."

They end up raising fifty-five dollars for Woodruff's trip. Now he can fulfill the promise he made to Dr. Clyde S. Campbell from his hometown after winning at the trials: "Tell the people back home in Connellsville that I'm going to Berlin to win. I'm going to do the best I possibly can so that they can be proud of my running because they've been pretty good to me." They have indeed been especially good to him.

He is the youngster, the kid on the team, and maybe that's why everybody seems to be drawn to him. Woodruff just celebrated his twenty-first birthday, and it feels as if this is his birthday present: a nine-day trip on a luxury liner. He shares an impressive stateroom with Ralph Metcalfe and Mack Robinson.

Woodruff doesn't feel a bit of seasickness, unlike some of the others. He needs to adjust those first two days, but he has his sea legs and considers himself a pretty good sailor. He enjoys dining, and walking on the decks outside talking with the other athletes. This feels like a vacation of sorts.

Woodruff has heard bits and pieces throughout the last year about Hitler and the treatment of Jews in Germany and the proposed boycott of the Olympics. He's never been interested in politics so he doesn't really know what the fuss is all about. The boycott is something he never discussed back at the university or at the YMCA where he lives. Metcalfe, on the other hand, who speaks so well and is so smart, seems to know a lot about the boycott, the Nazis, and what is happening. That's why Woodruff listens carefully to everything Metcalfe says related to the upcoming games—on how to compete, how to act, and how to conduct himself.

Both Metcalfe and Robinson give him lots of advice, and Woodruff takes in every valuable piece. Having been to the 1932 Olympics and narrowly missing out winning gold medals in both the 100 meters and the 200 meters, Metcalfe shares many things, especially how to be smart while running.

Woodruff enjoys hearing stories about Chicago and Wisconsin from Metcalfe and about California from Robinson. Both of those places feel as far off as Berlin, especially since the farthest he's ever traveled outside Connellsville was to Pittsburgh, then New York City for the trials.

With the trip well under way, Woodruff writes a letter to the editor of the News Standard back home, expressing his gratitude for the support he's been given.

Editor, News Standard
Uniontown, Pa.

Dear Sir:
I was certainly surprised to receive the letter from you and still more surprised to find the money enclosed with it. I wish to whole-

heartedly thank every individual who contributed any money toward raising this fine sum that you sent me.

The receiving of this money gave me the great feeling that the people back home are really rooting for my success. I'm going to try and return from Berlin with another victory for their sake as well as my own.

I'm only sorry that I can't do something directly for each individual who was so kind to help me like this.

The trip I enjoyed enormously, except the first couple of days out when I had a little difficulty adjusting myself to the rocking of the ship. But that situation was soon overcome about the third day.

The boys and girls on the trip were treated royally with plenty of good food and nice sleeping quarters. I didn't realize there was so much water on this earth: it seemed endless.

I will just say thank you again for what you all did for me and I hope to be able to do something for all you good friends in Berlin.

Sincerely yours,
JOHN WOODRUFF

CHAPTER TWENTY

THE OLYMPIC SPIRIT AND OLYMPIC PEACE
1936

THE TWENTY-ONE YEAR-OLD from Oakland, California, steps off the SS *Manhattan* to be greeted by the swell of a boisterous German band. The people in Hamburg welcome Archie Williams and the rest of the American Olympic team with smiles, applause, and excitement. He hears the Germans singing songs in their own language, serenading all the athletes, and the songs never seem to stop. Soon Archie finds himself boarding a bus and being driven to the city hall, known as the Rathaus, a building that appears to be hundreds of years old and steeped in tradition. The athletes pass through the immense entryway and up a grand flight of stairs, flanked by the upright, uniformed members of the honor guard of Hitler Youth, and then arrive at a reception hall with a gold-leafed, towering ceiling. The mayor of Hamburg welcomes the athletes in both German and English, with a procession of speeches from others to follow, some which Archie doesn't understand. After keys to the

The American team arrives on the docks of Hamburg, Germany, 1936.

city are passed out and a few words given by Avery Brundage, cigars, cigarettes, and fruit punch are shared among the men in suits while the athletes are served wine and orange juice.

The welcome feels sincere, though Archie wonders if they are welcoming everybody like that and if the Germans are being forced to do so. They want to roll out the red carpet, so that's exactly what they've done. Stepping over it feels unfamiliar for Archie.

From the first moment Archie arrives in Hamburg, he notices the Germans in military uniforms that stand out and the Nazi flags adorning the streets. It feels strange to have these tall, handsome, white foreigners being cordial and polite, greeting him with open arms.

Soon Archie and his teammates are on a bus again, this time shepherded to the Bahnhof, the station where their two trains to Berlin await. He doesn't fail to notice the obvious: Neither Archie nor any of the other African American athletes have to ride in the back of these buses.

• • •

The red, white, and blue U.S. flag stands out on the train station platform as it hangs over the two Nazi flags sporting the swastika. Thousands of Germans flock to the station to greet the arriving athletes and officials.

James LuValle watches Avery Brundage be the first to step off the train, greeted and kissed on the cheek by Dr. Theodor Lewald, the German Olympic Committee president. Soon after, he steps off the train not far behind Jesse Owens. A mob of young people that includes many young girls yells out "*Wo ist* Jesse? *Wo ist* Jesse?" They all know about his four world records, so they want to see the celebrity. Soon the girls circle around Jesse, snipping at his clothes with scissors. LuValle and the others can only laugh in disbelief. Poor Jesse has to turn around and get back into the train for safety.

LuValle and his teammates are ushered through the station by guides wearing clean, crisp white linen uniforms.

Is Hitler supposed to be showing up in a few minutes? LuValle jokingly wonders.

He keeps thinking about how good that twenty-five-year-old port tasted back at the Rathaus town hall in Hamburg. They were all served a small glass of the wine, and he never realized just how delightful wine could taste. LuValle is growing well acquainted with suddenly finding something new, such as boarding an ocean liner and dining in one of its immense halls. All because he happens to be fast. Very fast.

They board more massive buses, the women in one, the men in the others. They travel ten miles outside the city through some of the most beautiful landscape LuValle has ever seen. A forested area with ponds opens up to reveal a community full of brand-new buildings. This is the Olympic Village where all the men are staying. Soon LuValle and the others discover it is a world of its own, a massive mess hall that contains various chefs from every country preparing meals for the athletes. Each country has its own menu to order from. The Americans can order T-bone and filet mignon with their meals.

The German hosts could not have made their arrival any more pleasant and could not have been more personable. The political discussions are put on pause for the moment, and justifiably so.

• • •

Only twenty-two miles north of Berlin in the suburb of Oranienburg, past streets lined with plain houses, sitting in a modest pine forest, work begins on the Sachsenhausen concentration camp. Heinrich Himmler, who has been appointed by Hitler as Reichsführer SS and chief of German police on June 17, orders it built to serve as a model for future sites, calling it "a modern and progressive concentration camp." It will become the central office behind Hitler's sprawling labyrinth of concentration camps, the

A concentration camp inmate kneels in front of four SS henchmen, including commander Karl Otto Koch (second from right).

Prisoners at Sachsenhausen Camp haul logs as part of their assigned labor.

home base for the extermination of millions of Jews. Akin to the carefully constructed design and architecture of Olympia in Berlin, Sachsenhausen itself covers over 960 acres that includes comfortable houses for the SS guards, large warehouses, and a canal system with a small port. A quarter of the Berlin suburb is composed of this concentration camp.

As the top athletes from all over the world arrive in the pristine, shining city of Berlin to discover the welcoming Olympic Village and its training facilities, another training school is being developed in Sachsenhausen. It is slated for Hitler's SS leaders and junior officers, who will be trained and appointed to command the eventual two thousand concentration camps operated by the Nazis.

Starting in 1936 and operating for eight years, more than 200,000 people are imprisoned in Sachsenhausen. The first prisoners are political opponents of Hitler and his party, yet it will soon be full of men and women who are executed, die of starvation and disease, forced into unbearable labor, and subjected to medical experiments and torture. Before the Soviet Army liberates the camp, an estimated 30,000 to 35,000 prisoners die in Sachsenhausen.

* * *

The masterful ruse the Nazis pull on the rest of the world with its grand Olympics has a dress rehearsal earlier that year when they host the Winter Olympics from February 6 to February 16, 1936. It is only the fourth Winter Olympics ever held, and more than one thousand athletes from twenty-nine countries compete in the Bavarian Alps location of Garmisch-Partenkirchen. The goal for these games is to alleviate any international concerns for the coming Summer Olympics. A German official stresses the importance of these games, "The whole world will assess the prospects for a successful Olympic year according to our preparations for the winter event."

One overt step toward painting a peaceful picture to the world comes by Germany's inviting a Jewish athlete to compete on its team. Rudi Ball, who is only partly Jewish and played on the ice hockey team, serves to help dispel the belief that the Nazis won't allow non-Aryans on their team. Hitler also addresses President Henri de Baillet-Latour's concern about the anti-Semitic signs around Garmisch-Partenkirchen, promptly removing them from public view. Throughout the ten-day Winter Olympics, Hitler gives no speeches and the Nazis serve as gracious hosts. The only complaints come from the appearance of Nazi troops training in Garmisch, something Hitler remedies with the summer games.

With the Summer Olympics finally in motion, the German hosts have done their necessary preparations. Minister of Propaganda Josef Goebbels wants to do everything possible to cast Germany in the best and brightest light, so he strictly censors all media, including German press, radio, and film. Rules are sent out regarding any reports from the games. The Nazi minister of food and agriculture, Walther Darré, sends out a directive to the public that states, "In no case must Jewish provocateurs get a chance of creating incidents which will add grist to the mill of hostile propagandists abroad. For this reason all signs posted in the fight against Jewry must be removed for the period in question."

The cleanup of Berlin doesn't just include the streets and buildings themselves, nor is it simply getting rid of anti-Jewish signs. The anti-Semitic newspaper *Der Stürmer* is removed from the newsstands, though it continues to be published throughout the games. Along with Olympic banners hanging from storefronts all over Berlin, the red swastikas stand next to them in accompanying banners. The SS and SA troops are ordered to be personable and courteous hosts as well.

The world is being shown and not told that Germany has changed. Victor Klemperer, a German and Jewish literary scholar who goes on to pen and publish his diaries, *I Will Bear Witness,* states this about the Berlin Olympics:

Berlin is transformed into a world-class Olympic city,
complete with festive art and decorations.

"People at home and abroad are constantly being told that they are witnessing the revival, the blossoming, the new mind, the unity, the steadfastness and glory, of course also the peacefulness of the spirit of the Third Reich, that lovingly embraces the entire world."

Yet even though the crowds chanting Nazi slogans and language persecuting the Jews have all vanished, Klemperer notes that "still, day and night, the swastika flags are flying everywhere."

The German historian Arnd Krüger calls these three months the "Olympic pause," a time when "the darker aspects of the regime were cast into the background, (and) ordinary people in Germany could regain their common humanity and meet and converse with foreigners regardless of their ethnic or religious background." The authentic enthusiasm shown by the Germans truly does seem to be an indicator that they want peace with the rest of the world.

The athletes certainly share the optimism and belief that Ger-

African American athletes stroll through the Olympic Village. Berlin, 1936.

many has indeed changed. How can they not after being welcomed and treated in a manner that makes them forget any rumors or realities hovering around their hosts? For some, such as the black athletes, the welcome and treatment are better than the kind they receive back home.

• • •

Mack Robinson feels as if he is on a brand-new college campus. He's in one of the little cottages that contains from eight to twelve double bedrooms. His roommate is Johnny Woodruff. They pass a living room at the front of the building, and after examining their new home for the next week, Mack notes everything inside, from the telephone booth to toilets to the bath and shower. Their room has two beds, along with a table and chair. The layout of the Olympic Village is ideal, with pristine landscaping and manicured lawns. Mack notices Woodruff taking pictures of the village right after they arrived, using a little, old box camera he brought over to Berlin.

The American Olympic Team arrives at the Olympic Village, 1936.

Upon first arriving at the village, the athletes are welcomed to their assigned house with a printed message from their hosts:

Welcome to the Olympic Village!

This is your home during the weeks to come. Here you will dwell together with your friends and fellow participants, a community of comrades serving the same ideal, who are overjoyed to greet you, live with you and pass pleasant hours in your company.

Everything that has been provided here is for your comfort and convenience, and the regulations have been considered and drawn up in your interest so that you may be assured undisturbed enjoyment of your new home.

Over this Village waves the Olympic flag and the national banner of your native land. Each morning the chimes play the Olympic Hymn.

May the Olympic spirit and Olympic peace reign here from the first to the last day.

Help us to ensure and preserve this peace.

The German Army erected this Village for the Olympic guests. It performed its task gladly in the interest of sport and because it reveres the Olympic ideals. Thus the German Army as well as the German people extends to you, its guests, a hearty welcome.

The Reich War Minister, Field Marshal von Blomherg
The President of the Organizing Committee for the Eleventh Olympic Games, Berlin 1936, Dr. Th. Lewald

Two things in the village stick out to them. First, every country has its own dining hall, and since the U.S. had one of the largest teams, it has what Archie Williams calls "all the goodies." Tables are

Cornelius Johnson makes friends with athletes and visitors at the Olympic Village.

set up with a variety of items, from fruit to cookies to pitchers of milk. The food is exceptional, better than the food on the SS *Manhattan*. Someone tells them that the chefs from the SS *Bremen*, Germany's luxury liner, are the ones cooking the food for the American team.

The training facilities also impress Mack. The track can be used by all the athletes, so they find themselves running to keep in shape on the track next to competitors from India, Poland, and Japan all at the same time. The coaches train them hard, trying to get them back into some sort of shape after the long, buffet-infused cruise. It takes all of them a while to get their land legs back.

Every sort of facility they can imagine is housed in this village. Places like dentists and barber shops. They can send mail, go swimming, or watch movies in the theater. A small shopping mall contains everything they might want or need. Each athlete has a card

Mack Robinson poses for pictures in the Olympic Village with athletes and a German soldier. 1936.

along with an Olympic passport that will take them by train, free of charge, to anywhere in Berlin.

Mack can't get over all the Germans coming up and asking for

Jesse Owens and Fritz Pollard relax at the Olympic Village.

the athletes' autographs. Not just people like Jesse Owens but even Mack himself. They talk with them and invite them to have a cup of coffee. All this talk about the boycott and the politics of the games doesn't make sense when it comes to meeting all these warm, enthusiastic Germans.

The camaraderie among the American team members continues to grow while they are in the village. They visit each other in their dorms, talking and sharing thoughts about what they are going to do or want to go see in the city. They are under a certain amount of supervision and discipline, so they have to focus on their training and cannot wander offsite without reason.

Mack and the others know the rules, though they aren't spelled out specifically. They all have a responsibility to maintain themselves to the best of their ability so they can prepare for their races. Every athlete takes that responsibility seriously, and each one knows how to conduct himself with this goal in mind.

Tidye and Louise pose for photos in the Olympic Village.

• • •

While the men bask in the German glories of the newly constructed Olympic Village, more than four hundred women competitors from various countries are housed in dormitories known as the Friesenhaus. The dorms were located in the Reich Sports Field complex adjacent to the Olympic Stadium. As the Olympic official program states, though, "The most beautiful athletic fields and training grounds were directly in front of their doors." Friesenhaus is surrounded by woods, it "resembled a secluded island."

The woman in charge of running the dormitories is Baroness Johanna von Wangenheim, the wife to the late ambassador to Constantinople. She volunteered for Red Cross work for many years and had a perfect command of many foreign languages and worked hard to inspire a spirit of friendship, family, and collaboration among the female competitors. She was strict with the rules and protocol, and limited visitors.

Louise and Tidye remember the beautiful hotel they stayed at in Los Angeles four years earlier. In contrast, these dorms are simple and small. There are no separate kitchens and dining halls for each country like the men have at the Olympic Village. So far, they have been served a lot of boiled foods, such as potatoes, beef, and cabbage.

Being near the vicinity of the stadium doesn't diminish the fact that they are staying in rooms like barracks.

An information desk is in the hall of the lower floor. This is where a friendly young German woman from Hitler's Honorary Youth Service has been assigned to take Louise and Tidye around, showing them where to shop and arranging transportation for them. This courtesy is extended to all the female competitors from the various countries. Two girls stand at the entrance gate of the Friesenhaus, along with two at the entrance hall, there to provide any assistance they can.

• • •

The prelude to the Olympics could not have gone more smoothly for Hitler and the Nazis. Baron Pierre de Coubertin, the life honorary president of the Olympic Games, says in a radio address, "What is the difference whether you use the Games to advertise southern Californian weather for the sake of tourism, or a political regime? The most important thing is that the Games are celebrated in a decent manner."

Avery Brundage takes a victory lap before the competition occurs. He stamps his endorsement on the German hosts shortly after they arrive.

"Conditions in Berlin are the finest ever provided in modern sport competitions. We in the United States who pride ourselves on being first in so many fields cannot equal the facilities provided here. We owe a great debt to Germany for the development of modern sport because it was in the Fatherland that the first intensive physical training began in the Turnverein.

"Lastly, we know Germany's devotion to the Olympic sports and we are sure the same spirit of the ancient games which began in Greece will be preserved. We know that high standards of fairness and courtesy for which Germans are known throughout the world will prevail on the playing fields and makes the 11th Olympiad the finest and greatest ever held."

═══════════════════

IN THE GLOW *and awe of a transfixed Berlin beginning its grand Olympics, twenty-eight thousand members of the Hitler Youth assemble in rows at the Lustgarten in the center of the city. Many Nazi rallies in the past have been held in this place. Three hours before the opening ceremonies of the*

Olympic Games, an ocean of soldiers flanked by colossal Nazi flags stand at attention to hear Josef Goebbels talk about their duties.

As Goebbels speaks, a German runner runs down the center of the German Youth, carrying the Olympic torch to finish the ten-day relay. Earlier on that drab, overcast morning, at 8:00 a.m., the band of the Wachtruppe Berlin regiment march down the Unter den Linden Boulevard to rouse and awaken the city. One new event created for these Olympics is the Olympic torch relay and ceremony. The relay is portrayed as an ancient Greek tradition, yet the first ten official Summer Olympics never held such an event. Hitler and the Nazis create this purely for dramatic effect. The drama does indeed impress, enough to continue to be used in Olympics to come.

Originally proposed by the Nazi Propaganda Ministry and implemented by Carl Diem, the secretary general who oversees the committee to organize the Berlin Olympics, the Olympic flame relay provides a grand picture of Hitler's new Germany to a major portion of Europe. Linking the Aryan lineage from the Greek empire to the new German empire, Hitler seeks to paint a picture of a monolith to come. The path for the "sacred flame" itself begins in Greece and ends nearly fifteen hundred miles away in Berlin. The runners who carry it can only be blue-eyed and blond.

Leni Riefenstahl, the director capturing the games for her celebrated film Olympia, uses the Olympic flame and relay as a seminal part of the picture, providing more future propaganda for Hitler and Goebbels. The film starts with Greek ruins and out of those appear beautifully sculpted German athletes to carry on the ancient traditions.

With the Olympic flame lit in the Lustgarten, German and Olympic officials are taken to the Palace of the reich chancellor in Wilhelmstrasse, where Hitler greets them. Count Baillet-Latour gives a short speech honor and appreciation to Hitler: "All those who appreciate the symbolism of the sacred flame which has been borne from Olympia to Berlin are profoundly grateful to your Excellency for having not only provided the means of bind-ing the past and the present, but also for having contributed to the progress of the Olympic ideals in future years."

In his official greeting to the International Olympic Committee, Hitler states that "Germany gladly assumed the task of preparing for the present competitions in a manner which aspires to be in keeping with the ideals and traditions of the Olympic Games, and hopes that she has thereby contributed to the strengthening of the principles of international understanding upon which this Festival is based."

CHAPTER TWENTY-ONE

READY, WILLING, AND ABLE FOR WAR

1936

JAMES LUVALLE LOOKS out the top of the double-decker bus at the masses lining the Unter den Linden boulevard. He feels a sensation of both awe and apprehension as he waves his hat. Berliners line both sides of the street; they are well dressed and jovial after waiting for hours to see the spectacle commencing down this very avenue. Yet in front of them stands a double row of brownshirts, at attention in their full battle regalia, and then in front of those Hitler Youth stand the SA men in their black shirts.

They look like they're about to begin marching to war any minute.

The American men's team boards one of the many buses taking athletes from the Olympic Village to the twenty-eight acres of Maifeld lawn next to the stadium, where they wait for the opening ceremonies to commence. It seems as if the whole world has flooded into this German city.

After the slow progression through thousands of Berliners,

LuValle follows the rest of his teammates out of the bus and onto the lawn. Between 1:00 p.m. and 3:00 p.m., 170 buses unload competitors from all the countries to the field where they wait for Hitler and the Nazis to march in to start the ceremony. The stadium opens its gates at 1:00 p.m. as well to make sure it is at full capacity by the time Hitler makes his arrival.

LuValle hears the sounds of an orchestra floating from the stadium. The Olympic Symphony Orchestra congregates to play for the crowd while they wait. The group includes the Berlin Philharmonic and the National Orchestra as well as the Bayreuth Wagner Festival choir. In the sky above him, the massive *Hindenburg* zeppelin hangs overhead, bearing the five Olympic rings painted on its side and the swastika hanging on its tail wings. The sleek, glistening, massive airship resembles a long, foreboding cylinder. Operational

The LZ129 *Hindenburg* flies over the opening ceremonies of the 1936 Summer Olympic Games.

since March, the zeppelin has made seventeen round trips across the Atlantic that year, carrying up to seventy-two passengers each trip. For more than an hour that day, the *Hindenburg* flies approximately 750 feet above Berlin.

The official Olympic report states that the *Hindenburg* "greeted the thousands assembled for the Olympic Games as the symbol of German inventive genius and workmanship." In fact, the airship is simply another tool in the Nazi propaganda machine effectively orchestrated and used by Goebbels. It will be officially used for a three-day propaganda flight to support Hitler's remilitarization of the Rhineland despite not having completed all its initial trial flights. This flight is used to broadcast Hitler's support from loudspeakers along with dropping pro-Nazi leaflets to spectators below.

Moving his gaze down from the *Hindenburg* to the grandstand that stands between Maifeld and the avenue outside, LuValle wanders over to it, wanting a different view of his surroundings. After a few minutes of walking, he stands at the top of the structure. On the side he just came from stand rows and rows of athletes. There are several thousand athletes from dozens of countries represented. Officially, there will be 3,963 competitors from 49 different countries who compete in 129 events. Only 331 of those are women, and there are far fewer black competitors. Looking out to the other side of the grandstand, down to the Unter den Linden, LuValle sees thousands of German troops.

The sight is surreal. The several thousand athletes are here to see who can run the fastest and jump the highest and dive with the most beauty. The multiple thousands of soldiers are here for what? To stand at attention for Hitler? But why? For what bigger purpose? They appear ready, willing, and able to be sent off to war, a war no one in the world wants.

Quite a contrast, LuValle thinks.

• • •

Adolf Hitler and top IOC officials enter the stadium for the opening ceremonies.

The crowd grows hysterical as Hitler enters his stadium and walks down the Marathon steps flanked by Baillet-Latour and Lewald, presidents of the International Olympic Committee and the Organizing Committee, respectively. Having already passed through all the teams on Maifield, Hitler strides onto the field with "March of Honor" by Richard Wagner providing the soundtrack. In the center of the field, a blond, blue-eyed five-year-old girl waits, her left hand holding a bouquet of flowers while her right hand is extended in a Nazi salute.

"*Heil, mein Führer,*" the girl dressed in all white says as Hitler smiles and gently takes her saluting hand in his to shake. Gudrun Diem, the daughter of GOC general secretary Carl Diem, curtsies and presents Hitler with the bouquet. As Hitler and the Olympic notables take their places in the special Honor Loge made for the Führer himself, the chanting of "*Sieg Heil*" swells among the triumphant countrymen and women.

German troops march under the Brandenburg Gate toward the Olympic Stadium for the opening ceremonies.

After a moment of silence in the stadium, the thirty-thousand-pound Olympic Bell rings for the first time to commence the games and welcome the teams into the arena for the Parade of Nations. The country where the Olympics originated walks out first, followed by nations arranged alphabetically. Leading the way for each team is a German student in all white carrying a placard with each country's name on it, followed by the flag-bearer. The Greek flag is held by sixty-year-old Spyridon Louis, who won a gold for the marathon in the 1896 Olympics. Forty athletes proceed behind Louis along the track, marching the length of it and dipping their flags in salute as they pass in front of Hitler's box.

Hitler and the Nazi leaders watch as the different countries march directly below them, the athletes giving a salute to the seats of honor according to their own country's custom and their standing with the German government. Applause comes in the type of salute given. The Nazi salute and the Olympic salute look very similar, so it's not always simple to see which type of salute is being given. This happens to the Austrians, who give the Olympic salute of a raised right arm stretched out to the side while the audience cheers them, viewing it as the Nazi salute of an arm simply stretched out to the front.

As the Austrian athletes walk into the Olympiastadion with confidence and jubilation, like every other team, they can't imagine what the men they salute have planned for their country.

Josef Goebbels, alongside Hitler, stares down at the Austrian athletes. Less than two years after welcoming Austria into the stadium, Hitler will announce an "Anschluss" between the two countries, a union by which Austria is annexed by Germany. The Anschluss in 1936 will be capped off when Goebbels gives orders for an event called the Kristallnacht, or the "Night of Broken Glass," where rioters burn down 267 synagogues in Germany and Austria. Goebbels's Kristallnacht vandalizes and loots around seventy-five hundred establishments owned by Jews and desecrates many Jewish cemeteries.

The violence is particularly brutal in Vienna, Austria, where most of the synagogues are torched to the ground in front of an acquiescent public and fire department. Thousands of Jews are arrested and sent to concentration camps such as Dachau and Buchenwald.

Countries such as Afghanistan, Bermuda, Bolivia, and Iceland give Nazi salutes. Italy, where the fascist salute originated, proudly displays its support of Hitler.

For Poland, 127 men and 17 women walk in the Parade of Nations. None can know that Germany will invade their country in just a few years and effectively start World War II. In the course of six years, Poland will lose almost 18 percent of its population, with an estimated 4.9 million people killed, 3 million of whom are Jews. Hitler will give orders to "kill without pity or mercy, all men, women, and children of Polish descent or language" simply because Poland is meant to be "depopulated and colonized by Germans."

All of the forty-nine countries marching on this day will be affected by the war Hitler and his army will wage. France, for instance, receives a rousing cheer from the crowd, with one spectator saying,

"Never was the War threat on the Rhine less than during these moments. Never were the French more popular in Germany than on this occasion. It was a demonstration, but one of comradeship and the will for peace." But France will be defeated almost four years later by the Germans, along with Holland and Belgium.

As they march on, each lowers their flag out of respect to the host country. That is, except the United States. As they walk, the second-to-last team in front of Germany, the Americans choose to take their boater hats and place them over their hearts, staring at their flag as it remains at its high position. Despite this being considered a tradition since the 1928 games, they are still reprimanded by the Olympic Committee for not showing deference to the future destroyer of nations.

Midway through their march, the Americans hear the applause stop as the German national anthem begins to blare out through the stadium. The German athletes have entered the arena, and though it is the United States' turn to be showcased and greeted by the crowd, they receive a respectful hush as the German song plays.

> *Germany, Germany over all*
> *Over everything in the world!*
> *When it comes to protecting and defending,*
> *Our unity unites us.*

The Germans have adopted Austria's "Emperor Hymn" to be used as their national anthem. The words aren't subtle in their declaration of Hitler's new regime.

> *From the Maas to the Memel*
> *From the Etsch to the Belt,*
> *Germany, Germany over all*
> *Over everything in the world!*

• • •

Archie Williams stands fifty feet away from the Führer, watching Hitler, Hermann Göring, Goebbels, and all the Nazi big shots walk past them as they wait on the field to enter the stadium along with the other countries. He marches with the rest of the Americans, wearing the navy blue coat and white flannel pants along with the fancy shoes and straw hat. After the team refuses to salute Hitler as they file past him, then lines back up on another field, Archie surveys all the teams around him.

The variety in the attire of every nation is as interesting to watch as the rest of the rituals taking place on this day. The Germans resemble soldiers in their military-style uniforms. The Frenchmen wear berets while the Chinese and Bermudians wear white sun helmets. The team from India looks impressive with their turbans.

Dr. Lewald steps up to a podium to welcome the competitors. He speaks about an Olympic fire rising to heaven and creating a bond between Germany, Greece, and Nordic immigrants and a lot more sacred ideas that Archie doesn't know the foggiest thing about. After a lengthy speech, Adolf Hitler steps up to make a simple announcement:

"I proclaim open the Olympic Games of Berlin, celebrating the eleventh Olympiad of the modern era."

Right afterward, the Olympic flag is hoisted. Trumpets sound and guns go off, a burst of white exploding into the air. Pigeons are released, twenty thousand of them, out of several hundred cages on the edge of the arena. The terrified creatures hover above all the Olympic athletes, scrambling to figure out where they are supposed to go. All heads look up into the air.

Archie sees a splat of white land on top of one of the shot-putter's shoulders. Some of the athletes begin to duck, trying to avoid direct hits from the birds dropping their loads. Archie and the other boys around him start laughing, joking about everybody getting hit by bird poop.

Then a torch relay runner springs out of the Eastern Gate and jogs along the track to light the Olympic Flame. The massive bronze altar erupts into a blaze that appears impossible to ever put out.

. . .

All athletes in the stadium raise their right hands as the Olympic Oath is declared by the German flag-bearer:

"We swear that we will take part in the Olympic Games in loyal competition, respecting the regulations which govern them, and desirous of participating in them in the true spirit of sportsmanship for the honor of our country and for the glory of sport."

After the "Hallelujah" chorus is sung, the athletes finally file back out of the stadium. The spectators remain, however, awaiting the "Olympic Youth Festival" that commences that evening.

Frederick T. Birchall, writing for the *New York Times,* sums up the day with high praise: "These Olympic Games have had an opening notable even beyond expectations, high as they were. They seem likely to accomplish what the rulers of Germany have frankly desired from them, that is, to give the world a new viewpoint from which to regard the Third Reich: It is promising that this viewpoint will be taken from an Olympic hill of peace."

The view the rest of the world sees is an impeccable Berlin welcoming strangers with smiles and optimism, all while being engulfed by the sprawling and impressive German Reichssportfeld with its stadium, amphitheater, and bell tower. Like the very flame burning, these magnificent structures appear to be permanent fixtures that can never fall. Like the illusion brought by the formalities and fanfare of the opening ceremonies, these structures also have a purpose, at least as far as Hitler is concerned. The Nazi architect, Albert Speer, succinctly articulates Hitler's motivations years later:

"I concentrate on Hitler's architecture not only because it was my field, but because I believe at least one pregnant clue to this strange man lies there. It was not his avocation; it was his obsession. And long before the end I knew that Hitler was not destroying to build, he was building to destroy. I and others, caught in the act, were helping him."

═══════════════

HITLER'S HATRED OF *the Jews has been fully documented in both print and public speech by the time he becomes chancellor of Germany. His belief in a superior master race spreads like a virus to other groups as well, ones the Nazis consider to be bad genes. On July 14, 1933, Hitler declares the Law to Prevent Hereditarily Diseased Offspring, a law that allows the state to regulate human reproduction, effectively eliminating "impure genes," as the German propaganda states. The law mandates sterilization for individuals suffering from physical and mental diseases. Special courts of physicians and judges choose up to four hundred thousand men and women to undergo such sterilizations. A small population of black people living in Germany at the time are among those who are sterilized.*

Exact figures are unknown; however, estimates state that there are thousands of black Germans in Germany when Hitler ascends to power in 1933. The first Africans in Germany were brought as household servants around the seventeenth century. During WWI, the French deployed African soldiers to the Rhineland in part to prevent a build-up of black troops in France, and partly because the Germans had asked them not to be deployed. The Belgian, British, and French governments took control of Germany's colonies in Africa following the war. As a result of the Treaty of Versailles in 1919, Africans were encouraged to become citizens of their respective mandate countries, but most soldiers in Germany preferred to stay in Germany. Many of these black soldiers married German women. Their children, who were mostly teenagers by 1933, became known as "Rhineland Bastards" or the "Black Disgrace."

As with his statements on the Jewish population, Hitler is clear on his thoughts about Afro-Germans in his autobiography, Mein Kampf. *"It was and it is the Jews who bring the Negroes into the Rhineland, always with the same secret thought and clear aim of ruining the hated white race by the necessarily resulting bastardization, throwing it down from its cultural and political height, and himself rising to be its master." In another passage, Hitler writes, "The mulatto children came about through rape or the white mother was a whore. In both cases, there is not the slightest moral duty regarding these offspring of a foreign race."*

Hitler never considers allowing blacks to remain in his country. "It is a scarcely conceivable fallacy of thought to believe that a Negro . . . will turn into a German because he learns German and is willing to speak the German language and perhaps even give his vote to a German political party."

This vitriol only intensifies leading up to the Olympics in Berlin. While Hitler and the Nazis manage to suppress the Jewish athletes competing in those games, they can't do so with the black competitors coming from abroad.

CHAPTER TWENTY-TWO

THE SNUB

1936

THE MADMAN WATCHES from his own special box called "the Honor Loge" in the center of the southern area of the stadium. Seated around him are officials and aristocrats, some in uniform and others in suits, Germans all under his righteous sway. For several hours now, the 110,000 spectators have been under his gaze and command. Every single thing constructed in this arena came under his supervision. Every single action is happening for one sole purpose: for Chancellor Adolf Hitler and his Nazi Party and his country to awe the rest of the world.

Since arriving at Reich Sports Field Stadium on this Monday afternoon, Hitler had basked in the glories of his fellow Aryan victories. Hans Wolke breaks an Olympic record in the shot put for Germany, as does Tilly Fleischer with the women's javelin throw. He smiles, nods, and receives congratulations from the state officials and party leaders surrounding him in his box. The two early German victories don't sour the experience when Finland takes gold, silver, and bronze in the ten-thousand-meter run. All victors in these three events are called to his box to be personally greeted by the Führer himself.

Hitler is not there to see "the fastest man in the world" win his first two rounds of heats for the 100-meter dash at the start of the day. The crowd roars at the sight of Jesse Owens and applauds his speed on the cinder. Owens's time in the second round, 10.2, would have set a new world record, but it is not counted due to the strong tail wind that follows him.

The men's high jump is the last event of the day, lasting until sunset settles on the stadium. Twenty-two of the competitors will jump over the 1.85-meter height in the opening round in order to proceed to the finals. A pair of Germans will make it to the finals, but they won't last against the Americans on the field, who continue to soar above the bar with a confident ease.

Hitler notices two of the most talented American high-jumpers. Their names won't mean a thing to Hitler. He won't ever know that Cornelius Johnson is dubbed the "Black Grasshopper" and comes from Compton Junior College in Los Angeles. Or that Dave Albritton went to the same high school and college as Jesse Owens.

Corny Johnson wins with a high jump of 6 feet 7¹⁵⁄₁₆ inches, shattering the Olympic record. Johnson seems to win with ease, never even taking off his sweatsuit during the initial jumps. Dave Albritton finishes second, and another American from Los Angeles, Delos Thurber, finishes third.

The three medal winners never get to shake hands with Hitler. For a while, the world believes the story that Hitler refused to shake Owens's hand, yet the mighty sprinter from Ohio State hasn't yet won any medal. It's the other three Americans who win, two who are part of the colored contingent of athletes the United States has brought.

Hitler departs from his Honor Loge, leaving any honorable congratulations behind, as well as leaving the exact timing and the precise motivation in question for all history.

Cornelius Johnson sets Olympic record.

German officials later state that Hitler left in order to avoid the rush of the crowd exiting the stadium.

Some reporters, such as Henry McLemore, a United Press staff correspondent, have fun with this information. "When dusk fell over Reichsportfeld, the old fellow's crisp blond curls were down over his ears, his bright blue eyes were ready for a healing beefsteak, and his peaches and cream complexion was leoparded with bruises." Stating that Hitler stayed around for everybody else, "He didn't have time for Cornelius—so the first playing of 'The Star Spangled Banner' (and I am still tingling from the sound and sight of America's song and flag) had to be accompanied without him."

New York Times correspondent Arthur J. Daley writes that Hitler left his box five minutes before the ceremony honoring the Americans began. "Press box interpreters of this step chose to put two and two together and arrive at the figure 4. In this they may be correct,

Cornelius Johnson wins gold and Dave Albritton takes silver.

but there will be enough future Negro winners to warrant delaying passing judgment for the present."

The gold-medal winner shunned that day, Cornelius Johnson, tells his sister that after Cornelius won the high jump, Hitler got up and walked out of the arena. It's not difficult to imagine the man who believes the Jews brought blacks into Germany to help ruin their race becomes a little irked to see the final outcome of the first day of his mighty Olympics. For a ruler hell-bent on the eradication of all races not aligned with his own, a leader who proclaims his own views by writing, "Systematically these black parasites of the nation defile our inexperienced young blond girls and thereby destroy something which can no longer be replaced in this world," seeing two black victories on display surely angers him, heart and soul.

History will have to deduce Hitler's true motivation that evening, but it records his departure. Photographs will record another incident that occurs after he leaves.

During the medal ceremony for Americans Johnson, Albritton, and Thurber, as the U.S. flag is raised for all three podiums, it is clear to the athletes and everyone else in the stadium that Hitler has departed. The question of whether the Führer will invite Corny into his box has been answered, and the three athletes know this.

The president of the International Olympic Committee, Count Henri de Baillet-Latour, is incensed by Hitler's actions and later that night demands that he congratulate either all the winners or none at all.

While the ceremony won't be shown in Riefenstahl's *Olympia* film, a photograph of the three Americans is taken, showing them on the podium saluting the U.S. flag. The tall athletes stand at attention like soldiers, their right arms bent and their hands flat against their temples. Yet for the second time that day, something happens that won't be repeated for the rest of the games, something captured in a snapshot seen in the Olympic official report.

Only moments after giving their country's salute, the three Americans move their right arms outward facing toward the sky. From far away it might appear as though they are giving the Nazi salute like all of the others in the stadium, yet their hands show something else. Instead of saluting with their palm flat and facing the ground as their fingers point upward, as the Nazis and Fascists commonly do, their hands are turned with their wrists turned upward and their thumbs slightly cocked down. This is known as a Bellamy Salute, one that is more than thirty years old and is performed to accompany the Pledge of Allegiance.

Given the fact that Hitler deliberately snubbed them in very plain view, "It may well be that Johnson, Albritton, and Thurber purposely performed the Bellamy Salute as a public act of American solidarity and defiance."

Hitler, for the rest of the games, chooses not to invite any more athletes to his loge box and congratulate them, thus never publicly snubbing anyone again. In a similar manner, the Bellamy Salute isn't performed by anyone after these men.

Corny's confidence is as tall as his height. Albritton shares with Owens how nervous he has been in the finals, yet Corny shows no nerves at all. He is a high-jumper who a news writer said was "the greatest potential high jumper that ever lived." That same writer wrote, "Johnson is not only colorful in skin but in his antics as well. Indoors he has a habit of appearing amateurish after he clears the bar. He lands on his stomach and emits a dolorous 'oof.' But no one had to help him to his feet. He jumps up, bows all around and then takes his place in line for another leap. It is this touch of humor which keeps the crowd in high humor and brings prolonged applause when his marks are announced."

Did the "colorful" and fun-loving Corny Johnson decide to give Hitler and his party one giant "oof" in mockery and defiance? Did he and his teammates give the Bellamy Salute to show off and display some rebellion? The proof is in the pictures.

"I THINK THEY *wanted to see if the black would come off if they rubbed our skin," Archie Williams tells a reporter. "Jesse Owens . . . was a hero in the eyes of the Germans. They followed him around the streets like he was the Pied Piper."*

"To tell you the truth, I didn't pay any attention. He [Hitler] was just another guy as far as I was concerned. By the time we got on the victory stand, I don't know whether he was there or not," says David Albritton.

"I was so close to him that I could have reached out and touched his neck," Louise Stokes says about being seated so close to Hitler in the stands. Regarding the Germans who met her on the streets of Berlin, Louise says,

"They would just stare and stare and never stop looking. I have actually seen them staring so hard that an automobile has come up and hit them."

"I was just a young athlete concentrating on the competition," Mack Robinson says. "I didn't realize at the time that there was all that controversy. I wasn't really aware of it until I got home and read all about it."

"I didn't notice any discrimination when I arrived in Germany," Johnny Woodruff says. "I went downtown Berlin doing a little sightseeing of the city, and the people, the German people were very, very cordial. They just crowded around you for autographs. Very friendly."

CHAPTER TWENTY-THREE

THE STOP

AUGUST 4, 1936

THE GROUND UNDERNEATH Woodruff's spikes is dry, while the sky above his head is pocketed with scattered clouds. It's just over sixty degrees today, and the wind barely blows in the stadium. As he glances at the track, he thinks what a fine, beautiful track it is. Whatever it's made from, whether it's red dirt or red cinders, it has a glow to it that he will never forget.

So far, the Olympics have run with precision. Each event, starting with the opening ceremonies, has been on time. Woodruff heard the Germans were sticklers for detail, and it shows. Athletes don't have to wait and wonder when they will be competing. Some of the old-timers tell Woodruff and the others this is the finest Olympic Games they've ever witnessed. He has already grown familiar with seeing the American flag hoisted and hearing the national anthem. He knows exactly when Hitler is in the stadium and when he leaves by the crowd noise. The sounds and the feel of the stadium change every time Hitler moves or speaks.

John Woodruff running the finals of the 800 meters.

Two laps around the track; 800 meters; half a mile. This is why he is here in Berlin. For this one race only.

For the first preliminary race of the 800 meters on the opening day of the Olympics and the follow-up semifinal the next day, Woodruff runs as he always does: starting the race by bolting to the front and staying there the whole way. In the first heat, he finishes third, qualifying with a modest time of 1.58.7. The first four runners in each of the six races make it to the semifinals, so he doesn't worry. In the semifinal, Woodruff makes sure he is going to the final, winning the race with no problem and posting the fastest time, 1.52.7. Both of those races aren't even competitive for him.

For the final 800 race on the third day of the Olympics, Woodruff decides to try a different strategy.

I'm gonna lay back in second position and wait back there until hitting the last 300 meters. Then I'll kick it in to try to win the race.

Strategy is something Woodruff hasn't really bothered with before now.

The seventh lane is a long way from the edge of the track, but Woodruff feels confident. Phil Edwards from Canada, one of the favorites, is running in lane 1. Kneeling down, Woodruff waits with the others and feels the hush of the stadium, the spectators waiting like him for the gunshot. Then with a quick, short blast, they are off. Several of the runners sprint to be close to Edwards, who begins to set the pace. Woodruff glides through the first turn, passing several on the outside to then hover behind Edwards while going through the second turn.

Something is wrong, however.

Edwards is running slowly. Way too slowly.

Ten meters, then another 10, and another, and Edwards isn't picking up the pace. As they make a full circle and complete the first 400 of the race, Woodruff still feels as if he is lagging, his long legs not fully lunging as they usually do.

The voices in the stands, calling out and chanting and screaming, fold into him like the second turn. As he closes in on the Canadian in front of him, running in the second lane to avoid tripping, Woodruff sees one figure—no, two of them—accelerating past on his right. Soon a third runner slides beside him. He can't move ahead, not with the lagging Edwards hogging the edge and two runners in front of him, another beside, and the rest of the pack pressing in behind him.

I'm boxed in.

Woodruff surges for a moment, still having much more energy left to spend, especially with the pace so maddeningly sluggish. But he can't get ahead. The three runners are as solid as a wall.

Don't break through them, Big John.

Breaking through them will result in fouling someone and being disqualified.

Be careful.

Decisions on a track, even for a steady race circling around the stadium twice, come in mere fractions of a second, yet they are forged from years of being hammered and honed in place. From his childhood with two young parents and too many children barely scraping by, to being told to get a job as a teen but failing to find one. Then trying to join the Navy but failing to find any room there. All because of being black. But this didn't slow Woodruff down.

He's the first in his family to graduate from high school and the first to go off to college, somehow figuring out how to make it. All those hours of uncertainty, wondering how he'd be able to pay for everything, studying, working, and running. To finally being able to earn his way to Berlin by winning the races and by having the people of Connellsville help pay his way here.

Woodruff has been shaped, molded, and created for this moment.

Lots of things have stood in his way, yet he has simply sidestepped them all. Bypassing and moving around them, especially those that stopped him dead in his tracks.

So, Woodruff stops running.

For a brief moment, with a quick decision, he slows to a near halt, the runners all smoothly rounding by him and keeping their pace.

Woodruff does something unthinkable in the world of running. He basically stops, allowing all of his opponents to proceed ahead of him.

He bursts his stride.

He breaks his rhythm.

Then, for the second time that day, Woodruff starts the race again, this time seeing a clear path in sight.

Sure, that path is going to be longer and more difficult to advance down, but he doesn't have second thoughts or inner doubts. Shifting out to the third lane, Woodruff coasts by his fellow competitors: MacCabe from Great Britain and Backhouse from Australia.

Anderson, the Argentinian, and Kucharski from Poland. His two American teammates, Williamson and Hornbostel. Then moving ahead of the tough Italian runner Lanzi, and finally ahead of Edwards.

A shouting, stunned crowd watches the impossible happen. A runner has paused, waited, and surveyed the field from the back, then moved past all of them on the outside, running far more than a mere 800 meters when it's all over.

Edwards himself shoots a glance toward Woodruff in amazement.

Before the final turn, Edwards makes a valiant thrust ahead of him again, this time having to go around Woodruff. This time, the Canadian runner is quick, so Woodruff follows with ease. Yet rounding that curve, Woodruff moves on the outside and turns up his engine to soar.

Those long legs he is known for don't let him down. He sails, this steady moving structure seeming to be impassable and unstoppable. On the fourth day of August in 1936, John Woodruff is indeed that, winning the 800 meters despite a last-second surge from the Italian, Lanzi.

He started the race with a strategy, but it backfired. He literally has to backtrack in order to move ahead. Nevertheless, that has never stopped him before and it will not today, not in front of Hitler and with the world watching.

Everything happens so quickly, from the first time he ever ran to trying out for the Olympics to suddenly standing on the podium hearing them play "The Star Spangled Banner" and watching the American flag being raised. Feeling nervous and confused, wondering whether to do the Nazi salute or the American salute and for a moment doing neither until finally honoring his own country. He watches in amazement as the young German girls come over and present with him a gold medal. Later he is given a small oak tree like all the other medalists. He wonders how in the world he's supposed to get this tiny tree back home with him.

At the time, it's hard to process and know exactly how he feels. He's not surprised, since he had come to this country determined. Yet he still feels something he has never quite felt before stirring inside him.

Years later, with the passing of time and the wisdom to comprehend that moment, Woodruff shares his thoughts on this event, expressing the "special feeling of winning the gold medal":

"This particular event hadn't been won by an American in 24 years. So, I was very happy for myself as an individual, for my race, and for my country. . . . Hitler tried to play us down. He was advocating that master race theory, and of course, we destroyed that theory by being black and winning all those gold medals."

CONTROVERSY BREAKS OUT *amid the black boxers in Berlin.*

Jimmy Clark is eliminated after fighting the Polish middleweight, Chmielewski. The latter wins the crowd, yet Clark makes it a slugfest, knocking the Polish boxer down for several counts right after the start of the match.

Clark's controversy arises after the match, especially from Clark and his team, which claims that the referee held off Clark for the moment after putting him down on the mat. Otherwise Clark might have knocked Chmielewski out. The Pole sends Clark tumbling in the same round. In the second round, Chmielewski receives a warning from the ref about holding Clark. Ultimately they give the vicious fight to the Pole. The Associated Press states how Clark lost that match was a "mystery."

Howell King's Olympics becomes more ripe with controversy after the boxer is forced to leave shortly after arrival in Berlin. Joe Church, featherweight, and Howell King, welterweight, are the number-one candidates in their divisions on the American Olympic boxing team. King and Church are abruptly and secretly sent home.

Boxer Howell King and Jesse Owens enjoy camaraderie
with athletes from around the world.

*The American boxing coach cites homesickness as the reason. Yet, some
news stories report the dismissal came as a result of accusations that the
boxers stole items from a German store. Joe Church shared his version of
the story:*

*"Three other fellows and I went to a store and we decided to try and get
away with a camera apiece. King was not with us."*

*Howell King and his mother both speak with reporters, blaming politics
for the dismissal.*

*"The whole matter seemed a frame-up to get me off the team because I
objected to the actions of the officials," King says. "Church was sent home
along with me because he was only an alternate on the team and could
be sacrificed without weakening the team and also to cover up any racial
angle that might develop."*

*Alternate Chester Rutecki would replace Howell King and lose in the
second round.*

CHAPTER TWENTY-FOUR

THE SNEAKERS

AUGUST 5, 1936

L IFE IS ALL about preparation. As far as the twenty-two-year-old from Pasadena is concerned, he has prepared enough. He's ready.

Mack Robinson stands in the shadows for a moment, unseen from the crowd, off the track, waiting to be called for the 200-meter final. He can't help thinking of Jesse Owens, the one they're all writing about, the runner everybody is cheering. Owens deserves the praise and the hype. He's already won two gold medals.

He thinks back to his childhood in Pasadena, about outrunning all his siblings and friends when they played "chase the fox." Anytime he broke away from the circle and caused everybody else to try to catch him, they never could.

Today I'm going to be chasing the fox, Mack thinks. *And I'm gonna try to catch him.*

Nobody—or at least very few people—in this stadium has any idea of the state record he set in the high hurdles back in junior high. They don't know how close he's been on Jesse's heels all season.

This can be the day.

He doesn't want to think about Hitler and the rumored buzz that the top Nazi refuses to shake the hands of the black medalists on that first day. The American newspapers would run stories of Hitler snubbing Jesse on the opening day, confusing Jesse with his best friend Dave Albritton and seven-foot-tall Cornelius Johnson. The black athletes all know the finals hadn't been run yet and Jesse hadn't been the one to win that first gold medal. Corny did. Hitler probably will not shake any of their hands. Though it doesn't matter: Hitler is just another spectator as far as Mack is concerned.

There was an image in the German newspaper *Der Angriff* that showed the black athletes with curlicues on their backs resembling monkey's tails. People actually came up to them on the streets of Berlin asking what they had done with them. Then there was the German fellow who walked up to him and rubbed a wet finger on his arm to see if the color would rub off. Mack refused to let this bother him. A few Germans athletes and even a few soldiers wanted to take pictures with him and pose with locked arms. He knows it's just some innocent and ignorant sort of thing. Many of the Germans have truly never seen a black man or woman in person before.

While in Berlin, Robinson receives more insults and racist behavior from the boorish shot-putter on the American team than from anyone else. The teammate got drunk on German beer and insulted Mack and the other black athletes.

It doesn't matter.

When they're called, Mack steps onto the cinder and stares down at those trusty old spikes of his. Then he glances over and finds Jesse, who's wearing new shoes. But this doesn't bother Mack much, either.

He will learn after the Olympics that Owens is not only wearing new spikes, but he is wearing new cleats with a distinctive two leather strips on the sides created by a German shoemaker, of all people. One who is actually named Adolf Dassler, shortening it to Adi. He and his brother, Rudolf, started a shoemaking business in their mother's laundry room. Living in a Bavarian town called

Herzogenaurach, the brothers' business took off, yet their fighting and frustration with each other resulted in their parting ways. Adi is able to convince Owens during a stealth visit to the Olympic Village to wear his shoes in these Olympics, and as a result Adi's brand receives international exposure and explodes in sales. It eventually becomes known as Adidas, while his brother's shoe business becomes Puma. Jesse's win in the Adi-designed shoes spurred thousands of orders immediately. And, during the war, American troops choose not to destroy the factory because of the association with Jesse Owens, and many become customers.

Jesse beat me by a foot in New York. By a foot.

He knows he beat the mighty Ralph Metcalfe, preventing him from competing in the 200 meters at these Olympics. He can do the same with the unstoppable Owens. Their times in the opening rounds have both been fast. Jesse sets an Olympic record in the first round with a 21.1-second run, while Mack runs 21.6 but easily wins the heat. On the same day, the third day of the Olympics, they run a second round, with Jesse running another 21.1 and Mack improving to a 21.2.

The semifinals take place a day later, on August 5. Robinson runs a smooth 21.1, tying Jesse to earn an Olympic record while also beating the formidable Canadian, Orr. Three hours later, at 6:00 p.m., with dark skies above yet little wind, the temperature a light fifty-six degrees, Mack and Jesse face off for the first time in Berlin.

Mack sees Jesse in lane 3, right next to his lane 4.

Each time's gotten better. I gotta break 21 to win.

There is only goodwill between Mack and Jesse. Here they are, two young black men, running in front of the world. In front of a sea of white faces and red and black flags. They're the best in the world. Mack and Jesse. And now they're side by side.

Mack almost didn't make it to the New York trials because of the cost. The same went with these Olympics. He was a long shot to make the team but did. Jesse's gotten the acclaim. He's also gotten the coaching, having been able to study every runner he's facing. That includes Mack. The coaches on the Olympic team have been around only Jesse and the USC guys, since one of them was the coach.

You have to work with the things God gives you.

Fritz Pollard, Jr., the hurdler on their team, has told Mack that Jesse actually went down to Florida and Cuba to train that past winter, so he is in peak shape by the time the trials arrived. Everybody else is simply trying to catch up to him, not only with his times but with his conditioning as well.

Mack bends down and eyes the lane, then crouches into starting position with his hands carefully placed onto the smooth cinder.

The gun goes off.

Steps are all it takes. Mere steps. A dozen, maybe. Twenty. Mack is starting to make the curve when he sees Owens on his left side. By the time they're turning into the straightaway of the 200, Jesse is already a few inches ahead of him. As an audience of seventy-five thousand cheers him on, Owens whips around and propels ahead somehow. So smooth, so fast.

Mack's never seen speed like this.

He keeps going, not letting up, but so does Owens. Mack feels as if he's running a great race, but it's all too much.

As he earns a clear second place and congratulates Owens on his win and place in history, Mack realizes he was indeed right. Someone had to break 21 to win the gold. Unfortunately, on this particular day, Owens is the one to do it, breaking the Olympic and world record by running a 20.7.

Later in life, Mack will say, "I always thought if I'd had some help I could have beaten Jesse, or made it even closer than it was."

On this day of being the second-fastest runner in the world, he will learn how to accept being overshadowed.

It will help him down the road as another Robinson will become as noteworthy as Jesse Owens himself.

CHAPTER TWENTY-FIVE

THE FOOTNOTE

AUGUST 5, 1936

THE ELIMINATION ROUND and second round of the 80-meter women's hurdles are scheduled on the same day at 3:30 p.m. and 5:30 p.m. respectively, leaving little time between heats. Tidye stretches and readies herself with high knees on the damp grass. As starter Miller with his white coat moves toward the line, Tidye looks up at the overcast sky and knows it's time to shine. She draws her lot.

Three Americans will compete in the 80 meter. Tidye, her 1932 Olympic teammate Simone Schaller, and 1928 Olympian Anne O'Brien. For the first round, Tidye draws the second heat, Anne the third, and Simone the fourth. The three best qualify for the semifinals. Tidye, Anne, and Simone move to the semifinals.

Tidye takes advantage of the two-hour break before the semifinals, knowing she will run in the second of the two semifinal heats. At the starting line, the hurdlers take their lanes from left to right. Tiffen from Great Britain, Testoni from Italy, Eckert from Germany, Schaller, ter Braake from Holland, and then Pickett. The girls dart forward at the sound of the gun and start to the clear the hurdles.

The medics carry Tidye Pickett out of the stadium.

Her legs glide over the hurdles, one after another. Then the trailing foot that's been giving her so many problems catches the top of a hurdle.

She tries to land and keep going, but her leg gives out on her as she falls. On the side of the track, Tidye screams out in pain as the coaches examine her ankle. The tears in her eyes aren't from sadness but from the searing pain rushing through her entire body. Feeling them touch her foot is agonizing, with the slightest movement producing a shriek for them to stop.

It's over.

For the second time, her Olympic dream is finished.

Only half an hour after witnessing Jesse Owens earn another gold medal, Tidye can't finish the semifinals for the 80-meter hurdles. After all the races, and the coaching from John Brooks, and despite receiving advice from both Ralph Metcalfe and Jesse Owens, Tidye still clips another hurdle and loses the race. She doesn't get to finish the race this time.

The coaches carry her off the track, since she can't hobble to the grass. The medics will remove her from the stadium on a stretcher. After she is examined for a few minutes, they share their prognosis:

Tidye has broken her ankle.

The spectators in the Olympiastadion resemble a massive screen in a theater showing far-off people. They don't seem real. None of this seems real.

This feels worse than four years ago when she wasn't allowed to compete.

This time, she was able to compete. To at least try. To get through the first round and to make it to the semifinals. The experience has been a good one, too. Although none of the Americans girls advance to the finals.

"It was better in 1936 than in '32," Tidye says about these games. "The coaches and all of them in charge were different in 1936, and they were nicer to us."

The only mention of Tidye's appearance in the 1936 Olympics will be a footnote to a footnote.

"The three best of each heat qualify for the Final

1. Braake (Holland) 11.8
2. Eckert (Germany) 11.8
3. Testoni (Italy) 11.8
4. Schaller (U.S. A.)
5. Tiffen (Great Britain)
6. Pickett (U.S.A.) . . . . fell."

History records her last name, her country, and her fall.

The fall itself is not unusual. Evelyne Hall Adams, the Olympic star who had the controversial second-place finish behind Babe Didrikson in the 80-meter hurdles at the 1932 Olympics in Los Angeles, once described the impact of hitting a hurdle herself:

"One of the reasons I hit the hurdle in the 1931 races was that the hurdles were different at that time. They consisted of heavy tee

Five of the finalists of the 80-meter hurdles in 1936 Summer Olympics await their start. L to R: Ondina Valla, Doris Eckert, Anni Steuer, Kitty ter Braake, and Claudia Testoni.

standards with a frame-like hurdle that was bolted in on the sides. It would swing if you touched the top bar. That's what I did in that race. I touched the top hurdle and the bottom of the hurdle swung back and caught my trailing foot."

Even though the United States embraces a black athlete like Jesse Owens, and, in the last couple of years, cheers on others like Joe Louis, the notion of the world applauding a young African American woman still seems far off. Indeed, this notion would be shattered in Tidye's lifetime.

The footnote referencing Tidye proves that a twenty-one-year-old girl from Chicago is the first African American female to ever compete for the United States. Her presence at the Olympics, whether she won or lost, is a victory beyond measure.

CHAPTER TWENTY-SIX

THE JUNIOR

AUGUST 6, 1936

FRITZ POLLARD DOESN'T feel outnumbered or ostracized here in this stadium and in this country. With all the talk of the boycott and the bad Germans, Fritz feels accepted. Besides, his brothers are with him. Back at the University of North Dakota, Fritz often joked that he was probably the only black in the whole state.

It's a lot warmer here, too.

Those winters in North Dakota didn't just teach him how to deal with the extremities, they also allowed Fritz to train in various circumstances. After a blizzard when the snow made jogging outside impossible he still found a way. In those cases, with the snow nearby piled as high as the train cars themselves, he resorted to running on top of boxcars. They cleared small walkways on the tops of the trains, allowing Fritz to run. He wore his thick airplane hat and bit down on a towel as he ran to keep his lips from freezing shut due to the cold.

Louise Stokes and Mack Robinson watch the competition from the stadium.

When you run in conditions like that, these are simple.

Pollard doesn't need people to know his name as they know Jesse's. He doesn't need them to know about his famous father, or the fact that he has been competing in a variety of sports his whole life. He was a top golfer when he was twelve, and played football before his father encouraged him to go into track instead.

He also doesn't need anybody talking about how he's only run in five meets before today.

Pollard thinks of what Metcalfe, Jesse, and Albritton told him during the boycotting controversy and his week with reports of their being some kind of black auxiliary.

"We're gonna go show them what we've got," Metcalfe had said. "We're no auxiliary and we'll prove it to the world."

His job is to cross over hurdles, and for this final race in the 110-meter high hurdles, that's exactly what Pollard does. One after another, just as he's been doing, gliding and getting into first place and staying there. Jumping off his left leg, swinging with his right, then landing and running four steps, then jumping again.

Forrest Towns, his American teammate, begins to get ahead of him on his left, so Pollard pushes. And he pushes a little too hard, tapping the third and second-to-last hurdles with the side of his left foot and then outright plowing through the last one. The hurdles are weighted down so they don't simply knock over like the ones in the States, yet he's strong enough to simply be slowed down but not hobbled by them. He takes those final seven steps to the finish line and is overtaken by the British runner, Don Finlay.

Towns, who broke a world record earlier that afternoon in the semifinals with 14.1, wins the gold with a 14.2, while Don Finlay places second just a fraction in front of Pollard, who will earn a bronze medal. Both of them have a time of 14.4 seconds.

I tripped on a hurdle and still placed.

Pollard knew he'd been running a good race, too. He might've

Fritz Pollard accepts his bronze medal.

been able to beat Towns if he hadn't nicked those hurdles and bashed down the final one.

As he congratulates Towns with a handshake and then an arm around his back, the applause from the crowd smothers them. Fritz is happy to see the two American flags raised moments later, along with hearing their national anthem.

CHAPTER TWENTY-SEVEN

THE BLACK PANTHER

AUGUST 7, 1936

THE OLYMPICS SO far have been a struggle for survival for Archie Williams. On August 7, as he climbs into the backseat of the old touring car along with LuValle to be taken to the stadium, he feels the throbbing ache in his leg muscles. Every morning, they go through regular training, where Coach Brutus makes them do wind sprints and race short races, distances of 300 yards and less. The coach is aware that they are all tired, so Archie figures Brutus sees no point in using up the energy they have running full distances, especially since they have so many heats of the 400 to run in such a short time. They all know they have to ration their energy so it won't be completely gone by the time the finals come around.

The first round arrives at ten-thirty in the morning, when the first three of each heat qualify for the second round. Archie easily wins the heat in 47.8 seconds, the best time in that initial round. LuValle wins his as well, but with a time of 49.1. That afternoon, they have to run again, and both of the Americans win their heats for a second time. LuValle, however, has more energy in his tank, running a 47.6 this time.

The following day there are two semifinal races beginning at 3:00 p.m. to determine the finals. It's customary for a coach to accompany the athletes anytime they're competing in the finals, so Coach Lawson Roberson is with Archie and LuValle as they are being driven to the stadium. The sky is still overcast, with the wind mostly absent on this seventy-degree day.

Archie has grown used to the German drivers taking them to the stadium. So far, every day he has attended the events, cheering on his teammates. He wants to make sure he is there to see Corny, Albritton, and Jesse all break records, and since most finals are in the afternoon, he usually has time to see them. It's already past 2:00 p.m., so they don't have much time to delay in order to get onto the field.

The Berlin-Hamburg highway takes them to the Reich Sports Field, nine miles away from the Olympic Village. Most of the time they ride in the buses provided by the city, ones that run all day long. In this case, they sit in the backseat while a serious-looking older gentleman chauffeurs them. A very no-nonsense driver.

As they reach a fork in the road, Coach Robertson, sitting next to the driver in the passenger seat, points to his right and says, "Go that way." The German only shakes his head, and in broken English tells the coach, "No, that way, that way." The car pauses as the driver and Coach Robertson continue to go back and forth. "I know it's that way," Robertson says. The driver speaks some words in German and keeps refusing, saying they need to go the opposite way. Archie and LuValle sit in the back, looking at each other with obvious concern as the two men's voices continue to grow louder.

Soon the German raises his voice as if he's cursing at Coach Robertson. Then he shuts off the car, opens the door, and climbs out.

"Where's he going?" Archie asks.

The driver must have had enough of the bickering and simply said, *To hell with this.*

"He doesn't know where he's going," the frustrated coach in the front seat says.

"We gotta get to the stadium," Archie says to LuValle. "We're going to miss our race."

LuValle understands the situation and jumps out of the car to chase down the driver. Archie can hear LuValle speaking German since he knows a little. For about ten tenuous minutes, LuValle stands on the side of the road, talking and pleading with the German. Finally, the two of them walk back, and the driver shuffles back behind the wheel, saying nothing to Coach Robertson.

The car turns left, going the opposite way from that Robertson had told him to go, but this time the coach doesn't say a word. Archie gives LuValle a look that says *Thank you.* He can't imagine boating halfway across the world only to miss the finals because of a stupid argument.

● ● ●

Back in the States, LuValle and Archie and other runners never competed in more than one race on a given day. Running a single 400-meter race was certainly enough. Yet for the second day in a row, they have to run two races, mainly because there are so many athletes competing. By the time the final arrives that afternoon, it turns out that all six of the runners are English-speaking: he and Archie, then Brown and Roberts from England, and Fritz and Loaring from Canada.

Archie's body feels good, especially from the rubdown he just had, which made his legs feel nice and loose. He also feels good about his lane assignment. Usually he draws the outside lane, but today he beat the system somehow to be one away from the outside lane. It's an improvement at least. Coach Brutus has trained him to know his pace, to know if it's a slow race or a fast one, and to know how he's using his fuel when he doesn't have a clock beside him. Archie's developed a good sense of pace by now, never starting too fast. He always hits his spurt just as he is coming off the last turn.

Don't step out of your lane.

That's his biggest concern, edging out of his lane right as the curved lanes merge into one straight line. By then, he is usually coasting and many times leading a race.

Archie begins to dig into the track to get ready for the final race. He thinks of the last words Coach Brutus spoke to him.

"Go in and do it. Do it like you've always been doing it."

Archie feels anxious to simply get it on and race. In front of this crowd knowing this is *the* race he's here in Berlin for, he's scared as hell and wants it done.

. . .

"The final of the 400 meters," the British commentator narrates at the start of the race. "The spikes will have to do their job. This is a fierce race. Two Americans, two Canadians, and two representatives of Great Britain. Brown and Roberts of Great Britain. Williams and LuValle of America. And Fritz and Loaring of Canada.

"And here's Miller the starter taking the pistol. Getting ready for the great moment. And here it is. Brown's on the outside lane. Next to him, Williams, the American Negro."

The crack as the gunshot goes off.

"Look at Brown's tremendous stride, but he's taking it easy. He's holding his effort back rather unexpectedly. Williams is a beautiful mover. He's a black panther! He's not waiting—he's cutting loose. He's coming up on the backstretch. Very threatening. He's gaining, hand over fist. Brown's going well, but he's leaving it too late. That Negro's dangerous!

"Williams will bring it home before they go in the straight. Brown's gotta fight for it now. That Negro's got him. Fifty yards from the straight, Williams is ahead. He's going away. Brown looks beaten. There's Roberts and LuValle on the inside. LuValle is going strong. Roberts is challenging him, but Williams leads. He'll do it. No, look—Brown's sprinting!"

"First Williams of America. Second, Brown—no wonder he looks run out. And here's LuValle, very happy to have taken third place."

*   *   *

What am I doing here?

Archie feels numb standing on the winner's platform, as if all of this is some incredibly detailed dream.

When he was a kid he never imagined competing in these games. Even when he started breaking records in track, the idea still felt far

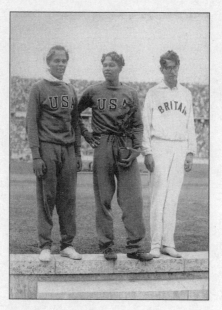

Archie and James finish the 400-meter race with gold and bronze medals, respectively, with Godfrey Brown of Great Britain taking second. L to R: LuValle, Williams, and Godfrey.

off. Archie only truly had the Olympics in his mind when he made the team. There were people he knew who had been practicing for these games ever since the last ones had ended, competitors like Metcalfe, Corny, Tidye, and Louise. This all felt like some kind of fantasy, all along, from the very first moment Coach Brutus brought up the possibility to right now congratulating the other racers. Deep down Archie wondered *what if?* Yet it'd never been some concrete goal.

At the ceremony, as he hears "The Star Spangled Banner" playing, Archie wants LuValle next to him to pinch him.

That's my name on the board.

But it still doesn't feel real.

That's my gold medal they're handing me.

But this doesn't feel real. The Frenchman handing out the medals tries to kiss him on the cheek, but Archie's not having any of that.

He thinks of the question a reporter asked right after he had bro-

Archie Williams speaks with reporters after winning the gold medal in the 400 meters.

ken the world record in the 400 meters back in Chicago: "How do you feel to be the best in the world?" All Archie could do was laugh.

"What the hell are you talking about?" Archie said to the man. "How do you know I'm the greatest in the world? There may be some guy down there in Kenya being chased by a lion that broke my record before breakfast. I just beat the ones that showed up that day."

CHAPTER TWENTY-EIGHT

THE GOLDEN CONCESSION

AUGUST 9, 1936

T HE RAGE INSIDE has been building since yesterday morning. Met-calfe always—always—manages to burst through this sickening feeling of helplessness. He always deals with realities head on, such as growing up not having much, being forced to work as a kid all the way up through high school and college. Figuring out how to attend Marquette University and stay there, run track, study, and work all at the same time.

I can control things I can act upon.

Yet certain realities of life come without the option of taking action—mainly being a black man in 1936. Or living through the Great Depression. Or even things like tying Eddie Tolan at the Olympics yet not getting the victory, regardless of whether it's a legitimate and obvious tie.

This decision feels worse than the Tolan decision.

On August 4, Coach Robertson says he doesn't know who will get to run the 4x100-meter relay, though he mentions he knows that Jesse Owens is out of consideration since he has already done enough in this Olympics. The coach assures two athletes of their spot on the relay before the Olympics: Marty Glickman from Syracuse and Sam Stoller from Michigan. Along with Foy Draper, the three men are certainties for the relay based on their trials a few days before the event. They have been practicing running and exchanging the baton along with Frank Wykoff every day leading up to the event, one of the last of the games.

Then, a day before the 4x100-meter relay, on the morning of the trials for the race, the seven sprinters on the team meet with the head track coach along with the assistant track coach. Among those in the meeting are Metcalfe and Owens. Coach Robertson tells all of them that they have heard rumors that the Germans are concealing their best runners in order to upset the Americans in the relay. So Glickman and Stoller are out and Metcalfe and Owens are in.

All of the athletes sit there in disbelief. Metcalfe looks at Stoller, who gives a blank stare and remains speechless. Glickman, an outspoken eighteen-year-old, thinks this is lunacy.

"Coach, you can't hide world-class sprinters," Glickman says.

Metcalfe knows right away what is happening.

"Look, Coach, I've won my three gold medals," Jesse says, always the gentleman and the valiant one. "I'm tired. I've had it. Let Marty and Sam run. They deserve it."

Coach Dean Cromwell, the assistant coach, snaps back at Owens, telling him they will do exactly what they are told.

"We're the only two Jews on the team," Glickman says to the coaches. "If we don't run there's gonna be a lot of criticism."

It doesn't matter. Suddenly, Metcalfe has another shot at gold, one he doesn't want. Not like this. Not this way.

He can't say a word or change a thing.

The injustice stays with him up to the seconds before the race. Lining up in his lane, careful to make sure he's starting off in the right spot to allow himself enough time to take the baton from Owens, Metcalfe knows Glickman's point is exactly why he and Sam aren't running.

They got tossed off the team to satisfy these Nazis.

This isn't what America is all about. This is exactly what they are supposed to stand against. This is what all those arguing for a boycott had protested, spotlighted, and warned about. After all that, the American team was suddenly folding.

Germany doesn't get to dictate who runs and who doesn't.

Nobody's been told that this was some command from the Germans, maybe from Hitler himself. But Metcalfe suspects the Americans received pressure.

We don't believe in their philosophy or their politics.

The U.S. shouldn't have fielded the best athletes to run this race. They should have fielded the *right* athletes, the ones designated to run this, the ones who have been practicing since arriving in Berlin.

Now Metcalfe just wants to rip up the track and get the race over with.

Jesse starts fast, as always, and he runs with perhaps a bit more energy and attitude than he might have otherwise had. Then Metcalfe begins sprinting when Owens reaches the handoff spot. The baton is passed flawlessly. He feels the cylinder in his hand and he launches ahead. Raw power explodes in front of the crowd, still excited, loud, and animated after over a week of games. The American team blows ahead of the other teams as Metcalfe runs a strong, steady race.

The world watches Metcalfe enact what Owens said about his being a locomotive.

It might be one of the fastest 100 meters Metcalfe will ever run.

His handoff is clean and perfect. Draper and Wykoff have a less-than-stellar exchange, with one rushing into the other and having to slow down, but it doesn't matter. The damage by Metcalfe and Owens is done.

Ralph Metcalfe stands on the podium to accept the gold medal in the 4x100-meter relay with his teammates—Jesse Owens, Foy Draper, and Frank Wykoff—by his side.

Their time is 39.8 seconds.

Yet again, Metcalfe sets a world record, and yet again, he earns himself a gold.

This time, however, he wants neither.

He wants to stand up for everybody who can't stand, who can't fight, and who can't race.

He knows where this lane goes. The path that lies ahead. He knows it's about battling against those who set the rules and allow racism of any kind to rear its ugly, repugnant head.

"We don't want compromising and patronizing concessions from anybody," Metcalfe admits years later. "We demand that which every self-respecting citizen should have and we are going to get it."

CHAPTER TWENTY-NINE

THE TEAM

AUGUST 9, 1936

WHEN THE TWO races are over, LuValle knows that he only made a mistake in one of them, the one in which he earns bronze.

During the tough 400 meters he runs with Archie, he makes two errors. He draws the inside lane, the second-closest to the field, so he can watch the rest of the pack ahead of him. LuValle stays in the lead for most of the race, but really it begins only after they round the turn and come into the stretch with 100 meters left. At the finish line, everybody runs on top of each other; it's that tight a race.

"You could describe the finish of that race as though we had been running on smooth ground and in the last 100 yards, all of a sudden, we were going up a vertical cliff and people were dropping rocks on us," LuValle says about the race.

His first error is looking around, which he knows is absolutely *verboten* for a runner. The second is he starts his sprint too early, resulting in his fade at the very end when the other runners are dashing to the finish line. Archie is unbeatable on this day, but

Brown storms back and makes it close. LuValle is just glad to come out with a medal.

Two days later, on August 9, the relay race's outcome tells a different story.

They all know about the nonsense that happened with the 4x100 relay, how assistant coach Dean Cromwell broke Glickman and Stoller's hearts by telling them they couldn't run. It was quite obvious to LuValle and Archie and everybody else that it was unfair. So when the same sort of plan suddenly presents itself when the coaches tell LuValle, Archie, and teammate Hardin they will be replacing the other three runners in the 4x400-meter relay, all three of them refuse to compete.

LuValle's UCLA teammate Bob Young is on the relay team. Hardin has a close friend on the team as well. So both of them, along with Archie, feel the right thing to do is to refuse to run.

"We weren't gladiators," LuValle says. "At least we didn't feel like gladiators. I think that some of those Olympic Committee people and Cromwell and some of the others had the wrong attitude entirely about things in those days."

The coaches are surprised, but since there are three of them standing together, there isn't anything they can do. If they try to force him, LuValle plans on telling them what they can do with their plans.

Therefore, the lineup remains the same. The 4x400-relay team takes the silver. LuValle and Archie watch the race in the stands.

"They didn't lose by much," Archie says to LuValle before the medal ceremony. "They were close. But they got to compete, right? Isn't that what this is all about?"

LuValle knows his friend is right, and he stands behind their decision. In fact, he's proud of it.

After all the talk of Hitler, the boycott, and the bad Germans, the only bitter aftertaste LuValle has when he leaves this country is from the situation with the coaches and the relay teams. The Germans have proven to be nice people, with a German colonel inviting him and a few others to his home for dinner with his wife and two daughters one night. LuValle hasn't interacted with any of the Nazis, but with the German people, who have proven to be very tolerant of African Americans.

Things will be different when we get back home, LuValle knows. *Just because we've won some medals doesn't mean the racism in the States has gone away.*

CHAPTER THIRTY

TWO LADIES
AUGUST 9, 1936

L OUISE STOKES AND Tidye Pickett wait for the race to start. On the track, the women are all taking their places, getting ready for the 4x100 relay. This event is always one of the highlights of the games and the reason they put it at the end of the track competition. Some athletes move around and stretch while others stare down the track or focus on the race.

Louise and Tidye sit and watch in the stands while the crowd roars around them. Both can imagine themselves on the track. Both have been on tracks like this and have won. Tidye was just on this track but broke her ankle, which now rests in a cast. For Louise, the only part of her body that's broken is her heart.

Hitler didn't snub Jesse Owens, but our coaches snubbed Tidye and me.

They don't protest because they can't. They can't complain to their own coaches because it is their coaches' decision to make.

Amid the splendor of the stadium and the sun, the flapping of the flags, the swell of the crowd cheering and clapping, Louise and

Tidye remain resolute. This is the way life is but maybe it won't always have to be this way.

Maybe black women won't only earn Olympic berths but perhaps they will have more opportunities to compete. Instead of simply showing up to be there, maybe they will stand on the podium like Jesse Owens and Cornelius Johnson.

The reality is one of the few things Louise will later state publicly about yet another dismissal of her talent:

"There were times that were not too bad and not too good."

Louise later sees this event through different eyes. The eyes of a grown woman, a wife, a mother, a grandmother. Those eyes would see the truth.

"I was just a cute little girl that hardly didn't know anything. It was a lot of fun, traveling around Europe was a beautiful time. But when we [the black girls on the American Olympic teams] went out to run, we found other runners in our places. We just had to stand there and I felt terrible."

All the time spent, having decided to pursue running and to make it back to the Olympics. Hours spent training instead of spending time with her friends or family. All those days and months.

"I just should have said something but, after it was done, what could you do?" Louise says. "Fred Steers, who was our manager, just passed us by and never said a word. That's the way they operated. They just passed the buck."

The German girls are the favorites for the relay since three of them have been in the 100-meter final, though Helen Stephens won the gold in that event. All week long, Louise has been running times that qualify her for this final. She knows she should be out there with Helen.

The ladies on the German team set a new world record in the second round, and when this race starts it appears they will easily take the gold. The crowd is euphoric, with Hitler seated next to Goebbels, standing up and cheering the girls on as if they were his own soldiers. The German runners tear down their lane with a vicious determination, their batons handed off with absolute precision. By the time the last exchange happens, the Germans have a lead of around 9 meters. The incredible speed of Stephens can't overcome that distance in such a short time.

Louise stands along with the rest of the crowd and witnesses the shock in this race: The last two German runners fumble the handoff, dropping the baton and suddenly stopping in disbelief. The other teams blast by, with Helen leading the United States to victory, followed by England and Italy.

Yet again, this U.S. victory is bittersweet for Louise and Tidye. Watching a team she could have been on win, seeing the gold medals handed out, seeing the women stand and salute the American flag raised in their honor: It is painful to experience. But she's known from a very early age that life can be painful. The death of her sister, Alice, taught her that.

The nagging guilt that more could have been done that day has always been there deep inside, and as the flags flutter and the swell of humanity surrounds her, she realizes that there is nothing she could do.

"I felt bad, but I tried not to show it," she says thirty-six years later. "I tried to keep it out of my mind and not to study it. I couldn't get an ulcer over it."

Louise knows there is the possibility of the 1940 Olympics. There are many other possibilities to look for down the road when she's back home. For now, she will choose to enjoy the rest of this Olympic experience alongside Tidye. They can roam (or hobble) around Germany for the remaining days they will be there.

She thinks of Coach Quaine and wishes he was here.

"Maybe if I had my manager at the Olympics, things would have been different. But I was a mere child."

CHAPTER THIRTY-ONE

THE VERDICT

AUGUST, 1936

B LACK NEWSPAPERS SING the praises of the eighteen black athletes, but the mainstream press focuses on Jesse Owens. His four gold medals become legendary and an important tool in America's propaganda campaign. The exploitative concentration on a single hero versus Hitler pushes his black teammates into the background, and ultimately out of the story. There is far more to the story, however.

Jesse Owens wins four gold medals, yet ten more medals are won by the other black athletes.

Cornelius Johnson wins gold while floating through the air, along with Jesse's friend and OSU teammate David Albritton. These high-jumpers are the two snubbed by Hitler in the dusk on opening day.

One of the greatest runners of all time, Ralph Metcalfe, finally wins his gold in the 4x100-meter relay, though it meant Marty Glickman and Sam Stoller were denied a chance to compete. He also wins the silver just seconds behind the unstoppable Jesse in the prime of his career.

The two unlikely 400-meter runners, Archie Williams and James

LuValle, win gold and bronze respectively. As they look to the future, both men are more focused on their studies than on sports, making their accomplishments in these Olympics all the more impressive.

Frederick Pollard, Jr., wins a bronze in the 100-meter hurdles, knowing he could have at least earned a silver had it not been for the knocked-over hurdle. Mack Robinson earns a silver in the 200-meter dash, knowing he might have earned a gold and beaten Jesse had it not been for his run-down track shoes.

Among the group of black men composing the boxing team, only Jack Wilson earns a medal, scoring a silver in the bantamweight class.

The other medal winner is the tall youngster from Pennsylvania, John Woodruff, perhaps the most unlikely winner of them all with his amazing and unorthodox 800-meter run.

The talented long-jumper John Brooks is among the African American athletes not to earn a medal. Three other boxers—Jimmy Clark, Arthur Oliver, and Willis Johnson—and the weightlifter John Terry, won't medal, either.

Jack Wilson knocks out boxer at in bantamweight contest at the 1936 Olympics.

Tidye and Louise leave Berlin carrying only their memories and mementos with them, but no medals to add to the others they had won over the years. Tidye knows the real reason why. "I knew I was better than some of them," she says. "It was politics. Politics and sports, sports and politics, they've always gone together."

The closing ceremonies of the Berlin Olympics end in glorious fashion, much like the opening ceremonies. Once again, nations all over the world watch in awe at the presentation Germany has prepared. "The world has not seen—nor is it likely to see again until 1940 at Tokyo—anything approaching the fanatical attendance at the Nazi Olympics," a newspaper reports. "The most astounding exhibition of all was saved for yesterday's closing ceremony when Chancellor Hitler attended the official quenching the flame. The mammoth concrete stadium was filled to the last foot of standing room by 110,000 of the faithful. Outside the stadium for six miles

Jesse Owens breaks the Olympic long jump record and earns the gold medal, defeating Germany's Lutz Long during the 1936 Summer Olympics.

into the heart of Berlin every foot of the route was lined with black-shirts and brownshirts. Back of them was the crowd, three or four deep all the way, waiting for a glimpse of Hitler."

The world will always have its share of madmen whom the masses will seem content to follow. Opposing them does not always mean standing up, reaching out, and scoring some kind of victory. Sometimes, it is simply showing up and making them know that times are changing.

EPILOGUE

THE SYMBOLS STILL stand many years later.

There is Jesse Owens versus Adolf Hitler. In the words of John Drebinger, writing in the *New York Times* in December 1936, "This most amazing athlete of all time confounded even Hitler, considered no mean achievement in itself." Four gold medals taking down the Third Reich. These iconic images would be used for American propaganda and would also unfortunately overshadow the other accomplishments of the African American athletes at the Olympics. Those seventeen others weren't ignored at the time, however; the African American tennis great, Arthur R. Ashe, Jr., writes that "in the midst of the Depression, the athletic exploits of blacks were touted as a viable way out of a dreary future."

The passage of time reveals the legacies left behind by Owens's teammates. Rather than being mere footnotes in the pages of tucked-away journals, there are many monuments to the other seventeen African Americans competing alongside Owens, the men and women who capture Germany's attention and cause the Nazis to create the following new label for them:

"If the American team had not had their black auxiliary tribes, the result would have been sad."

When the Nazi Party's propaganda magazine founded by Josef Goebbels, *Der Angriff* (meaning "The Attack"), coins the term black auxiliaries, there is an unfortunate shadow of truth behind it. The NAACP's magazine, *The Crisis,* weighs in on the German's verdict, stating that when America gets into a pinch, "He reaches down and uses his colored citizens-in-name-only. . . . In the hour of crisis they become American citizens, 'our fighters,' 'our athletes.'"

From the active African American participants in the Revolutionary War to the Second Confiscation and Militia Act of July 17, 1862, during the Civil War, authorizing President Lincoln "to employ as many persons of African descent as he may deem necessary and proper for the suppression of this rebellion . . . in such manner as he may judge best for the public welfare." Black citizens have indeed been called to serve during extraordinary times.

The Berlin Olympics in 1936 was no exception. Yet back at home, from 1936 to 1938, there are still twenty-two reported lynchings in seven different states. Ralph Metcalfe, John Woodruff, and the rest of the eighteen African Americans are Olympic athletes in Germany, yet when they come back home to a segregated America, they go back to being Negroes.

It would have indeed been sad if America hadn't used its "black auxiliary tribes." As the African American journal the *Southern Workman* states, the German Olympics should be remembered not only for Jesse Owens's performance but as the moment in history when "Negro athletes from the United States came to the front and showed superiority over the best athletes of all races from every quarter of the globe." Arthur Ashe explains sixty years later how "the victories of black Americans at Berlin served as a beacon for all Americans of African descent."

The black press at the time celebrated the athletes' successes in Germany while also demanding the African American community think outside of the sporting worlds to all other areas where they could make their marks, such as in art and science and business and government. As history shows in the lives of the eighteen black athletes from the 1936 American Olympic team, some find success off the field while others would go on to surpass expectations in many other fields.

All of them are symbols in some shape and fashion. Symbols that still stand strong today.

• • •

One symbol would be an oak tree only eighteen inches in height, a sapling from Germany's Black Forest. Every gold medal winner from the Olympics receives not only a medal but one of these gifts. Some of the U.S. athletes decide they don't need the accompanying prize the Germans gave to them on the ship ride back home, tossing them overboard the SS *Washington*.

Woodruff arrives back home with a particular pride in winning an event that hadn't been won by an American in twenty-four years, especially since it is an African American to finish first.

When Woodruff and the other athletes arrive back in New York, the city holds a ticker-tape parade for them and Mayor LaGuardia officially greets them. Several hundred thousand people line the streets and peer out from office building windows to celebrate the Olympians, who ride in one hundred vehicles. Out of nearly four hundred representing the U.S. in Berlin, only eighty-one are able to participate in the parade, with some having returned earlier and others staying overseas to compete in events throughout Europe.

"We are all Americans here and we have no auxiliaries in this country," Mayor LaGuardia tells all of the athletes. The athletes the mayor refers to receive a rousing welcome back when the parade goes through Harlem.

For John Woodruff, the celebration doesn't end in New York.

"When I got back to Connellsville, Pennsylvania, they had a big parade for me . . . the biggest parade that ever turned out for anybody in that small town."

It is indeed a happy time for Woodruff and his family and friends. The acclaim lasts for quite some time as he continues to compete along with speaking to kids at school about his experiences in Berlin. He wins every major event he runs in until he stops competing in 1940. Yet the reality of racism back at home quickly presents itself during his sophomore year at Pitt. For a track meet at the U.S. Naval Academy, the navy refuses to let Pitt come if they bring Woodruff with them. Traveling conditions with the team are no different, either, with Woodruff forced to stay apart from his white teammates.

The prevalent discrimination is most evident in the 1937 Pan-American Games, when Woodruff wins the 880-yard dash with a world-record time of 1:47.8. Yet the officials remeasure the race and find it to be six feet short, thus not allowing Woodruff's record.

"You know what happened," Woodruff says. "Those boys got their heads together and decided they weren't going to give a black man a white man's record."

World War II prevents Woodruff from competing in another Olympics, instead resulting in his joining the army in 1941 as a second lieutenant. After being discharged in 1945, Woodruff comes back to New York and finds jobs that include being a parole officer, a teacher, and a special investigator. His first marriage results in two children, and he remarries in 1970.

Starting in 1983, his hometown of Connellsville hosts an annual John Woodruff Day honoring the track star and raising money for college scholarships. In the 1990s, the University of Pittsburgh displays Woodruff's gold medal in the Hillman Library. It later celebrates Woodruff as "a symbol of racial reconciliation and racial change." The university officially apologizes to Woodruff in 2006 during the celebration of the seventieth anniversary of his gold-medal win when it makes him its guest of honor. The great athlete attends despite health conditions that take both of his legs. Woodruff passes away a year later, in 2007.

As for that tiny oak sapling Woodruff brought home with him from Berlin, it is first planted at the Connellsville Library, then later in 1939 it will be transplanted to the left corner of the Connellsville High School track and football field. The same small tree Woodruff held in his hands while standing on the medal podium between two other athletes giving the Nazi salute still stands, towering over runners at the stadium.

• • •

While John Woodruff and others experience the jubilation of a ticker-tape parade upon arriving back in New York, some of the Olympic athletes, such as Archie Williams, stayed in Europe for exhibition meets, where they find themselves running against local high school students. This means they can only see pictures of the ticker-tape parade.

"The whole team came back right after the Olympics," Williams says. "We were over there for almost a month. When we got back, there was nobody at the boat to meet us, not even the deckhands. But it didn't matter."

Archie and his gold medal win are celebrated soon after he sets foot back in America. While not being able to bring his German oak tree back with him, having lost it in customs, he is still honored in many ways.

"I got the real key to the city and I got a ride in a big fire engine. I got a gold watch from the city, and a lot of honors and things. People wanted me to make speeches and things. I really felt proud then, because I had a chance to go back to my old schools that I'd been to, high schools and all, and see a lot of people. And of course they were proud of me. I cherish those moments."

As was true for the other African American Olympic athletes, Archie's return home is a return to reality.

"When I came home, somebody asked me, 'How did those dirty

Nazis treat you?' I replied that I didn't see any dirty Nazis, just a lot of nice German people. And I didn't have to ride in the back of the bus over there."

Archie isn't the only one who feels that way. Jesse Owens, the American hero, experiences the same segregation.

"After I came home from the 1936 Olympics with my four medals, it became increasingly apparent that everyone was going to slap me on the back, want to shake my hand or have me up to their suite," Owens says. "But no one was going to offer me a job."

Jobs are still scarce for African Americans in 1939, the same year Archie Williams graduates with a degree in mechanical engineering from the University of California, Berkeley. Since they aren't hiring black engineers, he is forced to work jobs temporarily, such as digging ditches for the East Bay Municipal Utility District. Archie eventually finds work at a local airport, after earning his pilot's license right around graduating from college.

"I went to work for the fellow that ran the flying school . . . I worked for him as a kind of 'ramp rat'—gassing airplanes and washing windshields."

Despite receiving enough training to become a flight instructor, Archie realizes flight schools aren't going to hire an African American for that, either, so he begins giving lessons on his own and earning a living while doing that. This leads him in 1941 to become an instructor in the Army Air Corps training the first black pilots to ever be in the military, the Tuskegee Airmen. With his engineering training, Archie is called to attend meteorology school at UCLA. After being commissioned in 1943, he comes back to Tuskegee, working both as a meteorologist and as a flight instructor.

Williams retires from the air force in 1964 as a lieutenant colonel, then goes on to teach mathematics and computer science at Sir Francis Drake High School in Marin County for more than two decades while also owning a flying service.

The engineer, pilot, teacher, and Olympic gold-medal winner passes away in 1993, leaving his wife and two sons.

. . .

In the heart of the campus of UCLA, right next to the school of law and across from Perloff Hall, stands LuValle Commons. After coming back from Berlin in 1936 and graduating Phi Beta Kappa, James LuValle spends the next year at that university earning his master's degree in chemistry. There has never been a question about his goals after the Olympics.

"As far as I was concerned, the day I got off the boat in New York Harbor when we returned from the Olympics, I was finished with track," LuValle says. With no games held in 1940 due to World War II, he never has an opportunity to make another stab at earning an Olympic gold.

After earning a master's with a focus on photochemistry, LuValle spends another three years getting his doctorate at Caltech in chemistry and mathematics. The attitude among his peers at the time is that the only promising careers for African Americans are in medicine, law, dentistry, teaching, or preaching.

"I, being from the West and having quite a different attitude about things, was somewhat incensed about this," LuValle says.

Proving those expectations wrong, LuValle soon becomes the senior research chemist at Eastman Kodak in Rochester, New York. While working there for ten years, he marries another chemist, Jean, in 1946. They have two sons and a daughter, who all have careers in science, engineering, and math. In his successful career, LuValle holds various positions in the fields of chemistry or solid-state physics until eventually serving as scientific coordinator for Palo Alto Research and Engineering in California. In 1985, he is honored by the board of regents of the University of California with the construction of the James E. LuValle Commons.

Later in his life, LuValle is asked what he is most proud of, his scientific accomplishments or his Olympic experience.

"My kids," LuValle says.

James LuValle passes away on January 30, 1993, at the age of eighty. Years later, John, LuValle's son, articulates what his father stressed and how he lived his life.

"Regardless of both the color of their skin and their social standing and their economic status, they were all people and they're equal value. He never had any . . . high and mighty thing. He would be very friendly with the janitor, friendly with the president of a company, whatever. And that's something that I think all of us kids really took as a wonderful life lesson."

* * *

LuValle is among the more fortunate of the eighteen black athletes on his Olympic team, and among all African Americans at the time. "Sometimes we did very well and sometimes we didn't," LuValle says. "During that period I never had a problem getting decent work." The same can't be said about others, especially for the man who nearly prevented Jesse Owens from earning four gold medals. Mack Robinson and his silver medal in the 200 meters arrive back in his hometown of Pasadena, California, without any fanfare or welcome. No parade of any sort awaits him.

"If anybody in Pasadena was proud of me, other than my family and close friends, they never showed it," Mack shares. "I was totally ignored—the way I was ignored in Berlin—when I got home. The only time I got noticed was when somebody asked me if I'd race against a horse during an assembly at school."

Mack attends the University of Oregon for two more years, earning titles in national collegiate and Amateur Athletic Union track, yet he will have to leave school to support his family. With few job opportunities and no advantages from his Olympic triumph, Mack finds himself sweeping the streets of Pasadena, sometimes while wearing his Olympic sweatshirt. Later on, he will do other manual labor in the city.

"I really believe that if he were a white silver medalist coming home from Germany, he wouldn't be digging ditches or asphalt," Mack's wife, Delano, states. "He would not be getting pennies for that type of job."

While being overshadowed at the Olympics by Jesse Owens, Mack finds a larger shadow eclipsing him later in life as his younger brother shoots to fame. Jackie Robinson breaks the racial boundaries of baseball while playing with the Brooklyn Dodgers, and Mack remains one of his biggest fans. Later in his life, Mack works hard to lobby his city to honor Jackie for all his achievements, raising sixteen thousand dollars himself for a bronze statue of his brother at UCLA. By 2017, eight statues have been created honoring Jackie.

Mack never could have imagined that the same city whose streets he swept will one day honor both him and his brother with nine-foot-high bronze busts right across from City Hall. The sculptures are unveiled in 1997. Other acknowledgments of Mack's achievements come in the last two decades of his life. Pasadena City College names its stadium after Mack and Jackie Robinson, and a post office in Pasadena becomes known as the Matthew "Mack" Robinson Post Office. Mack himself has Olympic recognition in 1984 during the opening ceremonies of the Olympics being held in Los Angeles as he helps carry the Olympic flag into the L.A. Coliseum.

The athlete who carried a childhood heart condition and a pair of worn-down spikes with him to the Berlin Olympics passes away in 2000 at the age of eighty-seven. He leaves his wife, Delano, along with four sons and four daughters, twenty-five grandchildren, and eight great-grandchildren.

. . .

As Mack Robinson is overshadowed by a younger brother, Fritz Pollard, Jr., is always going to take junior status compared to his larger-than-life father, who went from playing football at Brown University to being first African American to play in the Rose Bowl to being one of first few African Americans to play and coach in the American Professional Football Association in the 1920s. Fritz Pollard, Sr., enters the Pro Football Hall of Fame in 2005. Breaking barriers is just part of being a Pollard.

Graduating from the University of North Dakota with a bachelor's in education, Pollard Jr. later serves in the army as a special services officer during World War II. He also eventually earns a law degree and works for the U.S. State Department. In 2003, at the age of eighty-seven, Pollard passes away and is buried in Arlington National Cemetery next to his wife.

While working under Mayor Richard J. Daley as Chicago's human relations commissioner, Fritz is groomed for a role in politics, yet it is a role he doesn't want. With Fritz Jr. ready to raise a family, politics isn't a reliable field he wanted to be in. Instead, that role goes to one of Pollard's best friends: Ralph Metcalfe.

Chicago-native Metcalfe comes back home from Berlin frustrated by the experience.

"There were too many managers and too much buck passing," Metcalfe says. "I'm disgusted the way things went."

He is among those deciding not to run as amateurs, though he hasn't decided about turning professional. Following the Olympics, Metcalfe teaches political science and coaches track at Xavier University in New Orleans. During that time, he earns a master's degree in physical education at the University of Southern California. In 1942, he joins the army, and after World War II becomes director of the civil rights department in the Chicago Commission on Human Rights as well as leading an athletic commission before heading into politics. During this period Metcalfe marries Madalynne Fay and has a son, Ralph Metcalfe, Jr.

After being elected as an alderman in Chicago in 1955, Metcalfe becomes a leading advocate for helping to shape the Democratic

Party's stance on civil rights. As an ally to Mayor Richard Daley of Chicago for many years, Metcalfe speaks truth to power, severing his relationship with the mayor's office after commissioning a report entitled "The Misuse of Police Authority in Chicago." The report condemns Daley's relaxed attitude toward the deaths of African Americans at the hands of the police. Metcalfe continues his rise in politics, being elected as a U.S. congressman and serving four terms, up to his death in 1978. While in Congress, he coauthors the resolution that creates Black History Month and helps establish the Congressional Black Caucus. Chicago honors him with the twenty-eight-story Ralph H. Metcalfe Federal Building downtown.

Fighting for the black community will be Metcalfe's legacy. Near the end of his life, he continues to inspire and lead African Americans toward breaking down racial barriers in this country.

"Let us answer them non-violently, with determination. Let us join hands, let us merge our hearts of our great love for each other. Let us summon those strengths of ours, let us stay together through the most violent retribution—let us win a victory on our terms."

Ralph Metcalfe, Jr., sums up the life of his famous father with this statement:

"Dad was a quiet and humble person who had a tremendous work ethic and was always striving for uplift, like when he built that track program at Xavier University—that impacted a lot of people. And he was always about progress and work."

• • •

After the death of Ralph Metcalfe, Jesse Owens calls his longtime childhood friend, Dave Albritton.

"We should all get together," Owens says to his fellow '36 Olympic team member. "It's later than you think."

Many of the black athletes of their generation have remained friends over the years, with Albritton calling them "an unnamed fraternity." Like Metcalfe's, Albritton's career eventually leads him to run for the Ohio Senate in 1960 and serve six terms in the General Assembly. Nine years later he makes history when he becomes the first African American to chair a House committee. Albritton passes away at eighty-one years old in 1994. In 2013, his Danville, Ohio, community recognizes the silver medalist in the high jump from the '36 Olympics with the creation of a historical marker. It won't be a shrine like the one down the road remembering his best friend, Jesse Owens, but it is still a permanent symbol.

Owens passes away at the young age of sixty-six in 1980. His Olympic success initially does not create stardom for him in the U.S., where he accepts paid races against horses and moving vehicles. But he becomes a celebrated hero, a global ambassador for sports, and a celebrated speaker until his death, inspiring others with advice on success.

"We all have dreams," Owens says. "But in order to make dreams into reality, it takes an awful lot of determination, dedication, self-discipline and effort. These things apply to everyday life." Two U.S. postage stamps have been issued in his honor, among other tributes.

Owens isn't the first of the eighteen Olympians to pass away. Cornelius Johnson, the first African American to win a medal at the 1936 Olympics in the high jump, dies of acute bronchial pneumonia at only thirty-two years of age. Johnson retires from the high jump soon after the games, then becomes a letter carrier for the post office in his home town of Compton. In 1945 he joins the U.S. Merchant Marine, working as a cook on a ship docked in San Francisco. Johnson becomes sick with pneumonia, without a doctor present to treat it, and dies on his way to the hospital. His German oak tree still stands behind his home in Los Angeles eighty years after he received the gift in Berlin.

Of the lesser-known African American members of the 1936 Olympic team who don't come home with medals or oak trees, many continue to compete and to find success in their fields. One such is Jimmy Clark, the talented boxer from Titusville, Pennsylvania, who is virtually unbeatable as an amateur yet didn't win in the Berlin Games. During the quarterfinals, Clark loses a controversial decision that a Detroit newspaper claims is "a complete jobbing by boxing officials." The boxer turns pro after the Olympics, eventually defeating world middleweight champion Tony Zale with a knockout in 1938. Yet the potential he displayed in his youth is never matched later in his career. Clark says in an interview, "They robbed me in the Olympics and I was rushed too fast as a pro." He passes away at eighty years old, as a World War II Army veteran and an Olympic athlete who makes it into the Buffalo Boxing Hall of Fame.

History doesn't record the full lives of these Olympians, such as Willis Johnson, a Detroit native, who makes his professional heavyweight debut as Walloping Willis in 1937 and goes on to fight in thirty-seven bouts. Fellow Detroit boxer Howell King turns pro shortly after being sent home from the 1936 Olympics. He continues as a professional boxer for ten years, winning forty-four bouts with twenty KOs. Arthur "Art" Oliver, the Intercity Golden Gloves heavyweight champ, loses in the second round of the heavyweight class in 1936. The World War II veteran and sparring partner for Joe Louis dies in Indiana in 1944 when the truck he is riding in collided with a passenger train. John Terry, one of the greatest ever at the deadlift pound-for-pound, goes on to set a world record for the deadlift with six hundred pounds in 1939. He passes away in 1970 after working many years for the York Barbell Company. Jack Wilson, the silver medal winner in the bantamweight class in 1936, becomes a sergeant in the U.S. Army during World War II, and is the first African American boxer to fight a main event at Hollywood Legion Stadium. He is ranked number two in the world at welterweight by *Ring* magazine in 1941. Wilson passes away in 1956.

For John Brooks, the multitalented athlete specializing in the long jump, sports always plays a big part in his life. Just as he did with Tidye Pickett, Brooks continues to coach along with finding new pastimes such as playing tennis and square dancing. He works for the park district for thirty-five years and readies generations of Olympians. Square dancing, in fact, becomes a true passion for twenty years. Brooks excels as one of the first African American callers to attend a square dance convention. Dr. Daria Brooks-Terrell recalls one of the mantras her father shared with her: "So if you say do you know so-and-so, my dad would say does he know me? It's not about always who you know, knowing whoever doesn't necessarily change your life, shape your life; you have to be yourself. "

• • •

"Silent courage." These are the two words Louise Stokes's son, Wolfie, uses to describe her. The lives of the two black women who compete in the 1932 and 1936 Olympics for the U.S. may be summed up with these two words. They remain mostly quiet about the travesties in Los Angeles and Berlin, yet that courage always resides deep inside them both.

When Louise Stokes returns to her hometown of Malden, Massachusetts, in 1936 without a medal, the town still greets her like an Olympic champion, with a parade and party for her. She eventually stops running, especially since the 1940 Olympics are canceled due to World War II. Later in her life, Louise becomes an elevator operator, while in her spare time she competes as a professional bowler. She helps to create the Colored Women's Bowling League in 1941 and competes in it for the next thirty years. She marries a cricket star from the Caribbean named Wilfred Fraser in 1944, and the couple have a son, Wilfred Jr. whom they called Wolfie, and later a daughter named Shirley. Louise retires in 1975 after working for almost two decades as a clerk for the Massachusetts Department of Corporations and Taxation.

Her hometown of Malden never forgets Louise, even after her death in 1978. They dedicate the field house at Roosevelt Park in her memory in 1980, and then seven years later, in 1987, a black iron statue is dedicated in her memory at her alma mater, Malden High School.

Wolfie Fraser sums up not only his mother but the other African American athletes at the time:

"She never spoke ill about anything. She never talked about it. . . . My mother was a very humble woman. She never had aspirations that high. And I don't even know if she'd have thoughts like that."

Tidye Pickett later tells a newspaper about the courage it took to go to both of those Olympic Games. "It's just a part of me I suppose. I wasn't ever afraid."

Tidye moves from the world of athletics to that of education after the 1936 Olympics. After graduating from Illinois State University, she teaches in the East Chicago Heights school district, eventually becoming an elementary school principal while earning a master's degree from Northern University. When she retires in 1980, East Chicago Heights names an elementary school after her.

"Oh, you just can't imagine the thrill when I found out," Tidye says about that honor. "It was a great moment."

Faye Walker, one of Tidye's daughters, reflects on her mother's life and legacy:

"Mother was fearless and she believed in herself and she had a depth of character that was also incredible. And I think she would say that first of all . . . do what you believe in.

"Stand up for what you believe in and never, never give up."

• • •

Eighty years after the 1936 Olympics, the African American athletes on that U.S. team are finally officially honored by the White House. President Barack Obama and First Lady Michelle Obama, along with Vice President Biden, welcome many of the family members of those legendary Olympians on September 29, 2016.

"Imagine what it means for a young girl or a young boy who sees somebody who looks like them doing something and being the best at what they do," President Obama says. "There's no kid in American who can't look at our Olympic team and see themselves somewhere."

Before young African American girls and boys have Jackie Robinson, Jim Brown, Chuck Cooper, and Althea Gibson to look up to, there are these eighteen athletes paving the way. Not just one athlete versus a dictator, but a group of so-called black auxiliaries providing symbols of hope. More than an alumni hall on a college campus, a federal building in downtown Chicago, an elementary school, a bronze statue in a park, or a towering tree next to a high school field, the most powerful symbols are the athletes themselves.

"It wasn't just Jesse," President Obama states "It was other African American athletes in the middle of Nazi Germany under the gaze of Adolf Hitler that put a lie to notions of racial superiority—whooped 'em—and taught them a thing or two about democracy and taught them a thing or two about the American character."

OLYMPIA AUSWEIS

№ 10513

Gültig bis 1. Oktober 1936

XI. Olympiade Berlin 1936

AUG 28 1936

JOHN WOODRUFF
VOLLER NAME

800m DASH
STRASSE UND HAUSNUMMER

GEBURTSTAG   GEBURTSORT

WOHNORT   NATION

ORGANISATIONSKOMITEE FÜR DIE
XI. OLYMPIADE BERLIN 1936 E.V.

OLYMPIA AUSWEIS

№ 10513

tig bis 1.Oktober 1936

XI.Olympiade Berlin 1936

Archie Williams

ARCHIE WILLIAMS

400m DASH

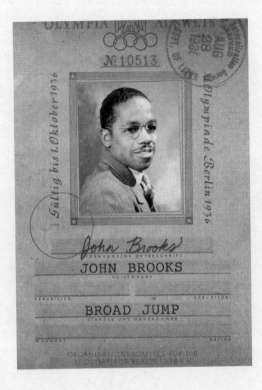

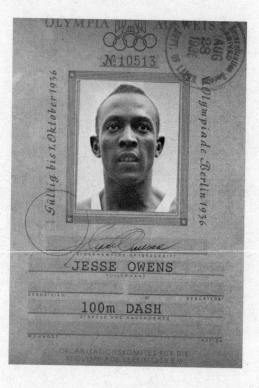

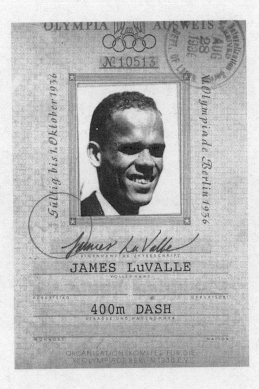

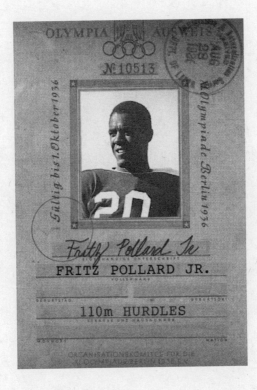

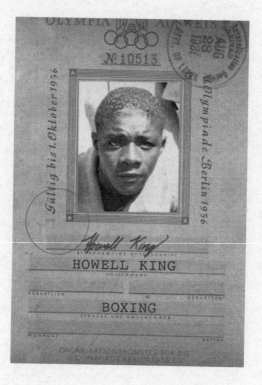

OLYMPIA ANWEIS

№ 10513

VI. Olympiade Berlin 1936

Gültig bis 1. Oktober 1936

AUG 28 1936

Howell King
EIGENHÄNDIGE UNTERSCHRIFT

HOWELL KING
VOLLER NAME

GEBURTSTAG   GEBURTSORT

BOXING
STRASSE UND HAUSNUMMER

WOHNORT   NATION

ORGANISATIONSKOMITEE FÜR DIE
XI. OLYMPIADE BERLIN 1936 E.V.

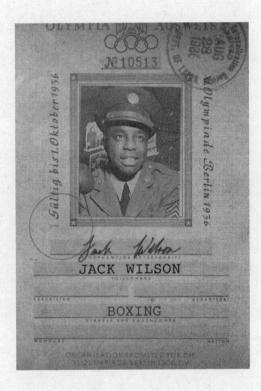

OLYMPIA AUSWEIS

№ 10513

Gültig bis 1.Oktober 1936

XI.Olympiade Berlin 1936

JACK WILSON
VOLLER NAME

BOXING
STRASSE UND HAUSNUMMER

ORGANISATIONSKOMITEE FÜR DIE
XI.OLYMPIADE BERLIN 1936 E.V.

OLYMPIA AUSWEIS

№ 10513

Gültig bis 1. Oktober 1936

XI. Olympiade Berlin 1936

James C. Atkinson
EIGENHÄNDIGE UNTERSCHRIFT

JAMES CLARK
VOLLER NAME

GEBURTSTAG   GEBURTSORT

BOXING
STRASSE UND HAUSNUMMER

WOHNORT   NATION

ORGANISATIONSKOMITEE FÜR DIE
XI. OLYMPIADE BERLIN 1936 E.V.

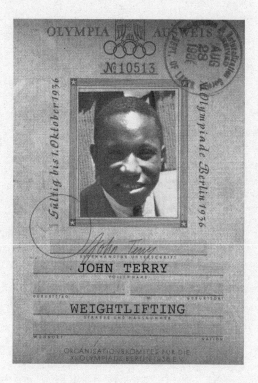

NOTES

INTRODUCTION

vii *Ninety percent of African Americans:* Dan Kopf, "The Great Migration: The African American Exodus from the South," *Priceonomics,* January 28, 2016, https://priceonomics.com/the-great-migration-the-african-american-exodus/, accessed March 22, 2017.

vii *He recalls the feel:* John Brooks: Deborah Riley Draper, Personal Interview with Dr. Daria Brooks Terrell and Wannetta Brooks, December 20, 2014.

viii *he meets a local girl:* Gerald R. Gems, *Before Jackie Robinson: The Transcendent Role of Black Sporting Pioneers* (Nebraska: University of Nebraska Press, 2017).

viii *David Albritton is just seven years old:* David Elwell, "Danville to honor its silver medalist: Community to unveil historic marker for 1936 Olympian Dave Albritton," DecaturDaily.com, July 11, 2013, http://www.decatur daily.com/news/danville-to-honor-its-silver-medalist/article_203fb1d6-eaa8 -11e2-9993-10604b9f7e7c.html, accessed March 3, 2017.

viii *barely remembers the lanky kid:* Wendy Wallace, "Tracking a Legend," *Lantern Oasis,* May 1, 1986.

PART ONE

CHAPTER ONE: THE GIRLS ARE FAST

3 *For many Americans in 1923*: History.com staff, "The Roaring Twenties," 2010, A&E Networks, http://www.history.com/topics/roaring-twenties, accessed June 12, 2017.

3 *whose membership grows to 5 million people*: Joshua Rothman, "When Bigotry

Paraded Through the Streets," December 4, 2016, *Atlantic,* https://www
.theatlantic.com/politics/archive/2016/12/second-klan/509468/, accessed
April 3, 2017.

4 *Popularizing the phrase "the New Negro":* Alain Locke, *The Works of Alain
Locke* (New York: Oxford University Press, 2012).

4 *"for generations in the mind of America, the Negro has been more of a formula":*
Alain Locke, "Enter the New Negro," *Survey Graphic,* March 1925: Harlem, NY.

4 *Locke sees a sweeping change occurring:* Ibid.

6 *Tidye's father, Louis Alfred Pickett, works as a foreman:* Gerald R. Gems, *Before
Jackie Robinson* (Lincoln, NE: University of Nebraska Press, 2017).

6 *The city's park system contains a number of facilities:* Ibid.

6 *The first day at the picnic:* Ron Grossman, "Tidye Pickett: Chicago track star
was first African-American female Olympian," *Chicago Tribune,* August 19,
2016, http://www.chicagotribune.com/news/opinion/commentary/ct-olym
pics-tidye-pickett-first-black-woman-flash-perspec-0821-jm-20160818
-story.html, accessed January 28, 2017.

6 *Her mother looks at the winnings with amazement:* Matt Osgood, "Sports History Forgot About Tidye Pickett and Louise Stokes, Two Black Olympians
Who Never Got Their Shot," Smithsonian.com, August 15, 2016, https://
www.smithsonianmag.com/history/sports-history-forgot-about-tidye-pickett
-and-louise-stokes-two-black-olympians-who-never-got-their-shot-glory
-180960138/#55yrezaAyw1bFISg.99, accessed January 24, 2017.

7 *house at 55 Faulkner Street:* Michael D. Davis, *Black American Women in
Olympic Track and Field: A Complete Illustrated Reference* (Jefferson, North
Carolina: McFarland & Company, Inc., 1992).

7 *She sprints and steps over every single railroad tie:* Deborah Riley Draper, personal interview with Wilfried Fraser, Jr., May 5, 2015.

7 *the railways at Malden square:* Elias Nason and George Jones Varney, *A Gaz-
etteer of the State of Massachusetts* (Boston: B.B. Russell, 1890), pp. 434–36.

7 *Her father, William H. Stokes:* Bob Duffy, "Stokes: Nowhere, Fast. Fast Malden Sprinter a Trailblazer, Though She Didn't Run," *Boston Globe* (Boston,
MA: Boston Globe Media Partners, LLC. 2000), accessed via www.high
beam.com, June 4, 2017.

7 *Louise's job is to pick up her younger brother and sisters:* Michael D. Davis,
*Black American Women in Olympic Track and Field: A Complete Illustrated
Reference* (Jefferson, North Carolina: McFarland & Company, Inc., 1992).

8 *Running doesn't allow her to escape the memory:* Duffy, "Stokes: Nowhere, Fast."

8 *After school, she routinely dashes over to Genevieve O'Mara's house:* Ibid.

10 *On the night of November 8, 1923:* "Adolf Hitler Attempts a Coup, 1923,"
EyeWitness to History, 2005, www.eyewitnesstohistory.com, accessed
March 10, 2017.

10 *A standoff ensues*: Peter Ross Range, *1924: The Year That Made Hitler* (New York: Little, Brown and Company, 2016).

CHAPTER TWO: A SINGLE INCH, A CROSS ON FIRE

11 *The cleaver cuts through the fish head with ease*: Vernon. Jarrett, "Ralph Metcalfe Had a Dream," *Chicago Tribune*, June 3, 1981.

12 *his older brother, Andrew, and younger sister, Lucy*: Deborah Riley Draper, personal interview with Ralph Metcalfe, Jr., December 20, 2014.

12 *Ralph's father, Clarence Metcalfe*: "Metcalfe, Ralph Horace," Scribner Encyclopedia of American Lives, Thematic Series: Sports Figures, https://www.encyclopedia.com/humanities/encyclopedias-almanacs-transcripts-and-maps/metcalfe-ralph-horace, accessed October 12, 2014.

13 *few examples he can follow*: Ralph Metcalfe, "Black Athletes Hall of Fame Induction Speech," March 14, 1974, metcalfecollection.org.

14 *They have been in the neighborhood for only less than a year*: Don Holt and Marcia Popp, *American Men of Olympic Track and Field: Interviews with Athletes and Coaches* (North Carolina: McFarland Publishing, 2004).

15 *His mother comes from a family of fourteen children*: Arnold Rampersad, *Jackie Robinson: A Biography*, (New York: Alfred A. Knopf, 1997).

16 *Burton, Mack's uncle, eventually persuades them to move West*: Rachel Robinson, *Jackie Robinson: An Intimate Portrait*, (New York: Harry N. Abrams, 2014).

17 *to buy a house at 121 Pepper Street*: Arnold Rampersad, *Jackie Robinson: A Biography* (New York: Alfred A. Knopf, 1997).

17 *with the help of a light-skinned relative*: Ibid.

17 *Kids in the neighborhood*: David Falkner, *Great Time Coming: The Life of Jack Robinson from Baseball to Birmingham* (New York: Simon & Schuster, 1995).

18 *"We didn't come all this way to let someone scare us. Especially like this"*: Holt and Popp, *American Men of Olympic Track and Field*.

18 *Adolf Hitler sits in the Landsberg Prison*: Ross, *1924: The Year That Made Hitler*.

19 *"Hitler Tamed by Prison"*: Associate Press, "Hitler Tamed by Prison," *New York Times*, December 21, 1924.

CHAPTER THREE: DISCIPLINE AND HEART

20 *He might've still been at his second school, Washington School*: Archie F. Williams, "Archie F. Williams, 1936 Olympic Games, Track & Field: An Olympian's Oral History," interviewed by George A. Hodak, June 1988, Amateur Athletic Foundation of Los Angeles.

21 *He'd already lived in west Oakland while attending his first school*: Archie F. Williams, "The Joy of Flying: Olympic Gold, Air Force Colonel,

and Teacher," oral-history interview conducted in 1992 by Gabrielle Morris, Regional Oral History Office, 1993: The Bancroft Library, University of California, Berkeley.

22 *Archie wonders what it would be like to attend CAL*: Ibid.

24 *But he can still remember the girl's words*: Dr. James E. LuValle, "Dr. James E. LuValle, 1936 Olympic Games, Track & Field: An Olympian's Oral History," interviewed by George A. Hodak, June 1988, Amateur Athletic Foundation of Los Angeles.

24 *James was born in San Antonio, Texas*: Ibid.

24 *His father, James A. LuValle*: Sibrina Nichelle Collins, "Unsung: James Ellis LuValle," *Undark*, August 15, 2016, https://undark.org/article/unsung -james-ellis-luvalle-olympics, accessed January 15, 2017.

25 *On Christmas Day, 1920*: Stanford University News Service, "Chemist James Lu Valle dies at 80," February 16, 1993.

26 *The mostly white Tilden Technical School turns out to be*: Timothy B. Neary, *Crossing Parish Boundaries: Race, Sports, and Catholic Youth in Chicago* (Chicago: The University of Chicago Press, 2016).

26 *"You have to put daylight between you and your nearest competitor"*: Robert Cross, "Docile No More," *Chicago Tribune,* November 28, 1976.

27 *He easily wins the race, but not only that*: "Tilden Victor in State Meet; 6 Marks Broken," *Chicago Sunday Tribune,* May 20, 1928.

27 *In 1928, the Summer Olympics is held in the Netherlands*: Bob Herzog, "'28 Games a breakthrough for women Track and field ban ended in Amsterdam," *Baltimore Sun,* April 7, 1996, http://articles.baltimoresun.com/1996 -04-07/sports/1996098157_1_betty-robinson-track-and-field-track-event, accessed 10 April 2017.

28 *One of those competing is Betty Robinson*: Frank Fitzpatrick, "Frank's Place: America's first female track hero deserves more attention," *Philadelphia Inquirer,* November 25, 2016.

28 *She arrives back home to ticker-tape parades in both New York and Chicago*: Frank Litsky, "Betty Robinson, a Pathfinder in Women's Track, Dies at 87," *New York Times,* May 21, 1999.

CHAPTER FOUR: DETERMINATION

29 *This time, she has company*: Glenn Stout, *Yes, She Can!: Women's Sports Pioneers (Good Sports)* (Boston: HMH Books for Young Readers, 2001).

30 *They played basketball together*: Matt Osgood, "Sports History Forgot About Tidye Pickett and Louise Stokes, Two Black Olympians Who Never Got Their Shot," Smithsonian.com, August 15, 2016. https://www.smith sonianmag.com/history/sports-history-forgot-about-tidye-pickett-and-lou ise-stokes-two-black-olympians-who-never-got-their-shot-glory-180960138 /#55yrezaAyw1bFISg.99, accessed January 24, 2017.

30 *Quaine started the Onteora Track Club*: Glenn, *Yes, She Can!*

31 *"A little thing like you doesn't have a chance"*: Glenn, *Yes, She Can!*

31 *She isn't quite five foot three, but surprisingly there is another player shorter than her on the team*: Deborah Riley Draper, personal interview with Bernita Echols and Fay Walker, December 20, 2014.

32 *Miss Pearl Greene notices Tidye*: "Berlin Olympics, 1936: Golden Memories," Northern Illinois University News, Summer 1984.

34 *It especially showed when he and his friends played Chase the Fox*: David Falkner, *Great Time Coming: The Life of Jack Robinson From Baseball to Birmingham* (New York: Simon & Schuster, 1995).

34 *"We discovered a heart murmur"*: Ibid.

36 *By March 1930, the unemployment rate more than doubles in the span of five months*: T. H. Watkins, *The Great Depression: America in the 1930s* (New York: Little, Brown & Company, 1993).

36 *"I am shaking with excitement"*: *The Goebbels Experiment*, directed by Lutz Hachmeister, First Run Features, 2005.

37 *The following day, Hitler speaks in Munich*: Sue Vander Hook, *Winston Churchill: British Prime Minister & Statesman* (Minneapolis: ABDO Publishing, 2009).

CHAPTER FIVE: DASHING TO THE TAPE

39 *"Boy, if I've gotta get on my hands and knees"*: Deborah Riley Draper, personal interview with Ralph Metcalfe, Jr., December 20, 2014.

39 *"Jimmy, I want you to run the 660 against Sam"*: Dr. James E. LuValle, "Dr. James E. LuValle, 1936 Olympic Games, Track & Field: An Olympian's Oral History," interviewed by George A. Hodak, June 1988, Amateur Athletic Foundation of Los Angeles.

40 *Outside of his job at the Los Angeles Public Library*: Edray Herber Goins, "A Lifetime Filled with Awards and Honors," *The History of Caltech's Underrepresented Students,* Purdue University, http://www.math.purdue.edu/~egoins/notes/caltechs_minorities.pdf.

40 *LuValle starts the race*: "Dr. James E. LuValle, 1936 Olympic Games, Track & Field: An Olympian's Oral History."

41 *As he marches into Soldier Field on September 3, 1930*: *Chicago Tribune*, August 25, 1930.

42 *Metcalfe sees only two other African Americans along with him*: "US Track Men Segregated," *Pittsburgh Courier*, September 6, 1930.

42 *In three short years, Ralph has been instrumental*: Reid Hanley, "Tilden's Metcalfe Led Way to Public League's Glory," *Chicago Tribune* March 23, 1990.

42 *From 1928 to 1930*: Kenneth T. Jackson, *Scribner Encyclopedia of American Lives, Thematic Series: Sports Figures* (New York: Charles Scribner's Sons, 2003).

43 *The anticipation for this event was dampened a couple days*: "US Track Men Segregated," *Pittsburgh Courier*, September 6, 1930.

43 *the crowd also stands and applauds Metcalfe*: Liam T. A. Ford, *Soldier Field: A Stadium and Its City* (Chicago: University of Chicago Press, 2009).

43 *The two black men won't race each other*: "US Track Men Segregated."

43 The *Pittsburgh Courier* writes of Metcalfe's victory: Ibid.

44 *On May 24, 1930, the entire country of Germany begins*: Organisationskomitee FÜR Die XI, Olympiade Berlin 1936 E. V., *The XIth Olympic Games Berlin, 1936 Official Report Volume 1* (Berlin: Wilhelm Limpert, 1937).

44 *Gathering in the town of Grünau*: Daniel James Brown, *The Boys in the Boat* (New York: Penguin Books, 2013).

45 *With the popularity of rowing in the 1920s and 1930s*: Doug Most, " 'Boys in the Boat' author discusses rowing's enduring appeal," *Boston Globe*, October 16, 2015.

CHAPTER SIX: THE UNDERESTIMATED

46 *Her cropped, straight brown hair makes her look tough*: Don Van Natta, Jr., *Wonder Girl: The Magnificent Sporting Life of Babe Didrikson Zaharias* (New York: Little, Brown & Company, 2011).

47 *Coach told the girls that Babe Didrikson*: Don Van Natta, Jr., "Babe Didrikson Zaharias's Legacy Fades," *New York Times*, June 25, 2011.

47 *Born in Port Arthur, Texas, Mildred Didrikson*: "Babe's Life," About "Babe" Didrikson Zaharias, http://www.babedidriksonzaharias.org, accessed March 17, 2017.

48 *Arthur Daley of the* New York Times: Arthur Daley, "Sport's Section Only," *New York Times*, July 26, 1931.

48 *With his eyes closed for a moment while recuperating in a hospital bed*: Dr. James E. LuValle, "Dr. James E. LuValle, 1936 Olympic Games, Track & Field: An Olympian's Oral History," interviewed by George A. Hodak, June 1988, Amateur Athletic Foundation of Los Angeles.

50 *LuValle takes their advice*: Ibid.

50 *"Well, what do you think you should do?"*: Ibid.

51 *"the Negro girl was practically unbeatable"*: Edward Bulger, "Malden Negro Girl Lowers 100-Meter Mark for Second Time This Season," *Boston Globe*, September 21, 1931.

52 *Four hundred people fill the stands*: Associated Press, *Indianapolis Recorder*, October 10, 1931.

53 *Tomorrow's* Boston Post *will write*: "Malden Girl Wins Mayor Curley Cup—Scores Places in Three Events in N.E. Title Events," *Boston Post*, September 20, 1931.

54 *While misspelling her name, the* Boston Post *states*: Ibid.

55 *His grandmother, Fannie Wall*: Archie F. Williams, "The Joy of Flying:

Olympic Gold, Air Force Colonel, and Teacher," oral-history interview conducted in 1992 by Gabrielle Morris, Regional Oral History Office, 1993: The Bancroft Library, University of California, Berkeley.

57 *Archie underwhelms them to death*: Archie Williams, "Archie F. Williams, 1936 Olympic Games, Track & Field: An Olympian's Oral History," interviewed by George A. Hodak, June 1988, Amateur Athletic Foundation of Los Angeles.

57 *"Our program is to purge Germany"*: Max Fraenkel, "Adolf Hitler 'Explains'," *Jewish Criterion*, January 23, 1931.

58 *At the end of 1931, one of America's most respected foreign correspondents, Dorothy Thompson*: Peter Carlson, "American Journalist Dorothy Thompson Underestimates Hitler," *American History*, October 6, 2015.

CHAPTER SEVEN: QUALIFIED AND CONFIDENT

60 *Chicago, the gritty metropolis by the lake*: Tracey Deutsch, "Great Depression," *Encyclopedia of Chicago* 2004, http://www.encyclopedia.chicagohistory.org /pages/542.html, retrieved March 16, 2017.

60 *John Brooks realizes the petite girl is special*: Gerald R. Gems, *Before Jackie Robinson: The Transcendent Role of Black Sporting Pioneers* (Nebraska: University of Nebraska Press, 2017).

61 *Standing in the newly completed Naval Armory*: Patricia Leeds, "Navy calls it quits at lakefront armory," *Chicago Tribune*, September 30, 1982.

62 *"New Playground Star Ties National 60 Yard Record"*: Betty Eckersall, "New Playground Star Ties National 60 Yard Record," *Chicago Tribune*, January 31, 1932.

62 *Days later, John Brooks visits the Pickett household*: Deborah Riley Draper, personal interview with Dr. Daria Brooks Terrell and Wannetta Brooks, December 20, 2014.

62 *Mrs. Pickett knows the impact a black girl*: Ibid.

63 *"Go get an education"*: Arlie W. Schardt, "Olympic Bridesmaid: Ralph Metcalfe, best sprinter of the early '30s, won everything but the race that really counted," *Sports Illustrated*, July 24, 1961.

64 *something he and Coach Con Jennings have worked on repeatedly*: Ibid.

65 *Newspapers all across the country announce his greatness*: Charles Dunkley, "Five World Marks Fall at Chicago; Indiana Wins—Gophers Get 31 Points To Finish Third," *Star Tribune*, June 12, 1932.

67 *From the moment the coach tells the Stokes family*: Deborah Riley Draper, personal interview with Wilfried Fraser, Jr., May 5, 2015.

68 *a local favorite named Ethel Harrington fails to qualify*: Richard Hymans, "The History of the United States Olympic Trials—Track and Field," *Track & Field*, 2008.

68 *Babe Didrikson continues to capture the crowd's attention*: Evelyne Hall Adams,

"Evelyne Hall Adams, 1932 Olympic Games, Track & Field: An Olympian's Oral History," interviewed by George A. Hodak, October 1987, Amateur Athletic Foundation of Los Angeles.

68 *"Ah'm gonna lick you single-handed"*: Susan E. Cayleff, *Babe: The Life and Legend of Babe Didrikson Zaharias* (Champaign, Illinois: University of Illinois Press, 1996).

68 *A block of ice*: Doris H. Pieroth, *Their Day in the Sun: Women of the 1932 Olympics* (Seattle: University of Washington Press, 1996).

69 *"Miss Pickett will have to thank George T. Donoghue"*: Ibid.

69 *"Coach Quaine is ecstatic, shouting how she's earned the right"*: Ann Chandler Howell, *In the Blocks: An Olympian's Story* (Chicago: Chandler/White Publishing Company, Inc., 1996).

70 *One reporter calls Babe's performance*: Cayleff, *Babe: The Life and Legend of Babe Didrikson Zaharias.*

70 *Metcalfe entered Stanford Stadium after sweeping every race*: Arlie W. Schardt, "Olympic Bridesmaid: Ralph Metcalfe, best sprinter of the early '30s, won everything but the race that really counted," *Sports Illustrated*, July 24, 1961.

71 *Tolan is seven inches shorter and thirty-five pounds lighter than Metcalfe*: "Fast Eddie Tolan Claims Double Sprint Gold," Olympic.Org, https://www.olympic.org/news/fast-eddie-tolan-claims-double-sprint-gold, retrieved February 10, 2017.

71 *Eddie Tolan set a record in 1929*: Eddie Tolan, "The Midnight Express," African American Registry, https://aaregistry.org/story/eddie-tolan-the-midnight-express/, retrieved February 10, 2017.

71 *Before the race, Metcalfe catches Tolan chewing gum*: Edward S. Sears, *Running Through the Ages,* 2nd ed. (Jefferson, North Carolina: McFarland, 2015).

71 *"the Black Panther of Marquette"*: Ibid.

71 *Metcalfe passes him with 20 meters left*: Richard Hymans, "The History of the United States Olympic Trials—Track and Field," *Track & Field* (2008).

73 *President Hoover faces off with veterans of World War I*: David Goldblatt, *The Games: A Global History of the Olympics*, (New York: W. W. Norton & Company, 2016).

73 *Hoover commands Army Chief of Staff and Major General Douglas MacArthur*: Wyatt Kingseed, "The 'Bonus Army' War in Washington," *American History*, 2004.

CHAPTER EIGHT: TOGETHER YET ALONE

76 *"I wonder if the bed above us ever pops open"*: "Pullman Sleeping Cars add Comfort to Overnight Travel," *Rails West*, 2010, http://www.railswest.com/pullman.html, retrieved February 3, 2017.

76 *a red, white, and blue banner*: Russell Freedman, *Babe Didrikson Zaharias: The Making of a Champion* (Boston: Clarion Books, 1999).

76 *Babe Didrikson whisks by*: Ibid.

76 *Jean Shiley is one of those teammates*: Jean Shiley Newhouse, "An Olympian's oral history : Jean Shiley Newhouse, 1928 & 1932 Olympic Games, track & field," 1988, LA84 Foundation.

77 *"She had no social graces whatsoever"*: Russell, *Babe Didrikson Zaharias: The Making of a Champion.*

77 *Evelyne Hall, the hurdler from Chicago*: Louise Mead Tricard, *American Women's Track and Field: A History, 1895 Through 1980, Volume 1* (Jefferson, North Carolina: McFarland, 1996).

77 *There is Elizabeth Wilde from Kansas City*: Doris H. Pieroth, *Their Day in the Sun: Women of the 1932 Olympics* (Seattle: University of Washington Press, 1996).

78 *Opening in 1892, the triangular red stone edifice*: Debra Faulkner, *Ladies of the Brown: A Women's History of Denver's Most Elegant Hotel* (Mount Pleasant, South Carolina: The History Press, 2010).

78 *guests look up to see the opulent atrium of the hotel*: Aldo Svaldi, "Historic Brown Palace Hotel in Denver sold to Trammell Crow affiliate," *Denver Post* March 5, 2014.

78 *Instead of walking into the grand lobby*: Glenn Stout, *Yes, She Can!: Women's Sports Pioneers (Good Sports)* (Boston: HMH Books for Young Readers, 2001).

78 *Tidye and Louise never enter the ballroom*: Deborah Riley Draper, personal interview with Bernita Echols and Fay Walker, December 20, 2014.

79 *The morning after the girls arrive*: Faulkner, *Ladies of the Brown: A Women's History of Denver's Most Elegant Hotel.*

79 *by playing her harmonica*: Newhouse, "An Olympian's oral history : Jean Shiley Newhouse, 1928 & 1932 Olympic Games, track & field."

80 *Years later, in 1984, Tidye will say*: "Tidye Pickett: Chicago track star was first African-American female Olympian," *Chicago Tribune*, August 19, 2016.

80 *Cold water rips Tidye awake*: Michael D. Davis, *Black American Women in Track and Field: A Complete Illustrated Reference* (Jefferson, North Carolina: McFarland, 1992).

80 *Babe's antics around the team and especially on the train*: Rich Wallace and Sandra Neil Wallace, *Babe Conquers the World: The Legendary Life of Babe Didrikson* (Honesdale, Pennsylvania: Calkins Creek Books, 2014).

80 *a Western Union bike*: Susan E. Cayleff, *Babe: The Life and Legend of Babe Didrikson Zaharias* (Champaign, Illinois: University of Illinois Press, 1996).

80 *getting into a pillow fight with Gloria Russell*: Evelyne Hall Adams, "Evelyne Hall Adams, 1932 Olympic Games, Track & Field: An Olympian's Oral History," interviewed by George A. Hodak, October 1987, Amateur Athletic Foundation of Los Angeles.

81 *Babe using the N word*: Cindy Himes Gissendanner, "African American

Women Olympians: The Impact of Race, Gender, and Class Ideologies, 1932–1968," *Research Quarterly for Exercise and Sport*, June 1, 1996.

81 *"That big girl from Texas"*: "Berlin Olympics, 1936: Golden Memories," *Northern Illinois University News*, Summer 1984.

81 *Waves of people, estimated at around 105,000*: The Official Report of the Xth Olympiad, Los Angeles, 1932 (Los Angeles: Wolfer Printing Company, 1933).

82 *The group photograph taken in front of the station*: Pieroth, *Their Day in the Sun: Women of the 1932 Olympics*.

82 *The newly built Village*: "The First-Ever Olympic Village Was Built in Los Angeles," *History & Society*, KCETLink Media Group, July 26, 2012, https://www.kcet.org/history-society/the-first-ever-olympic-village-was-built-in-los-angeles, retrieved February 10, 2017.

82 *the Chapman Park Hotel*: Hillel Aron, "The Story of Los Angeles' 1932 Olympics, When Everyone Was Poor," *LA Weekly*, August 13, 2016.

84 *"I came out to beat everybody in sight"*: William Oscar Johnson, "Babe," *Sports Illustrated*, October 6, 1975.

85 *President Herbert Hoover chooses not to attend*: Wallace and Neil Wallace, *Babe Conquers the World: The Legendary Life of Babe Didrikson*.

85 *slipping off her shoes*: Jean Shiley Newhouse, "An Olympian's oral history: Jean Shiley Newhouse, 1928 & 1932 Olympic Games, track & field," 1988, LA84 Foundation.

86 *the Chicago Defender announces*: Russ Cowen, "Tydia [sic] Pickett May Lose Olympic Spot," *Chicago Defender*, July 30, 1932.

87 *for unless Avery Brundage rules*: Ibid.

88 *NAACP sends a telegram to Jean Shiley*: Jean Shiley Newhouse, "An Olympian's oral history : Jean Shiley Newhouse, 1928 & 1932 Olympic Games, track & field," 1988, LA84 Foundation.

89 *After a series of struggles and shifting political moves*: Associated Press, "Hitler Fought Way to Power Unique in Modern History," *New York Times*, May 2, 1945.

89 *Hitler crafted his beliefs around indoctrination and publicity*: Ibid.

89 *his propensity for deception*: Michiko Kakutani, "From 'Dunderhead' to Demagogue," *New York Times*, September 28, 2016.

CHAPTER NINE: DEFEAT

91 *"God is watching everything you do"*: Arnold Rampersad, *Jackie Robinson: A Biography* (New York: Alfred A. Knopf, 1997).

91 *The favored runner in the 100-meter race*: Arlie W. Schardt, "Olympic Bridesmaid: Ralph Metcalfe, best sprinter of the early '30s, won everything but the race that really counted." *Sports Illustrated*, July 24, 1961.

91 *Metcalfe is so assured of the victory that he poses for the cameras*: Ibid.

92 *The electro-photographic timer used*: Arthur Daley and John Kieran, *The Story of the Olympic Games, 776 B.C. to 1968* (Philadelphia: Lippincott, 1965).

92 *his flawless physique slumping in defeat*: Schardt, "Olympic Bridesmaid."

92 *"I've never been convinced"*: "Olympics—1932 Los Angeles—Track Men's 100m—USA's Ralph Metcalfe & Eddie Tolan," *Imasportsphile*, retrieved April 14, 2017, https://www.youtube.com/watch?v=xmkXvi0cBpU.

93 *he tightens up*: Schardt, "Olympic Bridesmaid."

93 *"It was no question that I spotted the field"*: "Olympics—1932 Los Angeles—Track Men's 100m—USA's Ralph Metcalfe & Eddie Tolan."

94 *especially having to pay his way by serving as a waiter*: Keith McClellan, "Metcalfe, Ralph Horace," *Scribner Encyclopedia of American Lives*, 2002, https://www.encyclopedia.com/humanities/encyclopedias-almanacs-tran scripts-and-maps/metcalfe-ralph-horace, retrieved November 13, 2016.

94 *"There may be better sprinters in the world, but I doubt it"*: *2010-11 Marquette Media Guide—Cross Country/Track & Field*, Marquette Athletics, http://grfx.cstv.com/photos/schools/marq/sports/c-track/auto_pdf/2012-13/misc_non_event/TrackHistory.pdf, retrieved January 4, 2017.

95 *Coach Vreeland chose Mary Carew and Evelyn Furtsch to run instead of Tidye and Louise*: Michael D. Davis, *Black American Women in Olympic Track and Field: A Complete Illustrated Reference* (Jefferson, North Carolina: McFarland & Company, Inc., 1992).

95 *All they can do is stand*: Robert G. Weisbord, *Racism and the Olympics* (Piscataway, New Jersey: Transaction Publishers, 2015).

95 *They watch sweet Mary Carew start the 400-meter relay*: Daley and Kieran, *The Story of the Olympic Games, 776 B.C. to 1968*.

PART TWO

99 *He jumps to his feet, there he is*: Peter Longerich, *Goebbels: A Biography* (New York: Random House, 2015).

99 *the bone marrow disease osteomyelitis*: Anthony Read, *The Devil's Disciples: Hitler's Inner Circle* (New York: W.W. Norton & Company, 2003).

99 *After an operation at age ten*: Longerich, *Goebbels: A Biography*.

99 *his foot remains paralyzed for life*: *The Goebbels Experiment*, directed by Lutz Hachmeister, First Run Features, 2005.

99 *despising not only others but God himself*: Read, *The Devil's Disciples: Hitler's Inner Circle*.

99 *"driven by an exceptional craving"*: Longerich, *Goebbels: A Biography*.

100 *he witnesses the Jewish banking methods*: David Irving, "Revelations from Goebbels' Diary; Bringing to Light Secrets of Hitler's Propaganda Minister," *Journal of Historical Review*, vol. 15, no. 1, p. 2.

100 *Goebbels becomes impressed by Hitler's fervent belief*: Longerich, *Goebbels: A Biography*.

100 *"We need a firm hand in Germany"*: *The Goebbels Experiment*, directed by Lutz Hachmeister, First Run Features, 2005.

100 *"I'm ready to sacrifice everything for him"*: Longerich, *Goebbels: A Biography*.

101 *Hitler quickly recognizes Goebbels's gifts:* Ibid.

CHAPTER TEN: DO THE LITTLE THINGS WELL

103 *"The Rabbit"*: "Newspaper Clipping Peeved Metcalfe, so He Showed 'Em," *Chicago Defender*, July 30, 1932.

103 *Metcalfe lets doubt and discouragement*: Arlie W. Schardt, "Olympic Bridesmaid: Ralph Metcalfe, best sprinter of the early '30s, won everything but the race that really counted," *Sports Illustrated*, July 24, 1961.

103 *his stunning performance at Madison Square Garden*: Associated Press, "Ralph Metcalfe Dethrones Toppino in 60-Meter Dash," *Richmond Item*, February 26, 1933.

104 *"negro speed king"*: Associated Press, "Plan Welcome For Metcalfe," *Manitowoc Herald-Times*, February 27, 1933.

104 *"sable catapult"*: Grantland Rice, "The Spotlight," *Hartford Courant*, March 2, 1933.

104 *"sensational negro sprinter"*: Associated Press, "Metcalfe Sprints to World's Record in the 60-yard Dash," *Philadelphia Inquirer*, March 12, 1933.

104 *"colored dash star"*: Associated Press, "Normal Runners Cop C.I.C. Crown," *Lansing State Journal*, March 13, 1933.

104 *"ebon-hued"*: Alan J. Gould, "Sports Slants," *Kingston Daily Freeman*, March 15, 1933.

104 *"husky Marquette sprinter"*: Associated Press, "Cunningham Is Victor," *Cincinnati Enquirer*, March 16, 1933.

104 *"negro flash"*: Associated Press, "Ralph Beats Eddie," *Ogden Standard-Examiner*, March 19, 1933.

104 *Tolan turns in his amateur card*: Associated Press, "Eddie Tolan Is Discovered in Vaudeville Act," *Chicago Tribune*, November 29, 1932.

104 *Tolan tells reporters*: William Beatty, " 'What Price Glory?' Says Tolan As He Gives Up Chosen Career," *Decatur Herald*, January 24, 1933.

105 *"the sweetness of winning the battle"*: Ralph Metcalfe, "Black Athletes' Hall of Fame Induction Speech," Black Athletes Hall of Fame, March 14, 1974, Imperial Ballroom of the Americana Hotel, New York City.

105 *"giant negro"*: Associated Press, "Ralph Metcalfe Sets a New Mark in Indoor Race," *Shamokin Daily News*, March 22, 1933.

105 *"dusky Marquette University flier"*: Associated Press, "Metcalfe Runs 60-Yard Dash in 6 1-10 seconds," *Press and Sun-Bulletin*, March 23, 1933.

105 *"the colored midwestern runner"*: Associated Press, "Metcalfe Again Bests Toppino," *Salt Lake Tribune*, March 23, 1933.

105 *"Marquette University's negro speedster"*: Associated Press, "Metcalfe Wins Central A.A.U. 60-Meter Race," *St. Louis Post-Dispatch*, March 25, 1933.

105 *"Marquette University's ebony flyer"*: Associated Press, "Purdue Scores 4 Points in Relays," *Journal and Courier*, March 27, 1933.

105 *"the rangy Marquette negro"*: G.O. Gettum, "Thru Sportland," *Lebanon Daily News*, March 30, 1933.

105 *"sable cyclone"*: Associated Press, "Michigan State Flyers Hope to Smash Record," *Des Moines Register*, April 7, 1933.

105 *"Negro dash artist"*: Associated Press, "Drake Relays to Entertain Stars of Middle West," *Coshocton Tribune*, April 28, 1933.

105 *"Flying ebony"*: Wade Patterson, "Out on the Cinders," *Coe College Cosmos*, May 4, 1933.

105 *"crack colored sprinter"*: Associated Press, "After Dash Record," *Emporia Gazette*, April 29, 1933.

105 *"Marquette's colored dashman"*: Associated Press, "5 Lincolnite Trackmen in State Meet," *Daily Tribune* (Wisconsin Rapids), May 26, 1933.

105 *"Marquette's dark comet"*: Associated Press, "Dash Mark May Fall in Midwest Track Meet," *Manitowoc Herald-Times*, May 29, 1933.

105 *"midnight express"*: Associated Press, "Ralph Metcalfe Beats Owens in Race at Chicago," *New Castle News*, July 1, 1933.

105 *"Three Aces of Spades Star in AAU Games"*: Associated Press, "Three Aces of Spades Star in A.A.U. Games," *Marshfield News-Herald,* July 5, 1933.

106 *"Black Diamond Express"*: George Currie, "Here's the Man with the Softest Job in the World," *Brooklyn Daily Eagle*, July 6, 1933.

107 *Ralph Metcalfe has seared his name onto the world records*: G.O. Gettum, "Thru Sportland."

107 *Metcalfe's interest*: "The Conversion Stories of Knute Rockne and Ralph H. Metcalfe," Catholicism.org, http://catholicism.org/the-conversion-stories-of-knute-rockne-and-ralph-h-metcalfe.html, retrieved March 3, 2017.

108 *Yet Father Grace, noting Metcalfe's good grades*: Bill Gibson, "Hear Me Talkin' To Ya," *Afro-American*, February 11, 1933.

108 *"Ralph has the brains and the ability"*: "Newspaper Clipping Peeved Metcalfe, so He Showed 'Em," *Chicago Defender*, July 30, 1932.

108 *"Catholicity has opened my eyes"*: "The Conversion Stories of Knute Rockne and Ralph H. Metcalfe."

108 *Coach Jennings doesn't want Metcalfe to play football*: Deborah Riley Draper, personal interview with Ralph Metcalfe, Jr., December 20, 2014.

109 *The first part of Tarzan's prank*: Ibid.

109 *"The little things count"*: Damon Kerby, " 'Treat Little Jobs Like Big Ones,' Fastest Waterboy Says," *St. Louis Post-Dispatch*, November 17, 1933.

109 *The school prides itself*: Elisa Crouch, "Sumner celebrates its past amid worries about the future," *St. Louis Post-Dispatch* June 23, 2015.

110 *Sumner becomes notable for its excellence*: Caoimhe Ni Dhonaill, " 'Where Did They Go to High School?': A Brief History of the First High Schools in

St. Louis," *History Happens Here*, Missouri History Museum, October 18, 2013, http://staging.historyhappenshere.org/node/7470, retrieved May 23, 2017.

110 *Vashon High School, which opened in 1927*: "A History of Vashon High School," Vashon High School, Saint Louis Public Schools, http://www.slps .org/domain/2956, retrieved May 23, 2017.

110 *The students treat him like a celebrity*: Calvin C. Bailey, "Metcalfe, Ace Sprinter, Once Aspired to be a Quarterback," *African American*, September 23, 1933.

110 *"A fellow must be thinking about his team and his school"*: Ibid.

111 *That is what he did in Europe*: Associated Press, "Metcalfe to Europe," *Afro-American*, July 8, 1933.

111 *"Do the little things as well as the big things"*: Kerby, " 'Treat Little Jobs like Big Ones,' Fastest Waterboy Says."

111 *One of Hitler's first actions*: United States Holocaust Memorial Museum, "Nazi Propaganda," https://www.ushmm.org/wlc/en/article.php?ModuleId =10005202, retrieved February 13, 2017.

112 *"act as a firebrand"*: Peter Longerich, *Goebbels: A Biography* (New York: Random House, 2015).

112 *His plan is to "work on people"*: Ibid.

112 *"German sport has only one task"*: Jewish Virtual Library, "Nazi Perpetrators: Joseph Goebbels," http://www.jewishvirtuallibrary.org/joseph-goebbels-table -of-contents, retrieved March 23, 2017.

112 *"an infamous festival dominated by Jews"*: Carol Levy, "The Olympic Pause," *The Jewish Magazine* (2000, October High Holiday edition).

112 *"an invention of Jews and Freemasons"*: Max Fisher, "The Nazi Origins of the Olympic Flame Relay," *Atlantic*, May 10, 2010.

112 *In October 1933, Hitler and Dr. Lewald will visit the Olympic Stadium*: Tom Ecker, "Olympic Pride: Nationalism at the Berlin and Beijing Games," *Harvard International Review* (2014), November 10, 2014.

113 *in a speech at the end of 1933*: Max Domarus, *Hitler: Speeches and Proclamations 1932–1935* (Wauconda, Illinois: Bolchazy-Carducci Publishers, 1990).

CHAPTER ELEVEN: LOOKING AHEAD

115 *the only facility they have for sports*: Archie Williams, "Archie F. Williams, 1936 Olympic Games, Track & Field: An Olympian's Oral History," interviewed by George A. Hodak, June 1988, Amateur Athletic Foundation of Los Angeles.

116 *"Let's go back to school"*: Archie F. Williams, "The Joy of Flying: Olympic Gold, Air Force Colonel, and Teacher," an oral-history interview conducted in 1992 by Gabrielle Morris: Regional Oral History Office, 1993, Bancroft Library, University of California, Berkeley.

116 *"I'm going to be a dentist"*: Ibid.

117 *"Well, you're the coach"*: "Archie F. Williams, 1936 Olympic Games, Track & Field: An Olympian's Oral History."

118 *the small pink-gold compact*: Michael D. Davis, *Black American Women in Olympic Track and Field: A Complete Illustrated Reference* (Jefferson, North Carolina: McFarland & Company, Inc., 1992).

118 *On this Tuesday evening in April*: Associated Press, "Mercury A.C. Entertains for Miss Louise Stokes," *New York Age*, April 21, 1934.

119 *Hampered by a bad foot*: Associated Press, "Jinx on Girls at Brooklyn," *Afro-American*, April 21, 1934.

119 *Many other familiar faces are there*: Associated Press, "Women's National Track Champs on Tomorrow Night," *Brooklyn Daily Eagle*, April 13, 1934.

119 *the unlikely comeback for Betty Robinson*: Associated Press, "Betty Robinson Ready to Stage Track Comeback," *Indianapolis Star*, April 11, 1934.

119 *"I'd prefer being home listening to the radio"*: "Jinx On Girls at Brooklyn."

120 *promises that she will come back to New York*: "Mercury A.C. Entertains for Miss Louise Stokes."

120 *the president of the United States to openly address*: Paul M. Sparrow, "Eleanor Roosevelt's Battle to End Lynching," The National Archives: Forward With Roosevelt, February 12, 2016, https://fdr.blogs.archives.gov/2016/02/12 /eleanor-roosevelts-battle-to-end-lynching/, retrieved March 20, 2017.

120 *the county jail in Hazard, Kentucky*: Associated Press, "Probe Cemetery Lynching in Kentucky Town," *Jefferson City Post-Tribune*, January 25, 1934.

121 *First Lady Eleanor Roosevelt joins forces*: Sparrow, "Eleanor Roosevelt's Battle to End Lynching."

CHAPTER TWELVE: THE WORLD'S FASTEST MAN

123 *Staggering onto the train*: Dr. James E. LuValle, "Dr. James E. LuValle, 1936 Olympic Games, Track & Field: An Olympian's Oral History," interviewed by George A. Hodak, June 1988, Amateur Athletic Foundation of Los Angeles.

124 *"Brain Wonder" and the "Westwood Whirlwind"*: Irving Eckhoff, "Shoes Worry LuValle," *Los Angeles Times*, March 21, 1934.

125 *the speedy Al Blackman*: Bud Spencer, "Luvalle Races Blackman in Feature," *Oakland Tribune*, March 27, 1934.

125 *his new running shoes*: Eckhoff, "Shoes Worry LuValle."

126 *she also breaks a Canadian record*: Canadian Press, "Chicago Girls Win in Toronto Games," *Chicago Tribune*, July 13, 1934.

126 *a one-man track team*: Wilfred Smith, "Need a One Man Track Team? Just send for John Brooks," *Chicago Tribune*, May 4, 1932.

127 *Brooks just missed it*: Richard Hymans, "The History of the United States Olympic Trials—Track and Field," *Track & Field*, 2008.

127 *Tidye almost won her first hurdles*: Tidye Pickett nearly winning hurdling: Ron Grossman, "Tidye Pickett: Chicago track star was first African-American female Olympian," *Chicago Tribune*, August 19, 2016.

128 *Mack remains moved and inspired*: Larry Eldridge, "Mack Robinson—Overshadowed by Jackie," *Albuquerque Journal*, September 30, 1977.

129 *Metcalfe has had to nurse a bleeding muscle*: Associated Press, "Ward Scores 2nd Place at Drake Relays," *Michigan Daily*, April 29, 1934.

129 *"I thought I had you beat"*: Jacqueline Edmondson, *Jesse Owens: A Biography* (Westport, Connecticut: Greenwood Publishing Group, 2007).

130 *All legends have a starting point*: Timothy L. Hudak, "Looking Back at the OHSAA's Track & Field Championships," *Ohio High School Athletic Association*, Sports Heritage Specialty Publications, http://ohsaa.org/sports/history/tim-hudak-features/track, retrieved March 9, 2017.

130 *His jump breaks the Class A record*: Associated Press, "Piqua Track Team Easily Trounces Sidney Hi 83-39," *Piqua Daily Call*, May 25, 1931.

130 *Metcalfe has enough speed to beat the young and friendly-faced sprinter by a foot*: Charles Dunkley, "Bonthron Sets Record to Defeat Cunningham," *Independent Record*, July 1, 1934.

130 *"When I write that Ralph Metcalfe was the greatest sprinter of his day"*: Jesse Owens and Paul Neimark, *I Have Changed* (New York: William Morrow, 1972).

130 *These two victories at these AAU championships*: Chris Foran, "Ralph Metcalfe beats Jesse Owen at Marquette." *Milwaukee Wisconsin Journal Sentinel,* February 16, 1934.

131 *"Night of the Long Knives"*: United States Holocaust Memorial Museum, "Rohm Purge," *Holocaust Encyclopedia*, https://www.ushmm.org/wlc/en/article.php?ModuleId=10007885, retrieved May 16, 2017.

131 *Hitler states that fifty-eight men are killed*: Anthony Read, *The Devil's Disciples: Hitler's Inner Circle* (New York: W.W. Norton & Company).

132 *with any troublemakers or those deemed "degenerates" purged immediately*: Ibid.

CHAPTER THIRTEEN: THE NAZIS TAKE CONTROL

133 *Helene Mayer, considered the most gifted female fencer*: Susan D. Bachrach, *The Nazi Olympics: Berlin 1936* (New York: Little, Brown & Company, 2000).

134 *"My personal, but unofficial opinion"*: Ibid.

134 *As an athlete and self-made millionaire*: Frank Zarnowski, *All-around Men: Heroes of a Forgotten Sport* (Lanham, Maryland: Scarecrow Press, 2005).

134 *revolutionaries are not bred on the playing field*: Carolyn Marvin, "Avery Brundage and American Participation in the 1936 Olympic Games," *Journal of American Studies* 16 (1982), p. 83.

134 *"Where amateur sport with its high ideals flourishes"*: Ibid.

134 *Baillet-Latour later writes*: Ibid.

135 *He is told to make a decision on the spot*: Ibid.

135 *For six days, the Germans show Brundage around*: Marvin, "Avery Brundage and American Participation in the 1936 Olympic Games," pp. 81–106.

135 *the anti-Semitism raging through Germany like a wildfire*: Dr. Rafael Medoff, "Hitler on Trial," *Mishpacha Magazine*, April 5, 2014.

135 *the Germans promised "there would be no discrimination against Jews"*: Marvin, "Avery Brundage and American Participation in the 1936 Olympic Games," p. 83.

135 *Brundage gives his full-fledged support for the games to continue as planned*: Ibid.

135 *"In light of the report of Mr. Brundage"*: D.A. Kass, "The Issue of Racism at the 1936 Olympics," *Journal of Sports History* vol. 3, no. 3, winter 1976, pp. 223–35.

136 *In neither Brundage's report nor the AOC's resolution*: David Kenneth Wiggins, *Glory Bound: Black Athletes in a White America* (Syracuse: Syracuse University Press, 1997).

136 *two groups are largely responsible for the rising opposition*: Marvin, "Avery Brundage and American Participation in the 1936 Olympic Games," p. 83.

136 *Brundage disagrees with the legalists and ignores the moralists*: Ibid.

137 *"we're in for trouble, and plenty of it"*: Kass, "The Issue of Racism at the 1936 Olympics."

137 *The camp opens in March 1933*: Bachrach, *The Nazi Olympics: Berlin 1936*.

137 *conditions for the one thousand seven hundred prisoners*: New Republic staff, "The Harrowing First Report From Dachau Concentration Camp, in 1934," *New Republic*, https://newrepublic.com/article/119850/1934-report-dachau-concentration-camp, retrieved March 11, 2017.

138 *"Certain Jews must understand"*: Jeremy Schaap, *Triumph: The Untold Story of Jesse Owens and Hitler's Olympics* (Boston: Houghton Mifflin Harcourt, 2007).

138 *With Germany's full resources behind the Olympic preparations*: "The Berlin Olympics," The History Place, http://www.historyplace.com/worldwar2/triumph/tr-olympics.htm, retrieved April 3, 2017.

139 *the Olympiastadion*: "The 1936 Nazi Olympic Venues—Then and Now!" War History Online, https://www.warhistoryonline.com/world-war-ii/1936-nazi-olympic-venues-now.html, retrieved April 3, 2017.

139 *With Hitler's order that costs are of no concern*: Jason Pipes and Arvo Vercamer, "The 1936 Olympic Games in Germany," Feldgrau.com, https://www.feldgrau.com/Olympic-Games-Berlin-Germany-1936, retrieved April 13, 2017.

139 *Among the features of the Olympic Village*: Ibid.

139 *"Our first task in this ministry"*: Hans Fritzsche, "Dr. Goebbels and his Ministry," *German Propaganda Archive,* http://research.calvin.edu/german-propaganda-archive/goeb62.htm, retrieved April 3, 2017.

139 *Hitler will reveal the Aryan race*: Kass, "The Issue of Racism at the 1936 Olympics," pp. 223–35.

140 *On a brisk October eve in 1934 another mob of armed white men*: Ben Montgomery, "Spectacle: The Lynching of Claude Neal," *Tampa Bay Times,* October 20, 2011.

140 *The sheriff has Neal moved to several different jails*: Tameka Bradley Hobbs, *Hitler Is Here: Lynching in Florida during the Era of World War II* (Dissertation, Florida State, 2004).

141 *They bind their prisoner and then bring him back*: Montgomery, "Spectacle: The Lynching of Claude Neal."

141 *Thousands protest by writing to President Roosevelt*: Isabel Wilkerson, *The Warmth of Other Suns* (New York: Vintage, 2011).

CHAPTER FOURTEEN: ANYONE IS BEATABLE

142 *"They represent black pride"*: Ralph Metcalfe, "Black Athletes Hall of Fame Induction Speech," March 14, 1974, metcalfecollection.org.

142 *His five-foot-seven-inch height and weight of less than 150 pounds*: Bill Kashatus, "Plymouth's Ben Johnson once considered world's fastest sprinter," *Citizen's Voice,* May 25, 2014.

142 *On this night at the indoor championship at Madison Square Garden*: Bessye J. Bearden, "Ralph Metcalfe Beaten," *Chicago Defender,* March 2, 1935.

144 *Louise glances at the familiar quotation*: Ann Chandler Howell, *In The Blocks: An Olympian's Story* (Chicago: Chandler/White Publishing Company, Inc., 1996).

144 *Her senior school year*: Bob Duffy, "Stokes: Nowhere, Fast Malden Sprinter a Trailblazer, Though She Didn't Run," *Boston Globe,* September 10, 2000.

145 *"TYDIE STARTS RECORD BREAKING RELAY"*: Associated Press, "Tydie Starts Record Breaking Relay," *Chicago Defender,* April 6, 1935.

146 *The diminutive young woman, with bright and friendly eyes*: Associated Press, "Track Champion," *Chicago Defender,* May 4, 1935.

146 *They flew me across the country just so I could finish in fourth place*: Associated Press, "LuValle Leaves to Compete at Princeton," *Fresno Bee The Republican,* June 12, 1935.

146 *Eddie O'Brien, a sophomore from Syracuse, finishes with a blast in the final 80 yards*: Associated Press, "Sports," *Lead Daily Call,* July 13, 1935.

146 *LuValle never wanted to go east to run*: Dr. James E. LuValle, "Dr. James E. LuValle, 1936 Olympic Games, Track & Field: An Olympian's Oral History," interviewed by George A. Hodak, June 1988, Amateur Athletic Foundation of Los Angeles.

147 *Yet with his heavy fall class load*: Ibid.

147 *It is Independence Day, and more than fifteen thousand spectators*: Michael McKnight, "Faster Than the Fastest," *Sports Illustrated*, https://www.si.com /longform/peacock/index.html, retrieved March 10, 2017.

147 *On May 25, 1935, at the Big Ten Track and Field Championships*: Richard Rothschild, "Greatest 45 Minutes Ever in Sports," *Sports Illustrated*, May 24, 2010, https://www.si.com/more-sports/2010/05/24/owens-recordday, retrieved March 25, 2017.

148 *"He's Greatest Athlete of Modern Times"*: Conrad M. Jennings, "He's Greatest Athlete of Modern Times," *Shamokin News-Dispatch*, May 10, 1036.

148 *Metcalfe kneels in position*: McKnight, "Faster Than the Fastest."

149 *Peacock isn't completely unknown*: Ben Arogundade, "The 1936 Olympics: The Man Who Beat Jesse Owens," *Huffpost*, July 30, 2012, http://www.huff ingtonpost.com/ben-arogundade/1936-olympics-jesse-owens_b_1700705 .html, retrieved March 10, 2017.

149 *the school decided that he needed to drop football*: McKnight, "Faster Than the Fastest."

149 *Only recently, Metcalfe read an article with an Olympic coach*: Associated Press, "Robbie Says Metcalfe Can Not Beat Owens," *Brooklyn Daily Eagle*, May 28, 1935.

150 *Long, flowing flags of red, black, and white*: Peter Longerich, *Goebbels: A Biography*, (New York: Random House, 2015).

151 *Much of the success is due to the director's artistic flair*: David Clay Large, *Nazi Games: The Olympics of 1936* (New York: W. W. Norton & Company, 2007).

151 *Hitler asks her to film the upcoming Berlin Olympics*: Ibid.

CHAPTER FIFTEEN: THE BOYCOTT DEBATE

153 *He was friends with Avery Brundage*: John A. Lucas, "Judge Jeremiah T. Mahoney, the Amateur Athletic Union, and the Olympic Games," *Journal of Sports History*, Fall 2008.

153 *"While I can't attempt to speak"*: Davis J. Walsh, "Religious Persecution By German Government To Prompt Latest Action," *Evening News*, July 25, 1935.

154 *Avery Brundage answers publicly*: Associated Press, "Problem Faces Sports Leaders," *Times Herald*, July 26, 1935.

154 *"I regret to say that irrefutable proof"*: Associated Press, "Mahoney Again Suggests U.S. Shun Olympics," *Brooklyn Daily Eagle*, August 20, 1935.

154 *Mahoney writes a letter*: John A. Lucas, "Judge Jeremiah T. Mahoney, the Amateur Athletic Union, and the Olympic Games," *Journal of Sports History*, Fall 2008.

154 *Ralph Metcalfe gives his honest opinion*: W. Elaine Patton, "Playing the Field of Sports," *Indianapolis Star*, August 14, 1935.

155 *an open letter is written to these silent athletes*: "The 1936 Olympic Games—An Open Letter." *New York Amsterdam News*, August 24, 1935.

155 *"Refusal to participate would do untold good"*: David K. Wiggins, "The 1936 Olympic Games in Berlin: The Response of America's Black Press," September 21, 1982, *Research Quarterly for Exercise and Sport*, Vol. 54 , Iss. 3, 1983.

155 *The position that the black community*: Ibid.

156 *"the Olympic Games belong to the athletes and not the politicians"*: Heywood Broun, "It Seems To Me," *Reading Times*, October 28, 1935.

156 *Laws are announced on September 15*: "The Nuremberg Laws: Background and Overview," *Jewish Virtual Library*, http://www.jewishvirtuallibrary.org /background-and-overview-of-the-nuremberg-laws, retrieved April 14, 2017.

156 *The Nazis' definition of a Jewish man or woman*: "The Nuremberg Race Laws," United States Holocaust Memorial Museum, https://www.ushmm.org/out reach/en/article.php?ModuleId=10007695, retrieved April 14, 2017.

157 *blacks, Gypsies, or their offspring*: Ibid.

157 *Judge Jeremiah T. Mahoney demands*: Associated Press, "Judge Mahoney, AAU President, Calls For Ban On Olympics Declaring He Finds Discrimination Charge Proven," *Hartford Courant*, October 22, 1935.

157 *"I shall fight grimly to the very end"*: Carolyn Marvin, "Avery Brundage and American Participation in the 1936 Olympic Games," *Journal of American Studies*, 16 (1): p. 91.

158 *"If the result means my death, I care not"*: Associated Press, "A.A.U. Fight On Olympics Ban Raging," *Oakland Tribune*, December 8, 1935.

158 *Brundage argues every side he can*: Ibid.

159 *The slight margin of victory*: Associated Press, "Vote Taken on Boycott," *Los Angeles Times*, December 7, 1935.

159 *write in December of 1935 to Avery Brundage*: "Negro Athletes for Olympics," *New York Times*, December 5, 1935.

159 *"I have no reason to believe I would be mistreated"*: Associated Press, *Evening News*, December 3, 1935.

159 *the* Völkischer *are writing*: David Kenneth Wiggins, *Glory Bound: Black Athletes in a White America* (Syracuse: Syracuse University Press, 1997).

160 *The* Philadelphia Tribune *writes*: David K. Wiggins, "The 1936 Olympic Games in Berlin: The Response of America's Black Press," September 21, 1982, *Research Quarterly for Exercise and Sport*, Vol. 54 , Iss. 3, 1983.

160 *One example of this is showcased after Jesse Owens*: Ibid.

160 *a "scorching" letter*: Associated Press, "Scorching Notes Scores Nazis, U.S. Jim Crow," *New York Times*, December 13, 1935.

161 *Twenty-five cents*: John Woodruff, Interview by National Visionary Leadership Project, "John Woodruff: National Visionary," February 2, 2010, http:// www.visionaryproject.org/woodruffjohn/, accessed May 14, 2017.

161 *wonders if she watches him from Heaven*: Ibid.

161 *Born on July 5, 1915, in Connellsville*: Ibid.

162 *The Woodruffs are poor*: Don Holst and Marcia S. Popp, *American Men of Olympic Track and Field: Interviews with Athletes and Coaches* (North Carolina Jefferson, North Carolina: McFarland & Company, Inc., 2004).

162 *Connellsville's profitable coal and coke boom*: "Coke Ovens (Steel) Historical Marker," WITF, Inc., 2011, http://explorepahistory.com/hmarker.php ?markerId=1-A-233, accessed May 29, 2017.

162 *the population of Connellsville*: Mark Hofmann, "Connellsville boasts connections to Hollywood, history-making athletes," Trib Total Media, LLC, March 24, 2015, http://triblive.com/news/fayette/7531385-74/connellsville -river-youghiogheny, accessed February 9, 2017.

162 *home to more millionaires per capita*: J. R. Zaine, "Tuffy and the Comeback of the Coal Capital of the World," *Atlantic*, https://www.theatlantic.com /sponsored/chevron-ambu/tuffy-and-the-comeback-of-the-coal-capital-of -the-world/186/, retrieved January 11, 2017.

162 *In his first official competition, Woodruff*: "John Woodruff: National Visionary."

162 *Unable to find employment or enlist in the navy*: John Woodruff, interview by Randy M. Goldman, "Oral History Interview With John Woodruff," United States Holocaust Memorial Museum, May 15, 1996, https://collections .ushmm.org/search/catalog/irn504460, retrieved May 13, 2017.

CHAPTER SIXTEEN: BAPTISM BY FIRE

164 *Coach Brutus Hamilton*: Archie Williams, "Archie F. Williams, 1936 Olympic Games, Track & Field: An Olympian's Oral History," interviewed by George A. Hodak, June 1988, Amateur Athletic Foundation of Los Angeles.

164 *His own guidance counselor*: Archie F. Williams, "The Joy of Flying: Olympic Gold, Air Force Colonel, and Teacher," an oral-history interview conducted in 1992 by Gabrielle Morris, Regional Oral History Office, 1993: The Bancroft Library, University of California, Berkeley.

167 *Lucy, his younger sister, died*: Associated Press, "Sister of Ralph Metcalfe Is Dead," *Chicago Defender*, September 7, 1935.

167 *Then there was the terrible accident*: Associated Press, "Ralph Metcalfe in Automobile Accident," *St. Louis Star and Times*, November 29, 1935.

168 *die a couple of weeks later*: Associated Press, "Man Struck by Negro Track Star's Car Dies," *Des Moines Register*, December 15, 1935.

168 *dust all of those Germans*: Deborah Riley Draper, personal interview with Ralph Metcalfe, Jr., December 20, 2014.

168 *German military forces march into the Rhineland*: Guido Enderis, "Versailles Curb Broken. Hitler Smashes Locarno Citing Franco-Soviet Treaty As Reason," *New York Times*, March 8, 1935.

168 *the Franco-Soviet Treaty of Mutual Assistance*: History.com staff, "Hitler re-occupies the Rhineland," History.com, 2010, http://www.history.com/this-day-in-history/hitler-reoccupies-the-rhineland, retrieved April 13, 2017.

169 *"The German people is not interested"*: Associated Press, "Text of Chancellor Hitler's Speech to Reichstag, Denouncing Versailles Treaty," *New York Times*, March 8, 1935.

169 *The* New York Times *features a headline*: Edwin L. James, "German Conscription Alters Military Map: With Yearly Class of 300,000, Hitler May Soon Command Biggest Army in All of Europe," *New York Times*, March 17, 1935.

PART THREE

173 *Joe Louis is the son of a sharecropper*: "Joe Louis," Black History Now, May 24, 2011, http://blackhistorynow.com/joe-louis/, retrieved February 28, 2017.

173 *it is a foregone conclusion*: "Joe Louis," Box Rec, http://boxrec.com/media/index.php/Joe_Louis, retrieved February 28, 2017.

173 *the lack of ticket sales*: Lane Demas, "The Brown Bomber's Dark Day: Louis-Schmeling I and America's Black Hero," Department of History University of California at Irvine, Fall 2004, http://library.la84.org/SportsLibrary/JSH/JSH2004/JSH3103/jsh3103d.pdf

173 *"The fight won't go over three rounds"*: Bill Gibson, *The Afro American*, June 20, 1936.

174 *Maya Angelou writes*: Maya Angelou, *I Know Why the Caged Bird Sings* (New York: Random House, 1969).

174 *Reports of young black men looting*: David Clay Large, *Nazi Games: The Olympics of 1936* (New York: W. W. Norton & Company, 2007).

174 *"We all feel that the race"*: Arthur P. Davis, "Exit Joe Louis," *Norfolk Journal and Guide*, June 27, 1936.

174 *"Joe was overconfident in a big way"*: Bill Gibson, *The Afro American*, June 20, 1936.

174 *"Sure, I want to fight him again"*: Ibid.

174 *Joseph Goebbels congratulates Schmeling*: Large, *Nazi Games: The Olympics of 1936*.

174 *"Schmeling's victory"*: "The Louis-Schmeling Fight," United States Holocaust Memorial Museum, https://www.ushmm.org/exhibition/olympics/?content=louis_schmeling, retrieved February 13, 2017.

CHAPTER SEVENTEEN: TRIAL AND ERROR

175 *"the fastest field of women athletes ever"*: Louise Mead Tricard, *American Women's Track and Field: A History, 1895 Through 1980, Volume 1* (Jefferson, North Carolina: McFarland, 1996).

176 *the four thousand spectators*: Ibid.

178 *Tidye ends up being*: Jody Homer, "Pioneer from 1932 Remains Undaunted," *Chicago Tribune*, August 10, 1984.

179 *Heavy, bulky, and in the shape of an inverted-T*: "Hurdling," *Encyclopedia Britannica*, https://www.britannica.com/sports/hurdling, retrieved March 20, 2017.

180 *His grandparents, John and Amanda Pollard*: Deborah Riley Draper, personal interview with Fritz D. Pollard III, February 27, 2016.

180 *"highly respected"*: Afia Ohemena, "The Forgotten Pollards," *Rogers Park/West Ridge Historical Society*, July 24, 2014, https://rpwrhs.org/2014/07/28/the-forgotten-pollards/, retrieved March 20, 2017.

180 *Fritz Pollard Sr.*: "Fritz Pollard Biography," Biography.com, http://www.biography.com/people/fritz-pollard-9443774, retrieved March 20, 2017.

180 *the first African American to coach an NFL team*: "In Memoriam: Fritz Pollard," Fritz Pollard Alliance Foundation, https://fritzpollard.org/in-memoriam/fritz-pollard/, retrieved March 20, 2017.

180 *the National Football League unofficially segregates*: Al Harvin, "Fritz Pollard Dead at Age 92: Black Head Coach in N.F.L.," *New York Times*, March 31, 1986.

CHAPTER EIGHTEEN: THE OLYMPIC "BLACK GANG"

182 *"How's your coach doing?"*: Archie F. Williams, "The Joy of Flying: Olympic Gold, Air Force Colonel, and Teacher," an oral-history interview conducted in 1992 by Gabrielle Morris, Regional Oral History Office, 1993: The Bancroft Library, University of California, Berkeley.

183 *"Run faster than the others, and don't fall down, and don't run out of gas"*: Ibid.

183 *You can be anything*: Archie Williams, "Archie F. Williams, 1936 Olympic Games, Track & Field: An Olympian's Oral History," interviewed by George A. Hodak, June 1988, Amateur Athletic Foundation of Los Angeles.

183 *heading in the right direction and picking up speed*: Ibid.

184 *"Hey, Arch, slow down, you got it made"*: Ibid.

184 *University of Southern California*: "Cal's Gold Medal Runner Archie Williams: Hitler Wouldn't Shake His Hand Either," SBNation.com, July 25, 2012, retrieved February 3, 2017.

184 *graduate Phi Beta Kappa*: Stanford University News Service, "Chemist James Lu Valle dies at 80," Stanford, California: Stanford University, February 16, 1993.

184 *LuValle should have graduated in February*: "Archie F. Williams, 1936 Olympic Games, Track & Field: An Olympian's Oral History."

185 *Now, entering the National AAU Championships*: Randy Taylor, "Down at Princeton," *New York Age*, July 11, 1936.

185 *the only relief from the unrelenting sun comes underneath the bleachers*: "Archie F. Williams, 1936 Olympic Games, Track & Field: An Olympian's Oral History."

187 *Johnny-come-latelies*: Ibid.

187 *You just have to have the goods on the right day*: Ibid.

187 *This Sunday is the second day of competition*: Richard Hymans, "The History of the United States Olympic Trials—Track and Field," *Track & Field*, 2008.

187 *Just get out there and run it*: "Archie F. Williams, 1936 Olympic Games, Track & Field: An Olympian's Oral History."

187 *Only moments ago, he had to run his father out of the dressing room*: Dr. James E. LuValle, "Dr. James E. LuValle, 1936 Olympic Games, Track & Field: An Olympian's Oral History," interviewed by George A. Hodak, June 1988, Amateur Athletic Foundation of Los Angeles.

188 *New York is just too fast for James LuValle*: Associated Press, "Olympic Athletes Interviewed Briefly," *Atlanta Daily World*, July 15, 1936.

189 *he didn't have a dime to make the trip on his own*: Robert Petersen, "Hidden History: Mack Robinson, Jackie's long overlooked brother," *Off-Ramp*, May 19, 2016.

189 *Faded and battered, with the spikes worn down*: Brian Charles, "Mack Robinson ran into history, 76 years ago today," *Pasadena Star-News*, August 4, 2012.

190 *I didn't train enough*: Arlie W. Schardt, "Olympic Bridesmaid: Ralph Metcalfe, best sprinter of the early '30s, won everything but the race that really counted," *Sports Illustrated*, July 24, 1961.

190 *Only two-tenths of a second separate his time from the others*: Richard Hymans, "The History of the United States Olympic Trials—Track and Field," *Track & Field*, 2008.

190 *He can hear Coach Jennings*: Schardt, "Olympic Bridesmaid: Ralph Metcalfe."

191 *"Don't ask me how it feels to establish a world's record"*: Associated Press, "Olympic Athletes Interviewed Briefly."

191 *"I am glad I made this team"*: Alan Gould, "American Track Hopes Pinned on Sensational Frosh Squad," *Kingsport Times*, July 13, 1936

192 *"It's a great team we are sending over"*: Randy Taylor, "15 Negroes Make Olympic Team," *New Journal and Guide*, July 18, 1936.

192 *"My greatest regret"*: Associated Press, "Olympic Athletes Interviewed Briefly."

192 *a total of sixteen black men and two black women make the team*: Associated Press, "American Olympic Track and Swimming Teams Are Selected," *Evening News* July 13, 1936.

193 *"Mack Robinson, the Pasadena junior college negro boy"*: Associated Press, "Nineteen California Boys on U.S. Olympic Track-Field Team," *Chino Champion*, July 17, 1936.

193 *"John Brooks, former University of Chicago negro"*: Associated Press, "Owens Wins Two Events As Olympic Track Tryouts Open," *Palm Beach Post*, July 12, 1936.

193 *long-striding John Woodruff*: Alan Gould, "Ben Eastman, Bill Bonthron, and George Varaff Pass Abruptly From Olympic Picture," *Pantagraph*, July 13, 1936.

193 *"Before 19,152 enthusiastic fans Wednesday night"*: Associated Press, "Wilson Heads U.S. Olympic Boxing Squad," *New Journal and Guide*, May 30, 1936.

194 *"John Terry, Titan Weight Lifting"*: Randy Taylor, "John Terry, Harlemite, Makes Weight Lifting Squad on US Olympic Team in Princeton Meet," *New York Times*, July 11, 1936.

194 *"Misses Tydie Pickett and Louise Stokes"*: Associated Press, "Two Race Girls Win Olympic Medals," *Chicago Defender*, July 11, 1936.

194 *The* Chicago Defender *sums up*: Associated Press, "Owens Heads Large Group of Race Stars in Olympics," *Chicago Defender*, July 11, 1936.

CHAPTER NINETEEN: AN ALMOST COLOR-BLIND OCEAN

195 *the massive white flag*: Henry McLemore, "U.S. Olympic Team Sails For Battle Scene," *News-Herald*, July 15, 1936.

195 *Thousands line the docks around them*: Docents of the NJ Maritime Museum, "The role of the S.S. Manhattan in Olympic history," *Asbury Park Press*, September 22, 2016, http://www.app.com/story/news/history/2016/09/22/role-ss-manhattan-olympic-history/90849078/, retrieved February 2, 2017.

195 *Her pastor at Eastern Avenue Baptist Church*: Ann Chandler Howell, *In The Blocks: An Olympian's Story* (Chicago: Chandler/White Publishing Company, Inc., 1996).

196 *They raised enough to send along $75 for expense money and to keep another $105 for her homecoming*: Bob Duffy, "Stokes: Nowhere, Fast Malden Sprinter a Trailblazer, Though She Didn't Run," *Boston Globe*, September 10, 2000.

198 *Archie and his fellow black teammates link arms while posing*: Archie F. Williams, "The Joy of Flying: Olympic Gold, Air Force Colonel, and Teacher," an oral-history interview conducted in 1992 by Gabrielle Morris, Regional Oral History Office, 1993: The Bancroft Library, University of California, Berkeley.

198 *They're put up at the Hotel Roosevelt*: Archie Williams, "Archie F. Williams, 1936 Olympic Games, Track & Field: An Olympian's Oral History," interviewed by George A. Hodak, June 1988, Amateur Athletic Foundation of Los Angeles.

199 *The menu consists of chicken soup*: Alan Gould, "Baby Jack—Wants More To Eat," *Cincinnati Enquirer*, July 16, 1936.

200 *She takes a second to capture the vast ocean with a camera*: "US Olympic Team

Arrives in Germany for Summer Games," Getty Images, http://www.getty images.com/detail/video/manhattan-at-sea-the-ship-that-bears-us-olympic -athletes-news-footage/542772226, retrieved February 10, 2017.

201 *their room becomes the central gathering place*: Michael D. Davis, *Black American Women in Olympic Track and Field: A Complete Illustrated Reference* (McFarland & Company, Inc., Publishers, Jefferson, North Carolina).

201 *She only wishes she could train just a little*: Charles Grumich, "On The Sidelines," *Arizona Republic*, July 20, 1936.

202 *The camaraderie among the athletes*: Wilbur Young, "Olympic Team's Thoughts Turn to Spare-Ribs, Peas, and Rice," *Afro-American*, July 25, 1936.

203 *thus bringing respect to their country*: Ibid.

203 *Cornelius Johnson enjoys playing*: Randy Taylor, "Sports," *Cleveland Call and Post*, August 6, 1936.

203 *the story of the girl*: Associated Press, "Girl Stowaway on Ship," *St. Louis Post-Dispatch*, July 14, 1936.

203 *talk about who will be coaching Jesse Owens*: Taylor, "Sports."

203 *The 400-meter star from the University of California*: Henry McLemore, "400-Meter Ace Regains Health," *News-Journal*, July 17, 1936.

204 *Jesse Owens, has to shake off a head cold*: "Owens Works to Shake Cold," *Oakland Tribune*, July 20, 1936.

204 *the 4 x100-meter relay team*: Ibid.

204 *"Dark Battalion Best U.S. Bet"*: Charles Grumich, "Dark Battalion Best U.S. Bet," *News-Press*, July 30, 1936.

205 *"I think I've gained fifteen pounds"*: Williams, "The Joy of Flying: Olympic Gold, Air Force Colonel, and Teacher."

205 *eating or planning to eat*: Williams, "Archie F. Williams, 1936 Olympic Games, Track & Field: An Olympian's Oral History."

206 *Then there are athletes like Tarzan*: John Christian Hopkins, "The legend of Tarzan (Brown, that is)," *Four Corners Free Press*, August 23, 2014.

206 *Guys like Jack Torrance*: Williams, "Archie F. Williams, 1936 Olympic Games, Track & Field: An Olympian's Oral History."

207 *the good-looking swimmer Eleanor Holm Jarrett*: Williams, "The Joy of Flying: Olympic Gold, Air Force Colonel, and Teacher."

207 *trained on "champagne and late hours"*: John Bentley, "I May Be Wrong," *Lincoln Journal Star*, July 24, 1936.

207 *the team gossip on Harold Smallwood*: Henry McLemore, "Olympic Team Starts Long Trek to Berlin," *Ogden Standard-Examiner*, July 16, 1936.

207 *the athletes are issued a list of dos and don'ts*: Henry McLemore, "U.S. Team Gets List of Don'ts," *Oakland Tribune*, July 17, 1936.

207 *"The deportment and spirit of the team"*: Arthur J. Daley, "Brundage Praises US Athletes For Exemplary Conduct on Ship," *New York Times*, July 23, 1936.

208 *Ralph Metcalfe feels out of sorts*: Deborah Riley Draper, personal interview with Ralph Metcalfe, Jr., December 20, 2014.

208 *Tolan went to Australia last year and set a bunch of records*: "Midnight Express," Detroit Historical Society, July 13, 2012, https://blog.detroithistorical.org/2012/07/13/midnight-express/, retrieved March 25, 2017.

208 *Metcalfe is among the biggest names on the team*: Williams, "Archie F. Williams, 1936 Olympic Games, Track & Field: An Olympian's Oral History."

209 *Metcalfe gathers as many as possible*: Donald McRae, *In Black & White: The Untold Story of Joe Louis and Jesse Owens* (New York: Simon & Schuster, 2013).

209 *"We all know where we're going and what this means"*: Deborah Riley Draper, personal interview with Ralph Metcalfe, Jr., December 20, 2014.

210 *"Woodruff is a poor boy"*: Associated Press, "S-O-S For Johnny Woodruff," *Evening Standard*, July 13, 1936.

210 *"Tell the people back home"*: Associated Press, "Going to Berlin to Win, Woodruff Tells His Friends," *Daily Courier*, July 14, 1936.

211 *He's never been interested in politics*: John Woodruff, "John Woodruff: National Visionary," interview by National Visionary Leadership Project, February 2, 2010, http://www.visionaryproject.org/woodruffjohn/, accessed May 14, 2017.

211 *Both Metcalfe and Robinson give him lots of advice*: Wendell Smith, "Long John Woodruff Champion of the Olympic Games," *Courier-Journal*, June 27, 1971.

211 *Woodruff writes a letter*: Associated Press, "Woodruff Thanks Contributors to Standard Fund," *Evening Standard*, July 29, 1935.

CHAPTER TWENTY: THE OLYMPIC SPIRIT AND OLYMPIC PEACE

213 *The people in Hamburg welcome Archie Williams*: Archie Williams, "Archie F. Williams, 1936 Olympic Games, Track & Field: An Olympian's Oral History," interviewed by George A. Hodak, June 1988, Amateur Athletic Foundation of Los Angeles.

213 *city hall, known as the Rathaus*: Michael J. Socolow, *Six Minutes in Berlin: Broadcast Spectacle and Rowing Gold at the Nazi Olympics?* (Chicago: University of Illinois Press, 2016).

214 *cigars, cigarettes, and fruit punch*: Ibid.

214 *the station where their two trains to Berlin await*: Associated Press, "Berlin Gives Big Reception to Americans," *Press and Sun-Bulletin*, July 24, 1936.

215 *greeted and kissed on the cheek by Dr. Theodor Lewald*: Stuart Cameron, "American Olympic Team Arrives in Berlin, Germany," *Oshkosh Northwestern*, July 24, 1936.

215 *A mob of young people that includes many young girls*: Dr. James E. LuValle, "Dr. James E. LuValle, 1936 Olympic Games, Track & Field: An Olympian's

Oral History," interviewed by George A. Hodak, June 1988, Amateur Athletic Foundation of Los Angeles.

215 *twenty-five-year-old port*: Ibid.

215 *They travel ten miles outside the city*: Herbert H. Wildman, "Herbert H. Wildman 1932 & 1936 Olympic Games Water Polo: An Olympian's Oral History," interviewed by George A. Hodak, October 1987, Amateur Athletic Foundation of Los Angeles.

216 *Heinrich Himmler, who has been appointed by Hitler*: United States Holocaust Memorial Museum, "Heinrich Himmler," *Holocaust Encyclopedia*, https://www.ushmm.org/wlc/en/article.php?ModuleId=10007407, retrieved May 20, 2017.

217 *Sachsenhausen itself covers over 960 acres*: Mary Williams Walsh, "A Grand Design For Nazi Camp," *Los Angeles Times*, January 17, 1998.

217 *It is slated for Hitler's SS leaders and junior officers*: "You Can Never Forget the Concentration Camps," *Gaffney Ledger*, September 13, 1972.

217 *more than 200,000 people are imprisoned in Sachsenhausen*: "Sachsenhausen (Oranienburg): History & Overview," Jewish Virtual Library, http://www.jewishvirtuallibrary.org/history-and-overview-of-sachsenhausen-oranienburg-concentration-camp, retrieved May 20, 2017.

218 *when they host the Winter Olympics*: Susan D. Bachrach, *The Nazi Olympics: Berlin 1936* (New York: Little, Brown & Company, 2000).

218 *"The whole world will assess the prospects"*: David Clay Large, *Nazi Games: The Olympics of 1936* (New York: W.W. Norton & Company, 2007).

218 *Rudi Ball, who is only partly Jewish*: Bachrach, *The Nazi Olympics: Berlin 1936*.

218 *President Henri de Baillet-Latour's concern*: Ibid.

218 *Joseph Goebbels wants to do everything possible*: Sean Edgecomb, "Inharmonious Pursuits: Performing Racism at the Olympic Games," *Popular Entertainment Studies*, Vol. 2, Iss. 2, 2011, The University of Newcastle, Australia, pp. 5–20.

218 *Walther Darré, sends out a directive*: Duff Hart-Davis, *Hitler's Games: The 1936 Olympics* (New York: Harper & Row, 1986).

219 *The anti-Semitic newspaper* Der Stürmer: Bachrach, *The Nazi Olympics: Berlin 1936*.

220 *"People at home and abroad"*: Richard Evans, *The Third Reich in Power, 1933–1939: How the Nazis Won over the Hearts and Minds of a Nation* (New York: Penguin Press, 2005).

220 *the "Olympic pause"*: Anrd Krüger and William Murray, *The Nazi Olympics: Sport, Politics, and Appeasement in the 1930s* (Champaign, Illinois: University of Illinois Press, 2010).

221 *a brand-new college campus*: John Woodruff, "John Woodruff: National Visionary," interview by National Visionary Leadership Project, February 2,

2010, http://www.visionaryproject.org/woodruffjohn/, accessed May 14, 2017.

222 *Welcome to the Olympic Village!*: Organisationskomitee FÜR Die XI, Olympiade Berlin 1936 E. V., *The XIth Olympic Games Berlin, 1936 Official Report Volume 1*, (Berlin: Wilhelm Limpert, 1937).

222 *what Archie Williams calls "all the goodies"*: Williams, " Archie F. Williams, 1936 Olympic Games, Track & Field: An Olympian's Oral History."

223 *the chefs from the SS* Bremen: John Woodruff, "John Woodruff: National Visionary."

223 *Each athlete has a card*: Williams, "Archie F. Williams, 1936 Olympic Games, Track & Field: An Olympian's Oral History."

225 *Mack and the others know the rules*: John Woodruff, "John Woodruff: National Visionary."

226 *"resembled a secluded island"*: Organisationskomitee FÜR Die XI, *The XIth Olympic Games Berlin, 1936 Official Report Volume 1*.

226 *There are no separate kitchens*: Ibid.

226 *they have been served a lot of boiled foods*: Iris Cummings Critchell, "Iris Cummings Critchell, 1936 Olympic Games, Swimming: An Olympian's Oral History," interviewed by George A. Hodak, May 1988, Amateur Athletic Foundation of Los Angeles.

226 *a friendly young German woman from Hitler's Honorary Youth Service*: Ibid.

227 *"What is the difference"*: Arnd Krüger and Jim Riordan, *The International Politics of Sport in the Twentieth Century* (Abingdon, United Kingdom: Routledge, 2016).

227 *"Conditions in Berlin are the finest ever"*: Stuart Cameron, "American Olympic Team Arrives in Berlin, Germany," *Oshkosh Northwestern*, July 24, 1936.

227 *twenty-eight thousand members of the Hitler Youth*: Dorothea von Schwanenfluegel Lawson, *Laughter Wasn't Rationed: A Personal Journey Through Germany's World Wars and Postwar Years* (Medford, OR: Tricor Press, 2000).

227 *Three hours before the opening ceremonies*: Organisationskomitee FÜR Die XI, *The XIth Olympic Games Berlin, 1936 Official Report Volume 1*.

228 *the band of the Wachtruppe Berlin regiment*: Anton Rippon, *Hitler's Olympics: The Story of the 1936 Nazi Games* (Barnsley, England: Pen and Sword Books, 2006).

228 *the Olympic torch relay and ceremony*: Max Fisher, "The Nazi Origins of the Olympic Flame Relay," *Atlantic*, May 10, 2012.

228 *purely for dramatic effect*: Large, *Nazi Games: The Olympics of 1936*.

228 *Linking the Aryan lineage from the Greek empire*: Fisher, "The Nazi Origins of the Olympic Flame Relay."

228 *The runners who carry it can only be blue-eyed and blond*: Large, *Nazi Games: The Olympics of 1936*.

228 *Hitler greets them*: Organisationskomitee FÜR Die XI, *The XIth Olympic Games Berlin, 1936 Official Report Volume 1.*

CHAPTER TWENTY-ONE: READY, WILLING, AND ABLE FOR WAR

230 *James LuValle looks out the top of the double-decker bus*: Dr. James E. LuValle, "Dr. James E. LuValle, 1936 Olympic Games, Track & Field: An Olympian's Oral History," interviewed by George A. Hodak, June 1988, Amateur Athletic Foundation of Los Angeles.

230 *one of the many buses*: David Clay Large, *Nazi Games: The Olympics of 1936,* (New York: W.W. Norton & Company, 2007).

231 *the sounds of an orchestra floating from the stadium*: Ibid.

231 *the massive* Hindenburg *zeppelin hangs overhead*: Alan Taylor, "75 Years Since the Hindenburg Disaster," *Atlantic,* May 8, 2012, https://www.theatlantic .com/photo/2012/05/75-years-since-the-hindenburg-disaster/100292/, retrieved May 2, 2017.

232 *For more than an hour that day*: "LZ-129 Hindenburg: A Detailed History," http://www.airships.net/hindenburg/lz129-hindenburg-detailed-history/, retrieved May 4, 2017.

232 *"greeted the thousands assembled for the Olympic Games"*: Anton Rippon, *Hitler's Olympics: The Story of the 1936 Nazi Games* (Barnsley, England: Pen and Sword Books, 2006).

232 *dropping pro-Nazi leaflets to spectators below*: "LZ-129 Hindenburg: A Detailed History."

232 *he stands at the top of the structure*: LuValle, "Dr. James E. LuValle, 1936 Olympic Games, Track & Field: An Olympian's Oral History."

233 *The crowd grows hysterical as Hitler enters his stadium*: Frederick T. Birchall, "100,000 Hail Hitler; U.S. Athletes Avoid Nazi Salute to Him," *New York Times,* August 2, 1936.

233 *a blond, blue-eyed five-year-old girl*: Organisationskomitee FÜR Die XI, Olympiade Berlin 1936 E. V., *The XIth Olympic Games Berlin, 1936 Official Report Volume 1* (Berlin: Wilhelm Limpert, 1937).

233 *Gudrun Diem*: Large, *Nazi Games: The Olympics of 1936.*

234 *the thirty-thousand-pound Olympic Bell rings*: Organisationskomitee FÜR Die XI, *The XIth Olympic Games Berlin, 1936 Official Report Volume 1.*

234 *Applause comes in the type of salute given*: Birchall, "100,000 Hail Hitler; U.S. Athletes Avoid Nazi Salute to Him."

235 *Kristallnacht, or the "Night of Broken Glass"*: "Kristallnacht," *Holocaust Encyclopedia,* https://www.ushmm.org/wlc/en/article.php?ModuleId=10005201, retrieved May 4, 2017.

235 *The violence is particularly brutal in Vienna, Austria*: "Austria," *Holocaust Encyclopedia,* https://www.ushmm.org/wlc/en/article.php?ModuleId=10005447, retrieved May 4, 2017.

235 *Countries such as Afghanistan, Bermuda, Bolivia, and Iceland*: Birchall, "100,000 Hail Hitler; U.S. Athletes Avoid Nazi Salute to Him."

235 *For Poland, 127 men and 17 women*: "Poland at the 1936 Berlin Summer Games," Sports-Reference.com, https://www.sports-reference.com/olympics /countries/POL/summer/1936/, retrieved May 4, 2017.

235 *Poland will lose almost 18 percent of its population*: "Polish Victims," *Holocaust Encyclopedia*, https://www.ushmm.org/wlc/en/article.php?ModuleId=10005473, retrieved May 4, 2017.

235 *"kill without pity or mercy"*: Associated Press, "Portrait of Hitler," *Morning News*, November 26, 1945.

236 *except the United States*: Large, *Nazi Games: The Olympics of 1936*.

236 *the German national anthem begins to blare*: "1936 Olympics," narrated by Jack Martin, https://www.youtube.com/watch?v=WKvaE7Euevk, retrieved May 6, 2017.

236 *The Germans have adopted Austria's "Emperor Hymn"*: Large, *Nazi Games: The Olympics of 1936*.

237 *Archie Williams stands fifty feet away*: Archie Williams, "Archie F. Williams, 1936 Olympic Games, Track & Field: An Olympian's Oral History," interviewed by George A. Hodak, June 1988, Amateur Athletic Foundation of Los Angeles.

237 *The variety in the attire*: Ibid.

237 *Pigeons are released*: Ibid.

238 *the Olympic Oath is declared by the German flag-bearer*: Rippon, *Hitler's Olympics: The Story of the 1936 Nazi Games*.

238 *"These Olympic Games have had an opening"*: Birchall, "100,000 Hail Hitler; U.S. Athletes Avoid Nazi Salute to Him."

238 *"I concentrate on Hitler's architecture"*: James P. O'Donnell, "The Devil's Architect," *New York Times*, October 26, 1969.

239 *On July 14, 1933, Hitler declares the Law to Prevent Hereditarily Diseased Offspring*: Steven Luckert, Ph.D., "How Nazi Germany weaponized the race card against the US Army," *Medium*, https://medium.com/@Holocaust Museum/the-nazi-plan-to-divide-and-conquer-the-us-army-296a3c97fb54, retrieved March 9, 2017.

239 *The law mandates sterilization*: Susan D. Bachrach, *The Nazi Olympics: Berlin 1936*, (New York: Little, Brown & Company, 2000).

239 *thousands of black Germans in Germany*: Ibid.

239 *the French deployed African soldiers*: Hans Massaquoi, *Destined to Witness: Growing Up Black in Nazi Germany* (New York: William Morrow, 2001).

CHAPTER TWENTY-TWO: THE SNUB

241 *"the Honor Loge"*: Nicholas Whitlam, *Four Weeks One Summer: When It All Went Wrong?* (Melbourne: Australian Scholarly Publishing, 2017).

242 *Owens's time in the second round*: David Clay Large, *Nazi Games: The Olympics of 1936* (New York: W.W. Norton & Company, 2007).

242 *the "Black Grasshopper"*: Associated Press, "Owens Seeks Three Olympics Wins for America," *Oshkosh Northwestern*, August 3, 1936.

243 *"When dusk fell over Reichsportfeld"*: Henry McLemore, "Hitler Missed Best Bits of Action," *Oshkosh Northwestern*, August 3, 1936.

243 *Hitler left his box five minutes before the ceremony*: Arthur J. Daley, "110,000 See Owens Set World Record at Olympic Games," *New York Times*, August 3, 1936.

244 *Cornelius Johnson, tells his sister*: Gary Libman, "Pioneer Olympian Gold Medalist Helped Set Pace for Black Athletes," *Los Angeles Times*, July 15, 1984.

245 *This is known as a Bellamy Salute*: Raymond T. Stefani Ph.D., "Johnson, Albritton, and Thurber's Patriotic and Defiant Bellamy Salute in Response to Hitler's Snub at Berlin in 1936," *Sport Journal*, September 22, 2015, http://thesportjournal.org/article/johnson-albritton-and-thurbers-patriotic -and-defiant-bellamy-salute-in-response-to-hitlers-snub-at-berlin-in-1936/, retrieved March 24, 2017.

246 *chooses not to invite any more athletes to his loge box and congratulate them*: Steven J. Niven, "Cornelius Johnson and a Forgotten US Protest Against Hitler at the 1936 Olympics," *Root,* February 24, 2016, https://www.theroot .com/cornelius-johnson-and-a-forgotten-us-protest-against-hi-1790854343, retrieved March 24, 2017.

246 *"the greatest potential high jumper that ever lived"*: Bill Gibson, "Hear Me Talkin' To Ya," *Afro-American*, May 13, 1933.

246 *Albritton quote*: Gary Libman, "Pioneer Olympian Gold Medalist Helped Set Pace for Black Athletes" *Los Angeles Times*, July 15, 1984.

246 *"I was so close"*: Michael D. Davis, *Black American Women in Olympic Track and Field: A Complete Illustrated Reference* (Jefferson, North Carolina: McFarland & Company, 1992).

247 *"I didn't notice any discrimination"*: John Woodruff, "John Woodruff: National Visionary," interview by National Visionary Leadership Project, February 2, 2010, http://www.visionaryproject.org/woodruffjohn/, accessed May 14, 2017.

CHAPTER TWENTY-THREE: THE STOP

248 *It's just over sixty degrees today, and the wind barely blows in the stadium*: Organisationskomitee FÜR Die XI, Olympiade Berlin 1936 E. V., *The XIth Olympic Games Berlin, 1936 Official Report Volume 1* (Berlin: Wilhelm Limpert, 1937).

248 *whether it's red dirt or red cinders*: John Woodruff, interview by Randy M. Goldman, "Oral History Interview With John Woodruff," United States

Holocaust Memorial Museum, May 15, 1996, https://collections.ushmm .org/search/catalog/irn504460, retrieved May 13, 2017.

248 *have run with precision*: Ibid.

249 *I'm gonna lay back in second position*: John Woodruff, Interview by National Visionary Leadership Project, "John Woodruff: National Visionary," February 2, 2010, http://www.visionaryproject.org/woodruffjohn/, accessed May 14, 2017.

251 *From his childhood with two young parents and too many children barely scraping by*: "John Woodruff: National Visionary."

253 *Jimmy Clark is eliminated*: Associated Press. "Jimmy Clark One of Fighters To Be Eliminated." *Bradford Evening Star and The Bradford Daily Record* August 14, 1936.

253 *Howell King's Olympics*: Associated Press, "Church Explains His Dismissal from Olympics," *Chicago Tribune*, August 9, 1936.

254 *"King was not with us"*: Associated Press, "Ousted Boxer Returns Home," *New York Amsterdam News*, August 8, 1936.

CHAPTER TWENTY-FOUR: THE SNEAKERS

255 *Today I'm going to be chasing the fox*: Larry Eldridge, "Mack Robinson— Overshadowed by Jackie," *Albuquerque Journal*, September 30, 1977.

256 *black athletes with curlicues*: Jim Murray, "Mack Robinson Knows," *Courier-News*, June 22, 1978.

256 *rubbed a wet finger on his arm*: Bill Fleischman, "Sports People: Jackie's Brother, Mack Robinson, Is Worth Remembering," *Philadelphia Daily News*, August 2, 1984.

256 *the boorish shot-putter*: Murray, "Mack Robinson Knows."

256 *Owens is not only wearing new spikes*: Jennifer Barrett, "The History of Adidas and Puma," Newsweek.com, April 13, 2008, http://www.newsweek.com /history-adidas-and-puma-86373, retrieved April 14, 2017.

257 *Adi is able to convince Owens during a stealth visit*: Omar Akhtar, "The hatred and bitterness behind two of the world's most popular brands," March 22, 2013, http://fortune.com/2013/03/22/the-hatred-and-bitterness-behind -two-of-the-worlds-most-popular-brands/, retrieved April 14, 2017.

257 *Jesse beat me by a foot in New York*: Associated Press, "Owens teammate remembers tougher times for athletes," *Courier-Post*, July 13, 1984.

257 *The semifinals take place a day later*: Organisationskomitee FÜR Die XI, Olympiade Berlin 1936 E. V., *The XIth Olympic Games Berlin, 1936 Official Report Volume 1* (Berlin: Wilhelm Limpert, 1937).

258 *having been able to study every runner he's facing*: Frank Litsky, "Mack Robinson, 85, Second to Owens in Berlin," *New York Times,* March 14, 2000.

258 *The coaches on the Olympic team have been around only Jesse*: "Hidden History: Mack Robinson, Jackie's Long Overlooked Brother," *Off Ramp*, May 19,

2016, https://www.scpr.org/programs/offramp/2016/05/19/48971/hidden-history-mack-robinson-jackie-s-long-overloo/, retrieved March 3, 2017.

258 *Jesse actually went down to Florida and Cuba to train*: Deborah Riley Draper, personal interview with Fritz D. Pollard III, February 27, 2016.

258 *"I always thought if I'd had some help"*: Eldridge, "Mack Robinson—Overshadowed by Jackie."

CHAPTER TWENTY-FIVE: THE FOOTNOTE

260 *catches the top of a hurdle*: Richard Hymans, "The History of the United States Olympic Trials—Track and Field," *Track & Field*, 2008.

260 *despite receiving advice from both Ralph Metcalfe and Jesse Owens*: Jody Homer, "Pioneer from 1932 Remains Undaunted," *Chicago Tribune*, August 10, 1984.

261 *Tidye has broken her ankle*: Ibid.

261 *"The three best of each heat qualify"*: Organisationskomitee FÜR Die XI, Olympiade Berlin 1936 E. V. *The XIth Olympic Games Berlin, 1936 Official Report Volume 1* (Berlin: Wilhelm Limpert, 1937).

261 *"One of the reasons I hit the hurdle"*: Evelyne Hall Adams, "Evelyne Hall Adams, 1932 Olympic Games, Track & Field: An Olympian's Oral History," interviewed by George A. Hodak, October 1987, Amateur Athletic Foundation of Los Angeles.

CHAPTER TWENTY-SIX: THE JUNIOR

263 *he resorted to running on top of boxcars*: Deborah Riley Draper, personal interview with Fritz D. Pollard III, February 27, 2016.

264 *His job is to cross over hurdles*: "Remembering Fritz Pollard's Olympic legacy," *University Letter* (University of North Dakota blog), February 17, 2016, http://blogs.und.edu/uletter/2016/02/remembering-fritz-pollards-olympic-legacy/, retrieved April 23, 2017.

CHAPTER TWENTY-SEVEN: THE BLACK PANTHER

267 *Every morning, they go through regular training*: Archie Williams, "Archie F. Williams, 1936 Olympic Games, Track & Field: An Olympian's Oral History," interviewed by George A. Hodak, June 1988, Amateur Athletic Foundation of Los Angeles.

267 *Archie easily wins the heat in 47.8 seconds*: Organisationskomitee FÜR Die XI, Olympiade Berlin 1936 E. V., *The XIth Olympic Games Berlin, 1936 Official Report Volume 1* (Berlin: Wilhelm Limpert, 1937).

268 *so Coach Lawson Roberson is with Archie and LuValle as they are being driven to the stadium*: Williams, "Archie F. Williams, 1936 Olympic Games, Track & Field: An Olympian's Oral History."

268 *"Go that way"*: Ibid.

269 *By the time the final arrives that afternoon*: Dr. James E. LuValle, "Dr. James E. LuValle, 1936 Olympic Games, Track & Field: An Olympian's Oral History," interviewed by George A. Hodak, June 1988, Amateur Athletic Foundation of Los Angeles.

269 *especially from the rubdown he just had*: Williams, "Archie F. Williams, 1936 Olympic Games, Track & Field: An Olympian's Oral History,"

269 *Coach Brutus has trained him to know his pace*: Archie F. Williams, "The Joy of Flying: Olympic Gold, Air Force Colonel, and Teacher," an oral-history interview conducted in 1992 by Gabrielle Morris, Regional Oral History Office, 1993: The Bancroft Library, University of California, Berkeley.

270 *"The final of the 400 meters," the British commentator narrates*: "AGK Brown Wins Silver in 400m at 1936 Berlin Olympics," Youtube.com, October 25, 2013, https://www.youtube.com/watch?v=VQAEnPuOCU4, retrieved November 27, 2016.

271 *When he was a kid he never imagined*: Williams, "Archie F. Williams, 1936 Olympic Games, Track & Field: An Olympian's Oral History,"

272 *but Archie's not having any of that*: Williams, "The Joy of Flying: Olympic Gold, Air Force Colonel, and Teacher."

CHAPTER TWENTY-EIGHT: THE GOLDEN CONCESSION

274 *he knows that Jesse Owens is out*: David Clay Large, *Nazi Games: The Olympics of 1936* (New York: W. W. Norton & Company, 2007).

275 *So Glickman and Stoller are out*: "Jewish Athletes—Marty Glickman & Sam Stoller," United States Holocaust Memorial Museum, https://www.ushmm.org/exhibition/olympics/?content=jewish_athletes_more, February 23, 2017.

275 *"Coach, you can't hide world-class sprinters"*: Ibid.

275 *"We're the only two Jews on the team"*: Large, *Nazi Games: The Olympics of 1936*.

276 *Germany doesn't get to dictate who runs and who doesn't*: "Olympics—1932 Los Angeles—Track Men's 100m—USAs Ralph Metcalfe & Eddie Tolan," *Imasportsphile*, https://www.youtube.com/watch?v=xmkXvi0cBpU, retrieved April 14, 2017.

276 *The U.S. shouldn't have fielded the best athletes to run this race*: Arlie W. Schardt, "Olympic Bridesmaid: Ralph Metcalfe, best sprinter of the early '30s, won everything but the race that really counted," *Sports Illustrated*, July 24, 1961.

277 *"We don't want compromising and patronizing concessions"*: Ralph Metcalfe, "It's Never Too Late To Be Black," *Operation Push* (radio transcript), May 5, 1972.

CHAPTER TWENTY-NINE: THE TEAM

278 *LuValle knows that he only made a mistake*: Sibrina Nichelle Collins, "Unsung: James Ellis LuValle," *Undark*, https://undark.org/article/unsung-james-ellis-luvalle-olympics, August 15, 2016.

278 *"You could describe the finish of that race"*: Dr. James E. LuValle, "Dr. James E. LuValle, 1936 Olympic Games, Track & Field: An Olympian's Oral History," interviewed by George A. Hodak, June 1988, Amateur Athletic Foundation of Los Angeles.

279 *"We weren't gladiators," LuValle says*: Ibid.

279 *"Isn't that what this is all about?"*: Archie Williams, "Archie F. Williams, 1936 Olympic Games, Track & Field: An Olympian's Oral History," interviewed by George A. Hodak, June 1988, Amateur Athletic Foundation of Los Angeles.

CHAPTER THIRTY: TWO LADIES

281 *the only part of her body that's broken is her heart*: Bob Duffy, "Stokes: Nowehere, Fast Malden Sprinter A Trailblazer, Though She Didn't Run," *Boston Globe*, September 10, 2000.

281 *our coaches snubbed Tidye and me*: Pete Kearin, "She Qualified, But Couldn't Run . . . Louise Endures Olympic Snub," *Malden Evening News*, August 29, 1972.

283 *The German runners tear down their lane*: Organisationskomitee FÜR Die XI, Olympiade Berlin 1936 E. V., *The XIth Olympic Games Berlin, 1936 Official Report Volume 1* (Berlin: Wilhelm Limpert, 1937).

283 *The death of her sister, Alice, taught her that*: Duffy, "Stokes: Nowehere, Fast Malden Sprinter A Trailblazer, Though She Didn't Run."

283 *"Maybe if I had my manager at the Olympics"*: Pete Kearin, "She Qualified, But Couldn't Run . . . Louise Endures Olympic Snub," *Malden Evening News*, August 29, 1972.

CHAPTER THIRTY-ONE: THE VERDICT

286 *"It was politics"*: Jody Homer, "Pioneer from 1932 Remains Undaunted," *Chicago Tribune*, August 10, 1984.

EPILOGUE

289 *"This most amazing athlete of all time"*: Megan Gambino, "Jesse Owens Wins his First Gold," Smithsonian.com, August 3, 2011, https://www.smithsonianmag.com/smithsonian-institution/jesse-owns-wins-his-first-gold-42454053, retrieved July 11, 2017.

289 *"a viable way out of a dreary future"*: Jaime Schultz, *Moments of Impact: Injury, Racialized Memory, and Reconciliation in College* (Lincoln, Nebraska: University of Nebraska Press, 2015).

289 *had their black auxiliary tribes*: Ibid.

290 *"'our fighters,' 'our athletes'"*: Ibid.

290 *twenty-two reported lynchings in seven different states*: Frank Jacobs, "Chilling Maps of Lynchings in 1930s America," BigThink.com, April 16, 2018, https://bigthink.com/strange-maps/chilling-maps-of-lynchings-in-1930s -america, retrieved July10, 2018.

290 *superiority over the best athletes of all races*: Mark Dyreson and John Gleaves, "The 'Black Auxiliaries' in American Memories: Sport, Race and Politics in the Construction of Modern Legacies," *International Journal of the History of Sport*, vol. 27, nos. 16–18, November–December 2010.

291 *One symbol would be an oak tree*: John Woodruff, interview by Randy M. Goldman, "Oral History Interview With John Woodruff," United States Holocaust Memorial Museum, May 15, 1996, https://collections.ushmm .org/search/catalog/irn504460, retrieved May 13, 2017.

291 *the city holds a ticker-tape parade*: C.A. Lovett, "Manhattan Roars Welcome To Returning Olympic Stars," *Daily News,* September 4, 1936.

292 *the navy refuses to let Pitt come*: John Woodruff, Interview by National Vision-ary Leadership Project, "John Woodruff: National Visionary," February 2, 2010, http://www.visionaryproject.org/woodruffjohn/, accessed May 14, 2017.

292 *"a symbol of racial reconciliation and racial change"*: Dyreson and Gleaves, "The 'Black Auxiliaries' in American Memories: Sport, Race and Politics in the Construction of Modern Legacies."

293 *towering over runners at the stadium*: Sharon Capretto and John R. Malicky, "The Legacy of John Woodruff," Runnersgazette.com, http://www.runners gazette.com/results/woodruff11.htm, retrieved February 20, 2017.

293 *there was nobody at the boat to meet us*: Archie Williams, "Archie F. Williams, 1936 Olympic Games, Track & Field: An Olympian's Oral History," inter-viewed by George A. Hodak, June 1988, Amateur Athletic Foundation of Los Angeles.

293 *having lost it in customs*: Archie F. Williams, "The Joy of Flying: Olympic Gold, Air Force Colonel, and Teacher," an oral-history interview conducted in 1992 by Gabrielle Morris, Regional Oral History Office, 1993: The Ban-croft Library, University of California, Berkeley.

293 *"I cherish those moments"*: Williams, "Archie F. Williams, 1936 Olympic Games, Track & Field: An Olympian's Oral History."

293 *"How did those dirty Nazis treat you?"*: Noah Griffin, "Marin Voice: Remembering Archie Williams, Marin's Own Olympian," Marinij.com, August 8, 2016, http://www.marinij.com/article/NO/20160818/LOCAL1 /160819834, retrieved March 3, 2017.

294 *"After I came home from the 1936 Olympics"*: Tony Gentry, *Jesse Owens: Cham-pion Athlete* (New York: Chelsea House Pub, 2005).

294 *Archie eventually finds work*: Williams, "Archie F. Williams, 1936 Olympic Games, Track & Field: An Olympian's Oral History."

294 *he begins giving lessons on his own*: "Cal's Gold Medal Runner Archie Williams: Hitler Wouldn't Shake His Hand Either," SBNation.com, July 25, 2012, https://www.californiagoldenblogs.com/2012/7/25/3136179/cals-gold-medal-runner-archie-williams-hitler-wouldnt-shake-his-hand retrieved February 3, 2017.

294 *Williams retires from the air force*: Associated Press, "Archie Williams Is Dead at 78; Won a Gold at Berlin Olympics," *New York Times*, June 26, 1993.

295 *earning his master's degree in chemistry*: Dr. James E. LuValle, "Dr. James E. LuValle, 1936 Olympic Games, Track & Field: An Olympian's Oral History," interviewed by George A. Hodak, June 1988. Amateur Athletic Foundation of Los Angeles.

295 *"I was finished with track"*: Ibid.

295 *somewhat incensed about this*: Ibid.

295 *senior research chemist at Eastman Kodak*: Collins, Sibrina Nichelle. "Unsung: James Ellis LuValle." *Undark* 15 August 2016. https://undark.org/article/unsung-james-ellis-luvalle-olympics.

296 *"My kids," LuValle says*: Deborah Riley Draper, personal interview with Phyllis Ann LuValle, August 8, 2014.

296 *"I never had a problem getting decent work"*: Dr. James E. LuValle, "Dr. James E. LuValle, 1936 Olympic Games, Track & Field: An Olympian's Oral History," interviewed by George A. Hodak, June 1988, Amateur Athletic Foundation of Los Angeles.

296 *No parade of any sort awaits him*: Brian Charles, "Mack Robinson ran into history, 76 years ago today," *Pasadena Star-News*, August 4, 2012.

296 *"I was totally ignored"*: Robert Petersen, "Hidden History: Mack Robinson, Jackie's Long Overlooked Brother," *Off Ramp*, May 19, 2016, https://www.scpr.org/programs/offramp/2016/05/19/48971/hidden-history-mack-robinson-jackie-s-long-overloo/, retrieved March 3, 2017.

297 *"He would not be getting pennies"*: Ibid.

297 *Mack works hard to lobby his city*: Tim Wendel, "Another Barrier Broken," *USA Today Baseball Weekly*, February 26, 1997.

297 *nine-foot-high bronze busts*: Robert Weintraub, "Two Lives After Losing to Jesse Owens," *New York Times*, July 20, 2012.

297 *he helps carry the Olympic flag into the L.A. Coliseum*: Robert Petersen, "Hidden History: Mack Robinson, Jackie's Long Overlooked Brother," *Off Ramp*, May 19, 2016, https://www.scpr.org/programs/offramp/2016/05/19/48971/hidden-history-mack-robinson-jackie-s-long-overloo/, March 3, 2017.

298 *Graduating from the University of North Dakota*: Associated Press, "Pollard won bronze medal at 1936 Olympics," *ESPN Classic*, February 24, 2003, http://www.espn.com/classic/obit/s/2003/0220/1511897.html, retrieved January 2, 2017.

298 *He also eventually earns a law degree*: Wade Rupard, "Jesse Owens film brings back memories of UND track star Fritz Pollard Jr.," *Grand Forks Herald*, February 22, 2016.

298 *buried in Arlington National Cemetery*: Ron Rapoport, "Pollard Jr. left his mark, from playing to politicking," *Chicago Sun-Times*, February 20, 2003.

298 *"There were too many managers and too much buck passing"*: Associated Press, "Olympic Reception Flops," *San Bernardino Sun*, September 4, 1936.

298 *Metcalfe teaches political science and coaches track*: "Metcalfe, Ralph Horace," Encyclopedia.com, 2002, https://www.encyclopedia.com/humanities/en cyclopedias-almanacs-transcripts-and-maps/metcalfe-ralph-horace, November 23, 2017.

298 *Metcalfe becomes a leading advocate*: Chris Foran, "Ralph Metcalfe beats Jesse Owens at Marquette," *Milwaukee Wisconsin Journal Sentinel*, February 16, 1934.

299 *"let us win a victory on our terms"*: Ralph Metcalfe, "It's Never Too Late To Be Black," *Operation Push* (radio transcript), May 5, 1972.

299 *"We should all get together"*: Rebecca Teagarden, " 'Best Friend' Reflects on Jesse Owens," *Columbus Citizen-Journal*, April 1, 1980.

299 *"an unnamed fraternity"*: Ibid.

300 *the creation of a historical marker*: David Elwell, "Danville to honor its silver medalist: Community to unveil historic marker for 1936 Olympian Dave Albritton," DecaturDaily.com, July 11, 2013, http://www.decaturdaily.com /news/danville-to-honor-its-silver-medalist/article_203fb1d6-eaa8-11e2 -9993-10604b9f7e7c.html, accessed March 3, 2017.

300 *"We all have dreams"*: Frank Litsky, "Obituary: Jesse Owens Dies of Cancer at 66; Hero of the 1936 Berlin Olympics," *New York Times*, April 1, 1980.

300 *Owens isn't the first of the eighteen Olympians to pass away*: Gary Libman, "Pioneer Olympian Gold Medalist Helped Set Pace for Black Athletes," *Los Angeles Times*, July 15, 1984.

301 *"a complete jobbing by boxing officials"*: "Jimmy Clark," Chautauqua Sports Hall of Fame, http://www.chautauquasportshalloffame.org/jimmyclark.php, retrieved February 20, 2017.

301 *sports always plays a big part in his life*: Deborah Riley Draper, personal interview with Dr. Daria Brooks Terrell and Wannetta Brooks, December 20, 2014.

302 *When Louise Stokes returns to her hometown of Malden*: Chris Caesar, "BLACK HISTORY MONTH: Louise Stokes Fraser." Patch.com, February 14, 2012, https://patch.com/massachusetts/malden/black-history -month-louise-stokes-fraser, retrieved November 18, 2016.

302 *a black iron statue is dedicated in her memory*: Bob Duffy, "Stokes: Nowhere, Fast Malden Sprinter a Trailblazer, Though She Didn't Run," *Boston Globe*, September 10, 2000.

303 *the courage it took to go to both of those Olympic Games*: Jody Homer, "Pioneer from 1932 Remains Undaunted," *Chicago Tribune*, August 10, 1984.

303 *"Mother was fearless and she believed in herself"*: Deborah Riley Draper, personal interview with Bernita Echols and Fay Walker, December 20, 2014.

303 *Eighty years after the 1936 Olympics*: Marina Koren, "A White House Tribute at Last," *Atlantic*, September 29, 2016, https://www.theatlantic.com/news/archive/2016/09/white-house-olympicsberlin/502325/, retrieved July 6, 2018.

304 *"Imagine what it means for a young girl or a young boy"*: Associated Press, "Obama Welcomes Relatives of 1936 African-American Olympians," *USA Today*, September 29, 2016.

SELECTED BIBLIOGRAPHY

Bachrach, Susan D. *The Nazi Olympics: Berlin 1936*. New York: Little Brown, 2000.

Brown, Daniel James. *The Boys in the Boat*. New York: Penguin Books, 2013.

Davis, Michael D. *Black American Women in Olympic Track and Field: A Complete Illustrated Reference*. Jefferson, North Carolina: McFarland & Company, 1992.

Freedman, Russell. *Babe Didrikson Zaharias: The Making of a Champion*. Boston: Clarion Books, 1999.

Hillenbrand, Laura. *Unbroken*. New York: Random House, 2010.

Howell, Ann Chandler. *In The Blocks: An Olympian's Story*. Chicago: Chandler/White Publishing Company, 1996.

Hymans, Richard. "The History of the United States Olympic Trials—Track and Field." *Track & Field*, 2008.

Large, David Clay. *Nazi Games: The Olympics of 1936*. New York: W. W. Norton & Company, 2007.

Longerich, Peter. *Goebbels: A Biography*. New York: Random House, 2015.

Pieroth, Doris H. *Their Day in the Sun: Women of the 1932 Olympics*. Seattle: University of Washington Press, 1996.

Range, Peter Ross. *1924: The Year That Made Hitler*. New York: Little, Brown and Company, 2016.

Read, Anthony. *The Devil's Disciples: Hitler's Inner Circle*. New York: W.W. Norton & Company, 2003.

Schaap, Jeremy. *Triumph: The Untold Story of Jesse Owens and Hitler's Olympics*. New York: Houghton Mifflin Harcourt, 2007.

Stout, Glenn. *Yes, She Can!: Women's Sports Pioneers (Good Sports).* Boston: HMH Books for Young Readers, 2001.

Wallace, Rich and Sandra Neil Wallace. *Babe Conquers the World: The Legendary Life of Babe Didrikson.* Honesdale, Pennsylvania: Calkins Creek Books, 2014).

Watkins, T. H. *The Great Depression: America in the 1930s.* New York: Little Brown & Company, 1993.

ACKNOWLEDGMENTS

BLAIR UNDERWOOD

Several years ago, when I received an email from Deborah Riley Draper requesting I narrate her exquisite documentary, *Olympic Pride, American Prejudice*, about the 1936 Berlin Olympics—aka the Nazi Olympics—I was honored and immediately intrigued. Deborah and I had never met prior to that moment. I watched her ten-minute trailer and was thoroughly engaged. I was impressed by her deft handling of the material, her understanding of story, and her reverence for the individuals whose lives and pursuit of Olympic glory would become the beating heart of her full-length documentary, and our subsequent book.

Little did I know that I was embarking upon a journey filled with discovery, inspiration, and world travel, including Rio de Janeiro, Brazil, and even the White House! Deborah Riley Draper is the consummate professional. She is brilliant, driven, persistent, and relentless, but above all, humble and loyal. She is a visionary who epitomizes grace under pressure. I am eternally grateful that our paths have crossed. To see her brilliant documentary now living and breathing within these pages makes me gratified indeed.

I am also thankful to the entire Coffee Bluff Pictures team, most especially Deborah's husband, Michael Draper, for his never-ending support of the documentary, the book, and of course, Deborah. Your relationship and love story inspires all of us who have been fortunate enough to experience it.

Travis Thrasher, what can I say? It has been quite the journey. I have profound respect for your literary skills, and I am incredibly thankful that we all finally crossed the finish line together. It may not have been in our projected time, but right on time nonetheless! Your talent, work ethic, and patience are to be commended. And, speaking of patience, a special bow of gratitude to your wife and three beautiful daughters for sharing their family time as we persevered through the contours and breadth of this marathon.

Thank you, as always, to my extended family of friends, relatives, acquaintances, and loved ones for constantly preparing my path with prayers and immeasurable good wishes. Words cannot adequately express how grateful I am.

To my immediate family: Dad, Col. (Ret.) Frank Underwood Sr.; Mom, Marilyn Underwood; my siblings, Frank, Marlo, Mellisa; my wife, Désirée; and kids, Paris, Brielle, and Blake; thank you for endless encouragement, boundless love, and patience as I continue to eagerly pursue my various, ever-evolving creative endeavors.

No accomplishment is achieved in a vacuum or alone. Having a book published is certainly no exception. Thank you to my manager, Ron West, and attorney, Eric Suddleson, for always having my back and for trusting me as I continue to challenge myself by exploring new and different creative expressions, like book publishing!

Deborah Ainsworth and Maria Savoy, you two are phenomenal in every way, and I'm incredibly grateful to have you in my life, which could never run as smoothly without you.

Thank you, Lee Wallman, for always making sure we beat the drums loudly and extensively. Here we go again!

To Judith Curr, my former publisher at Atria Books, I will always be indebted to you, because you were the first publisher who shared my vision within the literary world. And you continue to do so. I am grateful for this, our sixth book together, that you initially green-lit.

Todd Hunter, many thanks for seeing the importance and value of these athletes' stories and for championing this book from its inception.

Thank you, Dawn Davis and Chelcee Johns at Simon & Schuster, for believing in our book and for picking up the reins of this project with grace and meticulous care. It's one thing to have a story (well written as it may be) created and constructed on a computer screen. It's another thing entirely to have that story printed, published, and marketed to the masses. Because of your particular focus and attention, *Olympic Pride, American Prejudice* will find its place in the literary canon of extraordinary African-American sports stories that defiantly refused to be buried and forgotten in the dustbins of history.

Most important, I'd like to thank the eighteen African American athletes who, through sheer determination, grit, and raw talent, stared down the fallacy and idiocy of white supremacy. Across the Atlantic Ocean, it loomed in the form of the devil incarnate: Adolf Hitler. In Jim Crow America, generations of black athletes had competed to win their respective competitions. In doing so, they often found themselves competing to win and maintain their dignity and humanity. In spite of it all, these young men and women defied the odds and shattered expectations, and yet, history had forgotten them all, except one: Jesse Owens. Though the much-heralded and very-deserving Jesse Owens broke records and brought home four gold medals, each and every one of them took their God-given abilities and melanin-rich skin into the belly of the beast: Nazi Germany 1936. They had the audacity to believe they could disprove Hitler's flawed notion of white supremacy and prove their worthiness through the objective metrics of athletic competition on the world stage.

As a creative person, when I am engaged in a project, it is always most gratifying when the story leaps from the pages or the screen and into people's hearts. In the best-case scenario, individuals are called to action in some way. Gold-medal winners and other Olympic champions are often invited to the White House after Olympic glory. The African-American athletes who competed in the 1936 Olympics were never afforded this rarified American honor. In the case of the *Olympic Pride, American Prejudice* documentary, through the perseverance and determination of Deborah Riley Draper, on September 26, 2016, remaining family members of the eighteen Olympic athletes were finally invited to the Oval Office of the White House. Eighty years later, those athletes were officially acknowledged and posthumously honored by the sitting commander in chief, President Barack Obama.

Though there will always be those forces that attempt to suffocate the ascendant hopes and dreams of others, righteousness and fairness have a stubborn way of showing up when least expected. History had forgotten them. Now, they will forever be remembered, and given their long-overdue respect, for time immemorial.

DEBORAH RILEY DRAPER

My mother and I loved to read. She thought books were always better gifts than toys. So as a little girl I had a lot of books, including a cherished leather-bound copy of *Little Women.* Throughout my childhood my mother and I spent countless hours in the massive Bull Street Library for fun. Later, when she was in graduate school, our library visits were very focused on researching and expertly navigating the microfilm and microfiche machines at Armstrong State University. I was quite a competent graduate assistant at eight.

To my mother, thank you for those experiences and skills, which served me well during the four years of making the documentary film *Olympic Pride, American Prejudice.* I scoured archival collections and primary source materials in libraries and special collections across Germany and the United States. I know you wanted me to become a teacher like you. In some respects, I did. The biography and history of black people are the inspiration for my storytelling. My hope is that this book and the film will serve generations to come as a vital history lesson, at once inspiring and educating. I love you and miss you every day!

To the executive producers of *Olympic Pride, American Prejudice*, Amy, Blair and Mike, thank you for believing in both me and the film that would spark this book.

To Dr. Amy Tiemann, thank you for your commitment to this story and believing that these eighteen athletes deserved a bigger medal stand. You were the very first person with whom I don't share a last name to invest in a film that I directed. Our list of shared firsts is extraordinary and transformative. From Berlinale to the Obama White House Christmas party to the DuSable Museum in Chicago, we have forged a path and friendship of which I am forever grateful.

To Blair Underwood, your star shines so brightly and so full of integrity, intelligence, and enthusiasm. I am still in awe that you chose to lend your Grammy Award–winning voice and Emmy Award–winning executive producer skills to my documentary and then steward the entire project into a book. Your talents and kindness are endless, and I am grateful to watch and learn. Thank you for saying yes to the film. Mike and I call you and your family "family" and are so excited whenever we get to bask in the joy and goodness that you all bring whenever you arrive.

To Michael A. Draper, my forever executive producer and loving husband, thank you for being there quietly and joyfully for this winding journey and not requiring me to have or know my destination but rolling with it. Your love for me is the greatest gift I have ever received. Thank you for cosigning my dreams and ensuring that I have the support and the resources to make those dreams come true. Thank you for being strong and secure, for creating a home filled with love and space for me to be me without compromise or sacrifice.

To Lacy Barnes, my BFF, thank you for always saying yes and always, always operating in excellence. You have been there through all of my "I have an idea" moments and have exuberantly jumped at 200 percent to make those ideas come to life. Those ideas have spanned the gamut, and as a result, we have experienced the most wonderful adventures. Thank you, and by the way, I have a few more ideas.

Tandi, thank you for your unwavering excitement about and commitment to excellence across everything we create, from films to books to events, and for always being ready to handle any situation with grace and great grammar.

To Twuanna Munroe Ward, thank you for being a lifelong friend, great cheerleader, and super publicist even though you are actually a soon-to-be CFO at a major company.

To Amber Carter, you are always in my corner with loads of love, a willingness to support in anyway and always ready to drop off a great pair of earrings and gumbo.

To Travis Thrasher, thank you for bringing the heart and hand necessary to get this book done.

And to Chelcee, who showed such patience and support for me as a freshman author, and to the entire Simon & Schuster family, I am so appreciative of this experience. It was one of the hardest things I have ever done. And I am a better person for it and hope that the book impacts everyone who picks it up and leaves them hopeful, triumphant, and active in creating a more collaborative, inclusive, and caring community wherever they are. This would not have happened without your hard work, vision, and trust. You are all truly the best in the game!

To everyone who helped make *Olympic Pride, American Prejudice* the film and the book a reality, I thank you.

To my incredible family members of the 1936 African American Olympians who shared their emotional and poignant stories in the documentary film and to those who represented their fathers, mothers, grandfathers, and spouse in 2016 at the White House, you have my love and greatest gratitude. You and your family have forever touched my life and enabled me to truly understand the power of film.

To the eighteen African American Olympic athletes who in 1936 dreamed, dared, and lived fearlessly and broke barriers during a notoriously complicated racial and political period— you changed sports on the world's stage and triggered a seminal movement in the fight for equality on and off the field. Thank you, Dave Albritton, John Brooks, James Clark, Cornelius Johnson, Willis Johnson, Howell King, Dr. James LuValle, Congressman Ralph Metcalfe, Art Oliver, Jesse Owens, Tidye Pickett, Fritz Pollard Jr., Mack Robinson, Louise Stokes, John Terry, Archie Williams, Jack Wilson, and John Woodruff. You and your contributions are forever remembered and recognized!

INDEX

NOTE: Bold page numbers refer to pictures.

PHOTO CREDITS

Courtesy of Farm Security Administration, Office of War Information
Photograph Collection, Library of Congress: x, xi
Courtesy of Faye Walker and Bernita Echols family collection: 5, 35, 61
Courtesy of Wolfie Stokes family collection: 8
Courtesy of Tilden High School Yearbook: 12
Courtesy of Jackie Robinson Foundation: 15
Courtesy of Malden High School: 32
Courtesy of UCLA Archives: 51
Courtesy of W. E. B. Du Bois Papers (MS 312). Special Collections and
University Archives, University of Massachusetts Amherst Libraries: 54
Courtesy of Marquette University, Special Collections: 65
Photo by Underwood & Underwood courtesy of Library of Congress, Prints
and Photographs Division: 72
Courtesy of UCLA Library Special Collections, Charles E. Young Research
Library, Golden State Insurance Company collection: 73
Courtesy of UCLA, Bartlett Papers: 83
Courtesy of LA84 Archives: 84, 87
Courtesy of Library of Congress: 86, 177, 190
Courtesy of Coffee Bluff Pictures Archives: 93, 106, 158, 166, 178, 198, 200,
202, 214, 305–22
Courtesy of Library of Congress/photo by International News Photo Co.: 121
Courtesy of Drake Relays Archives: 127
Courtesy of UCLA special collections: 124
Courtesy of Bundesarchiv, German Federal Archive: 114, 136 , 138, 152, 203,
219, 231, 234, 262

PHOTO CREDITS

Courtesy of John W. Mosley Photograph Collection, Charles L. Blockson Afro-American Collection, Temple University Libraries, Philadelphia, PA: 150
Courtesy of Fritz Pollard III family collection: 181
Courtesy of the Kathy Robinson Family Archives: 209
Courtesy of University of Pitt Special Collections; 249

ABOUT THE AUTHORS

TRAVIS THRASHER

Bestselling author Travis Thrasher has written more than fifty books and worked in the publishing industry for more than twenty years. His inspirational stories have included collaborations with filmmakers, musicians, athletes, and pastors. He has written fiction in a variety of genres, from love stories and supernatural thrillers to young adult series. He's also cowritten memoirs and self-help books. Travis lives with his wife and three daughters in Grand Rapids, Michigan.

BLAIR UNDERWOOD

Two-time Golden Globe nominee, Emmy, Grammy, and seven-time NAACP Image Award recipient Blair Underwood has distinguished himself as an award-winning actor/director/producer who continues to showcase his multitude of talents across virtually all media. He's had five books published, including his successful collaboration with Tananarive Due and Steven Barnes: *Casanegra, In the Night of the Heat, From Cape Town with Love* and *South by Southeast,* all released by Simon & Schuster's Atria Books. Visit his social media at Twitter: @blairunderwood, Instagram: Blairunderwood_official, and Facebook: BlairUnderwood.

DEBORAH RILEY DRAPER

Deborah Riley Draper is an award-winning director and writer known for the films *Versailles '73: American Runway Revolution* and 2017 NAACP Image Award nominee *Olympic Pride, American Prejudice*. In 2016, *Variety* named her one of 10 Documakers to Watch. In 2019, Draper penned the screen adaptation of the upcoming film *Coffee Will Make You Black*. Draper resides in Atlanta. Visit her social media at Instagram: @Versailles73.